D1566701

THE PERSISTENCE OF POETRY

THE
PERSISTENCE
OF POETRY

Bicentennial Essays on Keats

EDITED BY

Robert M. Ryan and
Ronald A. Sharp

University of Massachusetts Press
AMHERST

Copyright © 1998 by
The University of Massachusetts Press

ALL RIGHTS RESERVED
Printed in the United States of America

LC 98-7840
ISBN 1-55849-175-9
Designed by Steve Dyer
Set in Sabon by Graphic Composition, Inc.
Printed and bound by BookCrafters

Library of Congress Cataloging-in-Publication Data
The persistence of poetry : bicentennial essays on Keats / edited by
  Robert M. Ryan and Ronald A. Sharp.
     p.   cm.
  Includes bibliographical references (p.   ) and index.
  ISBN 1-55849-175-9 (alk. paper)
    1. Keats, John, 1795–1821—Criticism and interpretation.
  I. Ryan, Robert M., 1941– . II. Sharp, Ronald A.
  PR4837.P34   1998
  821'.7—dc21   98-7840
                                        CIP

British Library Cataloguing in Publication data are available.

Contents

ACKNOWLEDGMENTS

FOR THEIR ASSISTANCE in making the Keats Bicentennial Conference possible, we wish to acknowledge the generous support of the National Endowment for the Humanities, the Keats-Shelley Association of America, the Carl and Lily Pforzheimer Foundation, the Acriel Foundation, Kenyon College, Rutgers University at Camden, and the Houghton Library of Harvard University. For their encouragement and advice we would also like to thank Betty T. Bennett, William T. Buice III, Stuart Curran, Clark Dougan, Barbara Dupee, Dennis Marnon, Leslie Morris, Donald H. Reiman, Jack Stillinger, James L. Weil, Richard Wendorf, and Pam Wilkinson.

.

Introduction

ROBERT M. RYAN

THE JOHN KEATS Bicentennial Conference, held at Harvard University on September 7–9, 1995, was the most ambitious of many commemorations organized throughout the world to celebrate the two-hundredth anniversary of Keats's birth. Other events included local scholarly conferences in places ranging from Tokyo to Pretoria, the publication of books and special issues of journals, poetry readings, concerts, dramatic performances, television and radio programs, church services, wreath-layings, and a number of birthday parties of varying degrees of solemnity. In this miscellany of tributes one found a predictable commonality of pleasure in recalling the story of a young man without the advantages of birth, wealth, or education who made his way by talent and desire to a place among the English poets. There was also a common tendency to turn Keats's story into a celebration of the art of poetry itself, of its persistent vitality, its continuing power to bring delight and comfort in our fragmented, distracted postmodern culture.

A century ago, at the centennial anniversary of Keats's birth, not nearly so much energy was invested in commemoration. One event deserves to be recalled, since it provides perspective on the recent reassessments of the poet. On July 16, 1894, in anticipation of the centennial, a marble bust of Keats, the gift of a group of American subscribers, was placed in Hampstead Church. The bust was formally accepted on behalf of the English people by Edmund Gosse, whose speech on the occasion is worth remembering for what it says about the state of Keats's reputation at the time. Gosse remarked on how "singularly unattached" that reputation was:

It rests upon no privilege of birth . . . it is fostered by no alliance of powerful friends. He is identified with no progression of ideas, no religious, or political, or social propaganda. He is either a poet, or absolutely nothing—we withdraw the poetical elements from our conception of him, and what is left? The palest phantom of a livery-stablekeeper's son, an unsuccessful medical student, an ineffectual consumptive lad, who died in obscurity more than seventy years ago. . . . We honor in [Keats] a poet, and nothing but a poet.[1]

At the end of another century, admirers of Keats met at Harvard to honor again the ineffectual, consumptive lad who died in obscurity and whose fame is now more widespread than ever. And although today's Keats scholars are more aware than Gosse was of the progression of ideas that influenced Keats's writing, of the strength of his political allegiances and their consequences for his literary career, it may be said that we, too, gathered primarily to honor "a poet, and nothing but a poet," one whose fame rests centrally on his achievement in extending the linguistic and emotional reaches of English poetry. The John Keats Bicentennial Conference attempted to take stock of not only why Keats still matters after two hundred years, but also why poetry like his still matters in what has been called a "postliterate" age. Keats raises the question because he seems to epitomize the poetic character; indeed, he helped shape our culture's idea of what a poet is. His remarkable artistic achievement, especially when measured against the brevity of his life and the familial and economic disadvantages he confronted from early childhood, raises important questions about the nature of creativity, the relation of artistic talent to environment, and the role the poet plays in the life of a society.

For the project of assessing a poet's importance, cultural authority is broadly distributed throughout a society. It seemed to the organizers of the conference that the celebration of Keats's achievement should not be an academic exercise only, since his poetry's continuing life is not solely an academic phenomenon. Keats persistently attracts admiring attention from a heterogeneous audience of readers who continue to find pleasure, encouragement, and consolation in his verse. We hoped to understand why and how his poetry matters to the community of "ordinary readers," a capacious category that ranges from very young students to lawyers, physicians, financiers, and the clergy—all of which professions were represented among participants at the Harvard conference.

Drawing more than 250 individuals from the United States, Canada, Britain, Ireland, Italy, Israel, India, and Japan, the three-day conference differed from other academic gatherings in the variety of constituencies that were represented. Joining university scholars of international reputation were some of the most distinguished poets writing in English today, including Robert Hass (then poet laureate of the United States), Eavan Boland, Michael S. Harper, Philip Levine, Andrew Motion, and Alicia Ostriker. The poets were there by right: if Keats was killed by critics, as was widely believed in the nineteenth century, he was assuredly raised up again by poets—first by Shelley in *Adonais* and then, a decade later, by Tennyson, who demonstrated in his own writing Keats's vitality as a force inspiring and enabling new developments in poetry. This vitality has continued to be evident in our own century in the work of poets such as Wallace Stevens, Countee Cullen, and Amy Clampitt. Academic scholars tend to periodize Keats, finding him most intelligible as a man of the nineteenth century; poets are more likely to see him in the contemporary context of the literary tradition he helped to shape, as a living presence in the poetry being written now. The poets brought to the conference their personal experiences of the practice of versifying and of the intellectual, emotional, and economic concerns that make up a poet's life in every generation.

The conference was also notable for the participation of teachers from a broader range of educational institutions than is normally represented at academic conferences. Financial assistance provided by the National Endowment for the Humanities made possible the attendance of high school teachers and their inclusion in the conference program. In discussing their experience of what Keats means, or can be made to mean, to students reading him for the first time in the 1990s, the teachers conveyed a pragmatic sense of what is essential and what is perennial in the poet's work and reminded us that the most influential form of literary criticism is that which takes place daily in the classroom, still the primary environment determining poetry's impact on our society.

More than a hundred years ago, George Gissing wrote, "To like Keats is a test of fitness for understanding poetry."[2] If an appreciation of Keats is really a touchstone of critical acumen, then what was said about Keats at the Harvard conference ought to reveal much about the state of literary criticism in the 1990s, about our current preoccupations as scholars, teachers, poets, and readers of poetry. In general, there was broad agreement and remarkable collegiality among the heterogeneous group who came together to celebrate Keats's art. If there was a division perceptible among the participants, it was one that has been evident in criticism of Keats from the beginning: a divergence between those who are most impressed by the formal achievements of a brilliant and innovative verbal craftsman and those who respond more immediately to the intellectual and emotional meaning of the poetry and to the circumstances of the poet's life. This division became apparent in the very first session, a dialogue of senior scholars discussing "The Endurance of Keats," when M. H. Abrams regretted the tendency of critics to "disembody" Keats by overlooking what is most distinctively Keatsian in his poems—their linguistic novelty and concrete materiality as achievements in sound. Speaking from a different perspective, although not intentionally in rebuttal, Aileen Ward emphasized the emotional consolations to be found in the poetry and spoke of Keats's cultural role as a moral exemplar: "To approach the question of Keats's greatness from a moral rather than a critical perspective may seem a retrograde maneuver," she said, "yet it is validated by the response of many readers today—especially younger or nonacademic readers." The continuing value of such thematic criticism was later illustrated in Ronald Sharp's investigation of the poet's high ideal of friendship as a fundamental concern of the poetry, especially as an ingredient in his thinking about suffering and mortality. Some of the poets at the conference, who might have been expected to be most attentive to considerations of prosody and diction, also seemed to accentuate the poetry's moral resonance. Eavan Boland spoke of Keats's art as one which "values the human above the ornamental and the experience above the expression" and found his primary concern as a poet to have been "not the hubris of language but its responsibilities."

The division between formal and moral evaluations of Keats's achievement became apparent again in a panel discussion titled "The Art of Teaching Keats." Helen Vendler argued that the primary focus of classroom instruction should be the poet's formal accomplishments, his imaginative achievements in the invention of a distinctive style. Then Brenda Walton, a high school teacher from Florida, demonstrated the powerful appeal Keats has for her young students, who, although unsophisticated and inexperienced as readers, easily identify with a young poet troubled by insecurity, sexual embarrassment, and the secret feeling of being half in love with easeful death. When Vendler responded that she was not especially interested in these "therapeutic" uses of poetry, a discussion followed concerning the purpose and the audience for which poetry is written, raising questions as to whether Keats's high stature as a poet depends on what he tells us about human life or what he demonstrates about the craft of writing.

In one sense, of course, this is an artificial dichotomy; poetry has both a formal and a social identity, and Keats can be found in his letters arguing the importance of both. But the difference in emphasis has governed the history of Keats criticism from the start. Probably because poets were the first to "discover" him, early appreciation of Keats tended to emphasize the innovative craftsmanship, especially the invention of a new kind of sensuous imagery. This fascination with Keats's technique seemed to entail a corresponding lack of interest in or awareness of the intellectual content of the poems. "He questioned nothing," George Lewes said of Keats in 1848. "He strove to penetrate no problems; he was content to feel and to sing."[3] It is remarkable that Lewes made this observation in a review of Richard Monckton Milnes's pioneering biography of Keats, which made accessible many of Keat's most thoughtful letters. Nine years later, after Milnes issued the first printed text of *The Fall of Hyperion,* critics could no longer understand Keats merely as a receptor and articulator of beautiful sensations; they had to come to terms with him as a moralist and an aesthetic philosopher. In the past century, academic critics have been nearly unanimous in imposing on Keats's career a narrative that describes a movement from an early poetry of "sensation" to a maturer poetry of "thought," from sensuous escapism to humanist confrontation with what Keats called "the agonies, the strife of human hearts."

Although definitions and evaluations of Keats's achievement have varied with succeeding generations, no change in critical perception has been so remarkable as the one that has occurred since the late 1970s, when Marxist, feminist, and deconstructionist critics began a radical reassessment of the significance of Keats's poetry, asking accusatory questions about his alleged evasion of the social and political realities of his time, investigating the extent of his acquiescence in his society's subordination of women, and even disputing the validity of his judgment regarding the proper style and subject matter of his own verse. Critics have gone so far as to question the conventionally laudatory assessment of Keat's aesthetic and humanistic achievement by challenging the systems of authority and belief that have undergirded the enterprise of literary criticism since the nineteenth century. This suspicious scrutiny of Keats's ideological dispositions and those of the critical establishment that has defined the value of his poetry has produced strikingly new readings of Keats, evoking images of the poet that scarcely resemble the idealistic aesthete or the humanistic hero admired by earlier generations of readers.

This new Keats was much in evidence at the Harvard conference, confronting earlier versions of himself as the critical dialogue progressed. At least four generations of scholars were present, each articulating a different perspective on the nature and importance of the poet's achievement. At times there seemed to be as many Keatses present as there were participants. In his keynote address, Jack Stillinger identified this shift from unity to multiplicity in our perceptions of canonical writers as the most significant development in literary studies in recent years. Even within the various schools of criticism represented at the conference this multiplicity was apparent. Susan Wolfson observed that "as Keats continues to provoke a reading by gender, he resists unified interpretation, reflecting instead the multiple and often conflicting interests that shape its language." Historicists have also discovered a multiple Keats, including one who retreated from politics into insulated realms of art and beauty and another who demonstrates everywhere in his writing a troubled awareness of the historical and social realities conditioning his art.

Testimony to the power of historical investigation to illuminate Keats's poetry came from Debbie Lee, whose examination of contemporary relations between Britain and Africa situated Keats's *Lamia* within a context of imperial economics. In a different kind of historical study, Hermione de Almeida brought her broad knowledge of Romantic science to bear on the **Hyperion** poems, finding in them a convincing demonstration that, far from living isolated in the monastery of his imagination, Keats was in touch with the latest, most sophisticated scientific information available in his time. These studies make significant contributions to what Terence Hoagwood called the "inside story" of Keats's response to his historical circumstances, but Hoagwood also reminded the conference of the importance of the "outside story" of the poetry as a reflection of the socioeconomic forces that governed its production and reception.

The recent wave of historicist and feminist criticism was challenged by David Bromwich, who argued that the ideas on history, politics, and gender that have been absorbing the attention of Keats scholars are at best tangential in assessing his importance as a poet, which must rest primarily on his formal inventions. Recent criticism, Bromwich observed, has been searching assiduously for what Keats explicitly discountenanced in poetry—a moral purpose, a "palpable design" on the reader's conscience or creed. George Steiner offered an even more radical challenge to the comfort of Keats critics when he reminded the conference of the scarcity of good translations of Keats in other languages, an indication that Keats holds a rather lower position in the eyes of other linguistic cultures than he does in ours and, in fact, may not deserve the "major poet" status that the English-speaking world has awarded him.

The new consciousness of Keats's multiplicity comes accompanied inevitably, by a greater tolerance for ambiguity in our sense of the poet's artistic and social identity. Donald Reiman and Elizabeth Jones reminded the conference of the marginality of Keats's cultural position, as he moved uncertainly between the lower and middle classes, living in the suburbs when that social lifestyle was disdained as petit bourgeois and associating with what looks more like a third than a second generation of Romantics. It seems that if we do not know as surely as we once did who Keats was, we are coming to understand him more fully.

In all of the discussions and attempts at analysis and contextualization, the conference participants were aware that the impact of a poet like Keats in some sense eludes critical explanation. The sensuous precision of his verse demands no validation other than the immediate response it provokes; it proves itself, as he said, upon our pulses. Just as Keats was from the start a challenge, a stumbling block, a sign of contradiction that provoked a special kind of uneasiness among the defenders of political and cultural establishments, he continues to assert the claims of poetry against modern skepticism about the powers of language and the intellectual or emotional fulfillment possible in human life. We find ourselves, with all our sophistication, unable to resist his linguistic energy, his personal charm, his prodigal genius. Much of Keats's appeal might be termed "precritical." We are first captured by the sound and rhythm of his verse, by "the electric life which burns within his words"—to adapt Shelley's phrase. Conference participants tended to speak of their first encounter with the poetry as a liberating experience, a revelation of new possibilities of feeling and expression.

Walter Evert's account of his own youthful response may stand as exemplary:

> It was through Keats, now almost a half-century ago, that I
> learned how to *experience* poetry, not merely through emotional
> identification and intellectual analysis but as a miracle of rare
> device, a structure of associative elements in which the building
> blocks of rational order were reassembled to create something
> the mind could grasp and the tongue describe but which never
> existed before, and whose existence changed all the world
> around. . . . And through my fortuitous experience of Keats I
> can say that, for me, the primary experience of poetry is prior
> to all the agendas that poetry may touch upon or lend itself to.

The discovery of Keats is an especially revelatory and formative one for poets; many have had their vocations clarified and reinforced by the encounter, as Philip Levine reported in his moving account of Keats's impact on his life. All readers, whether poets, scholars, or impressionable teenagers, seem to stand equal at the moment of that primary, precritical experience of Keats, the first impression that binds us to him and permanently alters our conception of what poetry can be.

Our attempt to account for Keats, to explain him to ourselves on the two-hundredth anniversary of his birth took many forms; the papers included in this book suggest only some of what was said. The financial constraints of publishing forced on us the difficult task of selecting only a sample of the papers that were delivered. The collection at hand incorporates the thinking of a number of celebrated critics, young and old. It was important to include the insights of younger scholars who are approaching Keats from fresh perspectives; it seemed equally important to consider the tempered judgments of seasoned scholars, such as Walter Jackson Bate, who articulate a cultural wisdom that is gained only from long years of thinking, teaching, and writing about poetry. The conference papers are presented much as they were delivered, some longer than others, some taking the form of informal reminiscences, others presented as research papers with traditional scholarly apparatus. Despite their variety in tone and style, the papers cannot fully reflect the experience of those who attended the conference. To encourage genuine dialogue, panel discussions were scheduled to alternate with the formal delivery of papers. The drawback of this stimulating procedure is apparent now as we prepare the conference proceedings: the discussions that took place are not available in publishable form. The papers collected here can only hint at the range of presentations and the dialogues they provoked. Nevertheless, we are confident that the conversations will have permanent, tangible effects in the new era of teaching and criticism that inaugurates Keats's third century.

It was the Keats-Shelley Association of America that conceived of a Keats bicentennial conference and gave Ronald Sharp and me the privilege of imagining and organizing the event. From the beginning, the Association provided moral and financial support as well as continuing good advice. Jack Stillinger, in particular, has been a wise counselor, sharing his broad knowledge of Keats and the history of Keats criticism. The provost of Rutgers University's Camden campus, Walter K. Gordon, made funding available to support publication of this book. We wish also to thank the National Endowment for the Humanities for a liberal grant that made the conference possible. The John Keats Bicentennial Conference, in its broad-ranging discussion of issues of central cultural importance, demonstrated once again the Endowment's essential contribution to the intellectual welfare of the nation.

NOTES

1. *The Critic,* 4 August 1894, 78–79.
2. Quoted by George H. Ford, *Keats and the Victorians: A Study of His Influence and Rise to Fame 1821–1895* (New Haven, Conn.: Yale University Press, 1944), 174.
3. George Lewes, *British Quarterly Review* 8 (1848): 330.

Multiple Readers, Multiple Texts, Multiple Keats

Jack Stillinger

THE IDEA OF INCONGRUITY

MY TOPIC IS the multiple meanings of Keats's poems, the multiple Keats who created the multiple meanings, and what I think is the real reason for the yearlong tribute of admiration and affection that marked the bicentennial of his birth in 1995. My argument involves a notion of comic misfittingness, and I shall begin with three epitomizing examples in the form of a joke; a poem about Byron, Shelley, and Keats as the Three Stooges; and a typically zany passage from one of Keats's letters.

Here is the joke:

> Two fishermen are out in the middle of a reservoir in a rented boat, catching fish hand over fist, pulling them in as fast as they can get their lines back in the water.
> FIRST FISHERMAN: This is a great place to fish. Don't you think we should mark the exact spot?
> SECOND FISHERMAN: Sure, I'll put an X right here on the side of the boat. [Marks an X on the side of the boat.]
> FIRST FISHERMAN: That's a stupid thing to do, that's dumb. [Pause.] What if we don't get the same boat?

This will sound like something from a standup comedian on television, but in fact I have appropriated it from a piece by my colleague

Mike Madonick that appeared a few years ago in *Cimarron Review*.[1] In Madonick's telling, the fishermen are literary theorists named Jacques and Harold. As their dialogue continues, the two decide that the fish they have caught are not real fish at all, but merely linguistic constructs.

I use the joke to introduce the basic idea of incongruity. Everything funny has a central element of incongruity: something does not fit with something else. In Madonick's joke, the first incongruity is the idea of marking the spot with an X on the side of the boat. There is a second incongruity when the other fisherman thinks putting an X on the boat is dumb for the wrong reason: they might not get the same boat next time. When we add the implied identities of the fishermen—two of the most famous literary theorists of our time—the result is a still more complicated set of incongruities. Why would these two be out fishing together? Why would they say such dumb things?

The poem about Byron, Shelley, and Keats as the Three Stooges is by Charles Webb, who teaches writing at California State University at Long Beach. This was the final poem read at the concluding session of a Keats conference held at the Clark Library in Los Angeles in April 1995. It begins as follows:[2]

> Decide to temper Romantic *Sturm und Drang* with comedy.
> Keats shaves his head;
>   Shelley frizzes out his hair;
> Byron submits to a bowl-cut.
>
> *My heart aches, and a drowsy numbness pains*
>   *My sense, as though of hemlock I had drunk,*
> Keats sighs, his head stuck in a cannon.
>
> *Eternal Spirit of the chainless Mind!*
>   *Brightest in dungeons, Liberty!*
> Byron shouts, and lights the fuse.
>
> *O wild West Wind, thou breath of Autumn's being,*
> *Thou, from whose unseen presence the leaves dead*
>   *Are driven, like ghosts from an enchanter fleeing,*
> Shelley booms, and drops a cannonball on Byron's toe.

The poem continues with further slapstick intermingled with famous lines from the three poets, until—Webb says—

Until they die, too young, careening
  Into immortality covered with flour, squealing,
    Drainpipes on their heads—which explains why
For many years, the greatest poems

  In English have all ended *Nyuk, nyuk, nyuk,*
    And why, reading *She walks in beauty like the night;*
We are as clouds that veil the midnight moon;

  Season of mists and mellow fruitfulness,
    You may feel ghostly pliers tweak your nose,
And ghostly fingers poke the tear ducts in your eyes.

When Webb showed this poem to Beth Lau, his colleague at Long
Beach, she referred him to a similarly ludicrous passage about "Tee-
wang-dillo-dee" from the last of Keats's journal letters to his brother
and sister-in-law in America. In the passage, written on January 17,
1820, Keats is talking about his social life and the people he has seen
lately:

I know three people of no wit at all, each distinct in his excellence—A, B, and C. A is the foolishest, B the sulkiest, C is a
negative. A makes you yawn, B makes you hate; as for C, you
never see him though he is six feet high. I bear the first, I forbear
the second, I am not certain that the third is. The first is gruel,
the second ditch water, the third is spilt—he ought to be wiped
up. . . . Tee-wang-dillo-dee. This you must know is the Amen to
nonsense. I know many places where Amen should be scratched
out . . . and in its place "Tee-wang-dillo-dee" written. This is the
word I shall henceforth be tempted to write at the end of most
modern poems. Every American book ought to have it. It would
be a good distinction in society. My Lords Wellington, Castle-
reagh, and Canning and many more would do well to wear Tee-
wang-dillo-dee written on their backs instead of wearing ribands
in their buttonholes. How many people would go sideways
along walls and quickset hedges to keep their Tee-wang-dillo-
dee out of sight, or wear large pigtails to hide it. . . . Thieves and
murderers would gain rank in the world—for would any one of
them have the poorness of spirit to condescend to be a Tee-
wang-dillo-dee? "I have robbed in many a dwelling house, I have

killed many a fowl, many a goose, and many a man" (would such a gentleman say) "but thank heaven I was never yet a Tee-wang-dillo-dee." Some philosophers in the moon who spy at our globe as we do at theirs say that Tee-wang-dillo-dee is written in large letters on our globe of Earth. They say the beginning of the *T* is just on the spot where London stands. London being built within the flourish, *wan* reach[es] downward and slant[s] as far as Timbuktu in Africa, the tail of the *g* goes slap across the Atlantic into the Rio de la Plata, the remainder of the letters wrap round New Holland, and the last *e* terminates on land we have not yet discovered. However I must be silent; these are dangerous times to libel a man in, much more a world.[3]

At the conference in Los Angeles, Webb read this passage from Keats's letter and then recited his poem about the Three Stooges, adding "Tee-wang-dillo-dee" at the end:

> You may feel ghostly pliers tweak your nose,
> And ghostly fingers poke the tear ducts in your eyes.
> Tee-wang-dillo-dee.

Thus the celebration of Keats in Los Angeles concluded with a tweaking of the nose, tears in the eyes, and Tee-wang-dillo-dee. Everyone was delighted.

Just why was everyone delighted? What is it about such fundamental incongruities as the portrayal of the young Romantics as the Three Stooges and Keats's ridiculous excursus on Tee-wang-dillo-dee that gives people so much pleasure? At the same Los Angeles conference the day before, I had delivered a paper on multiple interpretations of *The Eve of St. Agnes*. When I heard Webb's poem in connection with the passage from Keats's letter, I thought I understood better than I had before why there are so many different and contradictory meanings in Keats's good poems and why these differences and contradictions are received as attractive rather than disturbing or displeasing. I wish to relate this comic misfittingness to some of the incongruities present in Keats's best-liked poems. There are many general names for the phenomenon: *difference, division, disjunction, disharmony, contrariness,* and so on. Whatever name we give it, it is the extreme opposite of the concept of unity that used to be central in our critical activity.

While literary art involves both unity and disunity, literary criticism until a couple of decades ago placed much more emphasis on the former and much less on the latter. We have been constructing unity in works, in groups of works, in single authors, in groups of authors, in whole periods and whole centuries, and making much of these unities, as if we had found them instead of constructed them. Throughout much of its history, the critical enterprise has depended on several kinds of oneness: a single author for each work; a single text of each work; a (hypothetical) single reader for the work—usually each critic individually, positing him- or herself as an ideal reader; and—what obviously follows from the concept of a single reader—a single interpretation of the work, which of course was the critic's own reading.

In more recent thinking, each of these onenesses has been supplanted by a plural. We now have multiple authors, rather than single solitary geniuses. We now acknowledge the existence of multiple versions of important works, rather than just one text per work.[4] Instead of a single real or ideal reader, we have multiple readers all over the place—classrooms full of individual readers in our college and high school literature courses, journals and books full of readers in our academic libraries, auditoriums full of readers at our conferences. All of these readers are constructing interpretations as fast as they read. As one might imagine, when it is a complex work that is being read, the interpretations differ from one another as much as the readers do. It is not possible that only one of the interpretations is correct and all the others are wrong.

I am interested in what happens when each of the principal elements of the literary transaction—author, text, and reader—is viewed as a complex of multiples. My aim is to explain, first, why there are so many different ideas of what a Keats poem means and, second, why we think Keats was a great poet and therefore why we expended so much energy in the celebration of his two-hundredth birthday.

MULTIPLE TEXTS

Keats is not one of the famous revisers of English poetry. Coleridge and Wordsworth, in contrast, were obsessive revisers all their lives; some eighteen separate versions of *The Rime of the Ancient Mariner* have been identified, all of them authored by Coleridge, and there are twenty or more separate texts of *The Prelude*. Keats never had the chance to revise over a span of decades or a succession of editions, the way Coleridge and Wordsworth did. But his practice during his brief life and his comments emphasizing the importance of spontaneity in writing make it seem unlikely that he would have produced radically altered versions of his major poems even if he had lived as long as the older poets.

Nevertheless, virtually all of Keats's poems do exist in multiple texts. For *Endymion*, there are three principal authorial versions: the text of the original draft; the text of the revised fair copy that Keats wrote out for the printer; and the first printed text, representing the words of the fair copy plus subsequent changes made by the publisher and the printer (as well as still further changes made by Keats in response). For each of the other complete long narratives—*Isabella, The Eve of St. Agnes,* and *Lamia*—there is the same array of draft, fair copy, and first printed text. For *La Belle Dame sans Merci,* we have two principal versions in manuscripts by Keats and his friends and the first printing of the poem in Leigh Hunt's *Indicator.* For *Ode to a Nightingale* and *Ode on a Grecian Urn,* there are the first published versions in a magazine, the next published versions in Keats's *Lamia* volume of 1820, and still other versions that differ from these in authoritative manuscripts. For the one hundred poems and fragments that were first published posthumously, there are almost always variant versions in the surviving sources—for example, two different endings of the *Bright Star* sonnet, one with the speaker living on forever and the other with the speaker dying.

Thus, even though Keats was not an obsessive reviser, still he—sometimes with help—created multiple texts of his poems. We are becoming increasingly sophisticated about these texts. We have long known about the two main versions of *La Belle Dame,* and recently Elizabeth Cook in her Oxford Authors *John Keats* printed an alternative text of *The Eve of St. Agnes* in an appendix. Nicholas Roe in his new Everyman *Selected Poems* of Keats is well aware of the existence of competing versions and makes some interesting departures from what has hitherto been the standard.[5]

This multiplicity of versions bears on the constitution of the Keats canon: how many *Eve of St. Agnes*es did Keats actually write, for example? It also has ramifications for the ontological identity—sometimes called the "mode of existence"—of any specific work in the canon: is *The Eve of St. Agnes* a single version of the work or all the versions taken together? If it is all the versions taken together, is the work constituted by the process of its revisions, one after another, or by all the versions considered as existing simultaneously? In addition, multiplicity of versions raises practical questions about the editorial treatment of the poems, the obvious one being which version to choose for reprinting in a standard edition or an anthology when we are allowed only one version per title. It certainly complicates the business of interpretation, as when critics expound composite rather than discrete versions of a work or cite one version to help interpret another (e.g., an earlier text to explain a later one). Finally, multiplicity of texts enters into matters of basic communication, as when critics argue about significant details in a work but in fact are using different versions of the work and therefore may be considered to be referring to different works.

But this is enough about multiple texts for present purposes. I wish to turn to a more problematic element of the transaction.

MULTIPLE READERS AND THEIR MULTIPLE READINGS

As everyone knows, there have been a great many readers of Keats's poems—many hundreds of thousands—over the past 180 years. What makes multiple reading a professional problem is that each reader has an experience of the poems that is different in some respects from the experiences of all the other readers; this produces many different personal readings. When the readings are publicly described, for example in classroom discussions, lectures, conference papers, and journal articles, many different interpretations are being launched into the air.

This situation has been widely acknowledged only recently. In the golden age of literary criticism, by which I mean the last couple of decades of the nineteenth century and the first sixty or seventy years of the twentieth century, virtually everybody's professional work was based on a simple notion of a single perfect text and a single ideal reader. The interaction of a single reader with a single text produced a single (most nearly correct) interpretation. As criticism progressed in its treatment of any particular work, the first ideal reader was supplanted by a second ideal reader, the first having been found to be wrong (or less nearly correct than the second), and then the second was supplanted by a third, and so on. The result, historically, has been that readers succeeded readers, one after another, but still there was always just one text and one reader.

I shall give some examples from criticism of *The Eve of St. Agnes*. For the first 130 years after it was published, readers viewed the poem mainly as a series of pretty pictures—a rich Romantic tapestry, as it was called by some critics, beginning with Leigh Hunt in Keats's own time.[6] The pretty pictures were the Beadsman praying in his chapel, Porphyro entering the castle, Porphyro and Angela sitting by the fireplace, Madeline and Angela meeting on the stairs, Madeline undressing in her bedchamber, Madeline praying before she gets into bed, Porphyro setting out the banquet, Porphyro and Madeline tiptoeing out of the castle.

Then in 1953 there appeared Earl Wasserman's brilliant and provocative reading of the poem as a metaphysical allegory based on two passages in Keats's letters.[7] In the first passage, Keats compares the imagination to Adam's dream of the creation of Eve in *Paradise Lost*: Adam "awoke and found it truth." This is a type of dreaming, or visionary, imagination, and for Keats it prefigures an earthly happiness repeated spiritually in a finer tone somewhere else. In Wasserman's application to the poem, Madeline is having just such a prefigurative dream when she practices her St. Agnes' Eve ritual: she dreams of the lover she will marry, and then she awakens to find he is there in truth. The other passage that Wasserman uses from the letters is the famous simile comparing human life to a "Mansion of Many Apartments." In Wasserman's interpretation, Madeline's castle represents human life, and Porphyro, passing upward to a closet adjoining her bedchamber and thence into the bedchamber itself, is progressing from apartment to apartment in the mansion of life, on a spiritual journey to join Madeline in some kind of higher (transcendental) reality.

There seemed at the time to be a number of things wrong with Wasserman's interpretation, and I launched my own career as a Keats critic by pointing them out in an essay first published thirty-five years ago called "The Hoodwinking of Madeline."[8] Madeline, when she awakens, is not happy to find a real Porphyro in her bed. Porphyro has been sneaking around the castle like a peeping Tom. Rather than experiencing spiritual repetition in a finer tone, leading to a higher reality, the two principals seem to be having sex, and only one of them is conscious of what is going on. The story is full of echoes of bad happenings in earlier works: the rape of Philomel, Satan seducing Eve, Lovelace raping the unconscious Clarissa Harlowe, and others. I went on in considerable detail, and my essay was well known for a while as the dirty-minded reading of *The Eve of St. Agnes*. When I republished the essay as a chapter in a book, a reviewer commented in verse in the Phi Beta Kappa *Key Reporter:*

> Alack for Madeline, poor hoodwink'd maid—
> By Porphyro then, now Stillinger betrayed.[9]

A decade after "The Hoodwinking of Madeline" first appeared, Stuart Sperry published his fine essay entitled "Romance as Wish-Fulfillment," in which he established Wasserman and me as two extremes of critical opinion on the poem. He charged Wasserman with being too romantically metaphysical and me with being too antiromantically realistic and skillfully steered a middle course between our interpretations.[10] Thus for the next two decades the standard opening for an essay on *The Eve of St. Agnes* was to recite a kind of Goldilocks and the Three Bears litany in which Wasserman was too high-flying, I was too down-to-earth, and Sperry was "just right." This was, of course, always followed by a "but": Sperry was just right in his way, *but* all previous critics, including Sperry, had overlooked such-and-such . . . , which then led into yet another new reading.

The notable thing about this activity is that each successive interpretation of the poem was intended to supersede all the previous interpretations—Wasserman making obsolete the idea that the poem is merely a rich Romantic tapestry; I making quite clear that Wasserman's reading was wrong in all the major particulars; Sperry showing how both Wasserman and I were oversimplifying the important points; and each subsequent critic again putting down an ever-growing body of predecessors. This was the era of single-meaning interpretation, which to some extent continues to the present day.

Since Sperry, there have been a great many readings of the poem. I identified some of them in my lecture in Los Angeles, in a handout titled "Fifty-nine Ways of Looking at *The Eve of St. Agnes*" (see the Appendix). I did not have time then, and of course do not have space here, to describe each reading individually.[11] The readings are grouped into nine thematic categories, each of which contains contradictory versions. Older readings of the poem appear in all of the categories; the more recent ones contributed by deconstructionist, Marxist, and feminist theory appear mainly in the last two sections.

I shall comment on just the final item, "politics of interpretation," as an example of the sort of complication that the list represents. Interpretation is not (primarily) political in the Marxist or feminist sense, but it is political in the more general sense of having to do with power—who gets to say what is going on in the poem. Take the storm that comes up just after Madeline loses her virginity. There are several different opinions about this storm. Madeline seems afraid of it; she thinks Porphyro will abandon her. Porphyro describes it as an "elfin-storm from faery land"—a timely "boon" to help hide their escape from the castle. The narrator says it is a real storm, calling attention to the wind, the sleet, and the icy cold. Then Madeline and Porphyro go out into the storm and have not been heard from since. At this point, the critics take over. One group thinks that Madeline and Porphyro perish in the storm. Another large group believes they live happily ever after in Porphyro's home across the moors. Another group argues that Madeline and Porphyro enter Dante's second circle of hell and are perpetually orbiting the world with other famous lovers who sinned carnally. Still other critics think it does not matter: Madeline and Porphyro would be dead now in any case, because this all happened "ages long ago." And so on.[12]

"Fifty-nine Ways of Looking at *The Eve of St. Agnes*" is just a token array of possible interpretations of the poem. Colleagues to whom I have shown the list and people in my lecture audiences have proposed still others. One freshman said at the end of a lecture that he had always thought the two secondary characters, Angela and the Beadsman, were having a sexual affair. There is nothing in the text to support such an idea, but I told him that it could be number 60 in my list, and later I thought of some reasons why it is not a totally worthless suggestion.

Now I shall try to explain why there have been so many different readings of *The Eve of St. Agnes*. In general, the explanation lies in the nature of the transaction between a complex work and a complex readership. On one hand, we have *The Eve of St. Agnes,* sending out many thousands of impulses of meaning in every direction, so many that the reader cannot possibly take in all of them and therefore has to make a selection. On the other hand, we have a readership that consists of, first, any individual reader (along with the complexity represented by the sum of that reader's personal knowledge and experience at the time of reading) and, second, the combination of all the readers who have ever read the poem taken together simultaneously. Each individual reader will be creative rather than passive while engaged in the activity of reading and will be creative in a way different from all the other readers. That is, each individual reader will assemble a unique combination of selected and emphasized meanings, adding and suppressing according to his or her own creative activity.[13]

So we already have two conditions producing multiplicity of meaning: a large number of readers over a long period of time and an excess of textual meaning. I shall use the opening stanza to illustrate this excess of meaning and what happens in the process of reading.

> St. Agnes' Eve—Ah, bitter chill it was!
> The owl, for all his feathers, was a-cold;
> The hare limp'd trembling through the frozen grass,
> And silent was the flock in woolly fold:
> Numb were the Beadsman's fingers, while he told
> His rosary, and while his frosted breath,
> Like pious incense from a censer old,
> Seem'd taking flight for heaven, without a death,
> Past the sweet Virgin's picture, while his prayer he saith.[14]

Twenty or more ideas and images are evoked by just the first four lines of this stanza. "St. Agnes" carries at least the ideas of saintliness, martyrdom, and virginity. There is "eve" in the sense of evening and nighttime, as well as the more specific sense of the night before a saint's day, and then come bitterness, chill, owl, feathers, cold, hare, limping, trembling, frozenness, grass, silence, flock, woolliness, and fold (this last both a farm structure and a social concept). The next four lines of the stanza contain fourteen more images: numbness, beadsman, fingers, telling (or counting), rosary, frostedness, breath, piety, incense, censer, oldness, flight, heaven, and death. The last line of the stanza has at least three more: Virgin, picture, and praying. Altogether, I count thirty-seven images, each with almost countless possible shades of meaning, in just the first nine lines of the poem.

An individual reader cannot possibly absorb and respond to all thirty-seven of these separate stimuli. So the reader selects some; overlooks, ignores, or suppresses others; and creates his or her own peculiar version of the content of the nine lines. Readers cannot help selecting and creating in this way; it is the main way that people read. And because each reader will put his or her spin on the images thus selected, when the work is complex in the manner of *The Eve of St. Agnes* each reader-constructed version will necessarily differ from every other reader-constructed version. The mathematical possibilities for variation are astronomical. And so we have significant differences in the readings and, if the readers write them up, a considerable accumulation of different readings in the critical literature.

With Keats's poems, there is still another condition in addition to large numbers of readers and the text's excess of meaning, and this is the characteristically Keatsian frequency of ambiguous and contradictory details in the texts. The opening description of the Beadsman can serve as an example. Certain details in the first two stanzas emphasize the Beadsman's piety, patience, and sympathy for the dead who lie about the chapel where he is praying; from these a reader might get the idea that the Beadsman is to be admired. Other details, tending to make him pitiable rather than admirable, stress the Beadsman's joyless self-denial and harsh penance; the fact that he is barefoot is an especially painful detail, given the emphasis on bitter cold in the opening stanzas. The different kinds of detail produce conflicting perceptions of the Beadsman, which in turn have a bearing on the reader's view of important matters that come up later in the poem, because the ritualistic, self-denying Beadsman prefigures the ritualistic, self-denying Madeline in the main narrative. What one thinks of the Beadsman to an extent carries over into what one thinks of Madeline.

For more complicated examples of contradictory detail in the poem, consider these statements about the two main characters:

Porphyro is Prince Charming, on a mission to rescue an imprisoned maiden.
He is a confederate of sorcerers, a worker of evil magic.
He is a peeping Tom.
He is an ardent lover.
He is a rapist.
He is Madeline's future husband.

Madeline is beautiful and desirable, the belle of the ball.
She is hoodwinked with faery fancy, shutting herself off from the real world.
She is a pious Christian.
She is a victim of self-deception.
She is a victim of Porphyro's stratagem.
She is Porphyro's happy bride.

About half of these statements are not congruent with the other half, yet each statement is true in the sense that there is support for it in the text and agreement among some of the readers and critics. Oppositions of this sort are central to the plot, characterizations, speeches, and descriptions. No wonder different readers have different ideas of what is going on in the poem.

In my lecture in Los Angeles I went on at some length concerning the reading process; how Coleridge's concept of unity underlies the activity; how Keats's various statements about reading support the idea of multiple interpretation; and how, despite the fact that we always expect new readings from students and critics, much of our current teaching and writing about literature continues to endorse the traditional goal of single-meaning interpretation. I set forth a practical theory of multiple interpretation and discussed the principal objection that arises whenever one favors a reader-response system of meaning and value: namely, the problem of the validity, or truth, of an interpretation. On what grounds does one decide what is correct and what is not correct? On what grounds does a teacher tell a student that the student's interpretation is wrong? How can literature be a field of knowledge when anybody and everybody can be a player? There are several defenses against this general objection, and I brought in all the ones I knew of, including one I invented myself—the concept of no-fault reading, whereby even the freshman who thinks that Angela and the Beadsman are having an affair is not really doing any damage and could actually, if the discussion were focusing too exclusively on Madeline and Porphyro, be making a positive contribution by shifting the focus to the minor characters and raising questions about what they are doing in the poem.

MULTIPLE KEATS

The remaining element of the transaction is the multiple of authorship, and here I shall be focusing on the responsibility for the excess of textual meaning and abundance of contradictory details illustrated in the preceding section.

Everybody is familiar with the poet's variety and versatility and therefore with the idea of multiple Keatses. There were several Keatses on view in 1995, at the Houghton Library, the Grolier Club in New York, the Dove Cottage Museum in Grasmere, and elsewhere: the Keats of the poetry drafts (produced as if by magic, he told his friend Richard

Woodhouse); the Keats of the boldly inscribed fair copies; the Keats first known to the public in the magazines and the three original volumes; the posthumous Keats, creator of the one hundred poems first published after his death; the personal Keats seen in the privacy of his surviving letters; the Keats who was the beloved friend at the center of what we now call the Keats Circle; the Keats of the various portraits; and the Keats who served as artistic collaborator, providing materials for subsequent nineteenth- and twentieth-century book designers, printers, and binders who created so many beautiful printings of his poems.[15]

These are just the most obvious types represented by the manuscripts, books, and memorabilia in the bicentennial exhibitions. To them we can add many more Keatses both from traditional criticism and scholarship and, more recently, from poststructuralist theory. These include aesthetic Keats, the champion of art for art's sake; sensuous Keats, who burst Joy's grape, with or without cayenne pepper on his tongue, and created some of the most palpable imagery in all of English poetry; philosophical Keats, who described "the vale of Soulmaking" and thought of life as a "Mansion of Many Apartments"; theoretical Keats, the formulator of "Negative Capability" and "camelion poetry"; topographical Keats, the well-traveled tourist who wrote a sonnet while dangling his legs from a precipice at the top of Ben Nevis; and theatrical Keats, the theater reviewer and unproduced playwright. There are also intertextual Keatses, including Spenserian Keats, Leigh Huntian Keats, Shakespearean Keats, Miltonic Keats, Dantesque Keats—the list goes on almost indefinitely. Other Keatses include political Keats, especially in his early poems and letters, but through the rest of his career as well; radical Keats, a more sharply focused political Keats; vulgar Keats, the only canonical male Romantic poet besides Blake who did not attend a university and the one with the lowliest upbringing; Cockney Keats, a more specific tag deriving from his lowly upbringing plus the "Cockney school" articles in *Blackwood's* and, 180 years later, Nicholas Roe's investigations;[16] suburban Keats, a variant of the preceding produced by the research of Elizabeth Jones;[17] effeminate Keats, identified first by reviewers who were his contemporaries and today by Susan Wolfson, Marjorie Levinson, and others;[18] masculine (even macho) Keats; and consumptive Keats, the one who dies movingly and heroically every time we read a biography or make our way to the end of the letters.

The list could go on and on. Still, these multiple Keatses are a random sampling of single Keatses—now one, now another, according to the approach, the method, the occasion, and the texts at hand. I am interested in something a little more complicated.

The phrase "Multiple Keats" in my essay title is meant to stand for an internal complexity in Keats that is constituted primarily by self-division—a sort of unresolved imaginative dividedness between the serious and the humorous, the straight and the ironic, the fanciful and the real, the high-flying and the down-to-earth, the sentimental and the satiric, the puffed up and the deflated. It manifests itself in many places, both in biographical anecdote and in Keats's writings—and in the writings, both in the letters and in the poetry, and in the poetry, both in the frivolous pieces tossed off for immediate amusement and in the most serious efforts that Keats hoped would earn him a place among the English poets. One way of representing this self-division is by referring to various kinds of comedy: the antic, the zany, the farcical, the ridiculous—for example, the illustrations of comic incongruity with which I began this essay.

Somebody in the NASSR (North American Society for the Study of Romanticism) user group recently raised the question of whether Keats had a sense of humor, and responses poured in to such an extent that one got the idea there were hardly any letters and poems in which Keats was *not* in some way being funny. Hundreds of passages in the letters contain puns, practical jokes, self-mockery, and comic description. Everyone has his or her favorite examples. One of mine appears in the last of the letters that Keats wrote during his walking tour in the summer of 1818. The letter is to Georgiana Keats's mother, Mrs. James Wylie, on August sixth:

> Tom tells me that you called on Mr. Haslam with a newspaper giving an account of a gentleman in a fur cap falling over a precipice in Kirkcudbrightshire. . . . I do not remember [any fur cap] beside my own, except at Carlisle—this was a very good fur cap I met in the High Street, and I dare say was the unfortunate one.

At this point, Keats invokes a bit of classical mythology to explain the newspaper account he has invented. The Three Fates, seeing two fur caps in the North, threw dice to eliminate one of them, and so the other fur cap, the one at Carlisle, went over the precipice and was drowned.

Then Keats imagines that it would not have been so bad if he himself had been the loser, provided he had been only half drowned:

> Being half drowned by falling from a precipice is a very romantic affair. . . . How glorious to be introduced in a drawing room to a lady who reads novels, with ". . . Miss So and so, this is Mr. So and so who fell off a precipice and was half drowned." Now I refer it to you whether I should lose so fine an opportunity of making my fortune; no romance lady could resist me—none. Being run under a wagon, side-lamed at a playhouse, apoplectic through brandy, and a thousand other tolerably decent things for badness would be nothing; but being tumbled over a precipice into the sea—Oh it would make my fortune, especially if you could continue to hint . . . that I was not upset on my own account, but that I dashed into the waves after Jessie of Dumblane and pulled her out by the hair.

Six weeks before Keats wrote this, Georgiana had left London to settle in America with her new husband, Keats's brother George. Emigration in those days was a serious disruption of family relationships—in most cases, the family members who stayed behind never again saw the ones who left—and Keats in this letter offers condolences to Georgiana's mother as if her daughter had died. "I should like to have remained near you, were it but for an atom of consolation, after parting with so dear a daughter. . . . I wish, above all things, to say a word of comfort to you, but I know not how. It is impossible to prove that black is white, it is impossible to make out that sorrow is joy or joy is sorrow" (*L*1:358–60). It is at this point in the letter that, without any transition whatsoever, Keats launches into his account of the gentleman in the fur cap falling over a precipice in Kirkcudbrightshire.

This oscillation between seriousness and hilarity, which we find throughout the letters, is one of their chief attractions to readers. Even in his last known letter, written from Rome two-and-a-half months before he died, when he was already leading what he called a "posthumous existence," Keats mentions punning: "I ride the little horse, and, at my worst, even in quarantine, summoned up more puns, in a sort of desperation, in one week than in any year of my life." He ends this letter with a poignantly comic gesture: "I can scarcely bid you good bye even in a letter. I always made an awkward bow" (*L*2:359–60).

There are numerous poems and passages that are openly funny—the early lines about Keats's trinity of women, wine, and snuff; the sonnet celebrating the grand climacteric of Mrs. Reynolds's cat; the whimsical self-description beginning "There was a naughty boy"; the lines about the cursed gadfly; the lines about the cursed bagpipe; the silly dialogue between Mrs. Cameron and Ben Nevis; the Spenserian stanzas making fun of his friend Charles Brown; and the extended self-parody in *The Jealousies,* to name just a few. The comedy in these pieces regularly depends on some kind of incongruous juxtaposition, as in the overthrow of expectation with a punchline. It is characteristically Keatsian to put together things that do not themselves go together.[19]

Keats wrote about this juxtaposing of contraries in the well-known lines that begin "Welcome joy, and welcome sorrow" and are sometimes printed under the title *A Song of Opposites:*

> Welcome joy, and welcome sorrow,
>   Lethe's weed, and Hermes' feather,
> Come to-day, and come to-morrow,
>   I do love you both together!
>   I love to mark sad faces in fair weather,
> And hear a merry laugh amid the thunder;
>   Fair and foul I love together. (1–7)

There are many such comic juxtapositions in poems that are not primarily funny. The opening of the fragmentary *Calidore*—"Young Calidore is paddling o'er the lake"—could be an early smokeable (as Keats would say) example, if we remember that Keats almost always took an ironic view of chivalric trappings. This was the time of the early poetry-writing contests, and it is easy to imagine a situation in which Keats was challenged to write a length of rhymed couplets following from the opening "Young Calidore is paddling o'er the lake." In fact, he wrote 162 lines before coming to a halt, still plotless.

Take the phrase "O bliss! / A naked waist" toward the end of the second book of *Endymion.* This is sometimes cited to illustrate Keats's vulgarity or bad judgment. Endymion has been wandering from cave to cave underground until he arrives at a bower and finds

> The smoothest mossy bed and deepest, where
> He threw himself, and just into the air

Stretching his indolent arms, he took, O bliss!
A naked waist: "Fair Cupid, whence is this?" [Endymion asks]
A well-known voice sigh'd, "Sweetest, here am I!"
At which soft ravishment, with doating cry
They trembled to each other. (II.710–16)

That "Sweetest, here am I!" is pure Chaucer, like something lifted from *Troilus and Criseyde*. Keats is recounting a passionate episode in the poem, with detailed physical description; but even though the narrator gets extremely worked up over what he is describing—he has to stop to invoke Helicon and the Muses—there is no question about the intentionally comic mixture of irony and literary allusion in "O bliss! / A naked waist. . . . 'Sweetest, here am I!'"

Another example from the same poem comes in the middle of book IV, when Endymion is in bed with his newly beloved Indian maiden and his heavenly love Phoebe rises and glares down on the couple:

O state perplexing! On the pinion bed,
Too well awake, he feels the panting side
Of his delicious lady. He who died
For soaring too audacious in the sun,
When that same treacherous wax began to run,
Felt not more tongue-tied than Endymion. . . .
Ah, what perplexity! (IV.439–47)

There are the grotesque images of the dream or nightmare at the beginning of the verse epistle to John Hamilton Reynolds:

Things all disjointed come from north and south,
Two witch's eyes above a cherub's mouth,
Voltaire with casque and shield and habergeon,
And Alexander with his night-cap on—
Old Socrates a tying his cravat;
And Hazlitt playing with Miss Edgeworth's cat. (5–10)

This ridiculous set of allusions leads into one of Keats's most serious considerations of the dangers of overinvesting in visionary imagination. In *The Eve of St. Mark*, another serious poem exploring the pros and cons of imaginative investment, similarly grotesque images adorn both the ancient volume that Bertha reads and the fire screen across the room. The earlier description ends anticlimactically with angels and mice; the latter passage has, among its "many monsters," not only mice again but several kinds of bird and, at the end of the list, the traditional enemy of both mice and birds, a fat cat.

Less central images that are not in accord with their surroundings but probably are there for the value of the incongruity include Porphyro's Pink Panther–like tiptoeing across Madeline's bedroom to check whether she is asleep and the redness of Hermes's blushing ears when, in the first paragraph of *Lamia,* he thinks of the beautiful nymph he is pursuing. (An early writer on the humor in *Lamia* remarks, "There are many other parts of the body which can be described as turning red when the tone is serious—the cheeks, the forehead, the throat, all these can burn with dignity. But not the ears. Red ears are funny.")[20] In *The Fall of Hyperion,* Keats describes himself and the goddess Moneta, standing side by side, as "a stunt bramble by a solemn pine" (I.293).

It does not require a major leap of criticism to go from local incongruities of the sort I have just exemplified to more serious mismatches that are central to our experience of the most important poems. I have already mentioned some that pervade the goings-on in *The Eve of St. Agnes:* Porphyro is the hero of the poem, an ardent lover, a Prince Charming to the rescue, and Madeline's future husband; at the same time, he is associated with images of sorcery, peeping-Tomism, cruel seduction, and rape. Madeline is the beautiful heroine, the belle of the ball, Sleeping Beauty, a pious Christian, and Porphyro's bride; she is also a foolish victim of both Porphyro's stratagem and her own self-deception.

There are statements and situations of doubtful compatibility everywhere one turns in Keats's good poems. Consider the speaker's musing about death in the sixth stanza of *Ode to a Nightingale:* "Now more than ever seems it rich to die, / To cease upon the midnight with no pain, / While thou art pouring forth thy soul abroad / In such an ecstasy!" The richness of this thought is immediately nullified by the realism of mortal extinction: "Still wouldst thou sing, and I have ears in vain— / To thy high requiem become a sod" (55–60). Consider the situation in the fourth stanza of *Ode on a Grecian Urn:* there is a lovingly described procession of townspeople on their way to some green altar—so far so good. Immediately, however, comes the realization that these people will never get to their destination, they will never go back to the town they came from, and their "little town" will be desolate "for evermore." Or take the lines about the happy/frustrated lovers two stanzas earlier in the same poem:

> Bold lover, never, never canst thou kiss,
> Though winning near the goal—yet, do not grieve;
> She cannot fade, though thou hast not thy bliss,
> For ever wilt thou love, and she be fair! (17–20)

These lines do not have to be paraphrased to make the point. In the ode *To Autumn* we get, first, a series of statements about how beautiful the season is; then the realization that all this beauty is dying; and finally (perhaps), if we put these two contrary notions together, the idea that somehow death is beautiful.

At this point it might seem that I am coming dangerously close to the old New Criticism of forty and fifty years ago—the "mystic oxymoron" of Kenneth Burke, for example, and "oxymoronic fusion" of Earl Wasserman.[21] Well, why not? We all learned to read from the New Critics, and we constantly use New Critical methods in the privacy of our classrooms and personal reading. Maybe "mystic oxymoron" and "oxymoronic fusion" are not such bad terms for the kind of authorial and textual complexity I am trying to describe.

The Idea of Canonical Complexity

For conclusion, I shall just point out the obvious: what happens when the two sides, author and reader, are brought together by the text. On one side we have the Keats of the whimsical incongruities and the more serious disjunctions, contraries, and mystic oxymorons: surely a complex multiple authorship, even if it resides almost entirely in the single historical entity John Keats, born two hundred years ago. On the other side we have an incredibly complex readership: all those multiple readers whom I referred to earlier. And we of course have multiple interpretations, the only possible outcome when you combine complex authorship and complex readership.

Physicists these days are writing about complex adaptive and evolving systems.[22] These are not bad terms for the model of reading I am developing. The authorship side of the literary transaction can be considered a complex adaptive system. Authors do read in the process of writing, interpret in the process of reading, and constantly interact with the works they are creating. The text, in the middle of the scheme, is not complexly adaptive. It doesn't do anything; it just sits there (in a manner of speaking) and is done to. But, obviously, it can be considered a complex evolving system, in the sense that it undergoes change every time somebody does something to it. The readership side is an infinitely expanding activity of further complex adaptive systems. Each individual reader is a center of virtually infinite possibilities for imaginative response in the process of reading, and there is an infinite number of individual readers (past, present, and future), each responding differently from all the others.

When we combine these complexities, what we have, to get back to the terminology of English departments, is nothing less than a canonical work and a canonical author. It is the nature of canonical works to have more meanings than any one reader can possibly take in at a reading and therefore to be, for all practical purposes, interpretively inexhaustible. In physics, the complexity of something is defined by the number of words (or propositions or equations) that are required to describe it: the simpler the entity, the shorter the description; the more complex, the longer the description. My "Fifty-nine Ways" is just a tip-of-the-iceberg example of what it would take to describe the meaning of *The Eve of St. Agnes*.

Who is ultimately responsible for this grand complexity of author, text, and reader? I believe the one indispensable element is the author. The reader's interpretive constructions, however infinite and inexhaustible, have to begin with materials already in the text waiting for the reader to come along. It is the author who put them there. I think it is above all because Keats provided so many, and such complicated, details—the starting materials for the fifty-nine (fifty-nine hundred?) ways of reading *The Eve of St. Agnes* and the rest of the good poems—that we made so much of him in the celebrations of his two-hundredth birthday. It is not a bad achievement for somebody who had to quit writing entirely at the age of twenty-three.

APPENDIX

Fifty-nine Ways of Looking at *The Eve of St. Agnes*

Love, Sex, Marriage

1. Human love (a celebration of love overcoming all obstacles)
2. Keats's love life

3. Keats's love specifically for Fanny Brawne
4. Celebration of sexual love
5. Celebration of Christian marriage
6. Erotic love versus religious purity
7. Sexual politics I: Porphyro as the peeping Tom/rapist, Madeline as the victim
8. Sexual politics II: Madeline as the seducer, Porphyro as the victim (a husband caught at last!)

Magic, Fairy Tale, Myth

9. Romance, enthrallment, enchantment
10. Sleeping Beauty
11. Porphyro as liberator of Madeline
12. Porphyro as vampire
13. The triumph of fairy over Christian religion
14. Initiation and transformation of maiden into mother
15. A version of Joseph Campbell's monomyth
16. The Fortunate Fall
17. Masturbatory ritual

Imagination

18. Authenticity of dreams
19. The visionary imagination succeeding (celebration)
20. The visionary imagination failing miserably (skepticism)
21. Porphyro's creative (seizing, adaptive) imagination
22. Contrast (or conflict) of two kinds of imagination
23. The hoodwinking of *everyone* (Beadsman, Angela, Madeline, Porphyro, the kinsmen and revelers)

Wish-Fulfillment (subhead of the preceding)

24. Narrative of desire
25. Fantasy of wish-fulfillment
26. Successful merging of romance and reality, or of beauty and truth

Poetry, Art, Creativity

27. Parable (allegory) of literary creativity
28. Antiromance; illustration of the limitations of romance

29. Remake of *Romeo and Juliet* I: imitation
30. Remake of *Romeo and Juliet* II: modernization ("tough-minded 'modern' recasting" as in *Isabella*)
31. Exercise in Gothicism
32. Satire on (parody of) Gothicism
33. Completion of Coleridge's *Christabel*
34. Rich Romantic tapestry
35. Pure aestheticism: art is the only thing that matters

Religion

36. Religion of experience
37. Religion of beauty
38. Love as a religious sacrament
39. Keats's attack on religion
40. Ironic version of the Annunciation
41. Parody of a saint's life
42. Paganism versus religion; the triumph of old religion over Christianity

Human Experience More Generally

43. Mortality and Madeline's fall from innocence
44. Tragedy
45. The inconsequentiality of human life (death takes all)

Epistemology, Ambiguity

46. Uncertainty of the phenomenal world
47. The semiotics of vision (looking, gazing); scopophilia
48. Ambiguousness of idealism and reality
49. Poem of disjunctions, equivocation—open-endedness in the extreme
50. Poem about speech, language, communication (and their unreliability)
51. Poem about the weather, the seasons, day and night, etc. (phenomenological reading)

Politics

52. Family politics (the *Romeo and Juliet* situation, with emphasis on social conflict)

53. The rottenness of aristocratic society (*Hamlet* theme)
54. The crisis of feudalism (feudal decay, mercantile ascendancy, disruption of the class system)
55. Dynastic oppression (Madeline the victim)
56. Patriarchal domination of women (ditto)
57. Keats's disparagement of women (characters and readers alike)
58. Poem about escape—from the castle, from family and/or society, from reality (etc.)
59. Politics of interpretation: who gets to say what things mean (Madeline? Porphyro? the narrator? the critic? the teacher? the reader?)

NOTES

This essay is the basis of a book just completed, entitled *Reading "The Eve of St. Agnes": The Multiples of Complex Literary Transaction.*

1. Michael David Madonick, "The Pirate Map," *Cimarron Review* 103 (April 1993): 83–85.
2. Charles H. Webb, "Byron, Keats, and Shelley." I am much obliged to the author for permission to quote from the version read at Los Angeles.
3. *The Letters of John Keats: 1814–1821,* ed. Hyder E. Rollins (Cambridge, Mass.: Harvard University Press, 1958), 2:245–47. Quotations of Keats's letters are from this edition, abbreviated *L* in text; volume and page numbers are given in text. I have slightly modernized quotations from the letters, partly in the interest of readability and partly to promote a new way of presenting old letters. A brief rationale may be found in my foreword to *John Keats: Letters from a Walking Tour* (New York: Grolier Club, 1995).
4. For recent examples of these newer lines of thinking, see my *Multiple Authorship and the Myth of Solitary Genius* (New York: Oxford University Press, 1991) and *Coleridge and Textual Instability: The Multiple Versions of the Major Poems* (New York: Oxford University Press, 1994).
5. *John Keats,* ed. Elizabeth Cook (Oxford: Oxford University Press, 1990), 544–54; *John Keats: Selected Poems,* ed. Nicholas Roe (London: J. M. Dent, 1995).
6. Reviewing Keats's 1820 volume in the *Indicator,* Hunt described the poem as "rather a picture than a story" (*Keats: The Critical Heritage,* ed. G. M. Matthews [New York: Barnes and Noble, 1971], 172). The idea gets general support from Keats's own comments in a letter to John Taylor dated November 17, 1819, concerning "colouring" and "drapery" in the poem (*L*2:234).
7. Earl R. Wasserman, *The Finer Tone: Keats' Major Poems* (Baltimore: Johns Hopkins Press, 1953). Wasserman drew especially on Keats's letter to Benjamin Bailey dated November 22, 1817, and his letter to John Hamilton Reynolds dated May 3, 1818 (*L*1:183–87, 275–83).
8. "The Hoodwinking of Madeline: Skepticism in *The Eve of St. Agnes,*" *Studies in Philology* 58 (1961): 533–55; reprinted in *The Hoodwinking of Made-*

line and Other Essays on Keats's Poems (Urbana: University of Illinois Press, 1971), 67–93.

9. Richard Harter Fogle, *Key Reporter* 38 (Fall 1972): 5.

10. Stuart M. Sperry, "Romance as Wish-Fulfillment: Keats's *The Eve of St. Agnes,*" *Studies in Romanticism* 10 (1971): 27–43; revised in Sperry's *Keats the Poet* (Princeton, N. J.: Princeton University Press, 1973), 198–220.

11. Each item represents a considered statement of what the poem is about, and most have been developed at article or book length in the accumulating criticism. Proper documentation, even without explanatory discussion, would double the size of this essay; many of the items have multiple sources (another multiple!). I shall remedy the omission in my forthcoming book.

12. The question of closure was first raised significantly by Herbert G. Wright, "Has Keats's 'Eve of St. Agnes' a Tragic Ending?" *Modern Language Review* 40 (1945): 90–94. Scores of critics have registered their opinions on the matter since then.

13. The principal critics whom I draw on are the usual array of now-classical reception theorists—Stanley Fish, Norman Holland, David Bleich, Wolfgang Iser, Umberto Eco, among others—but especially Louise M. Rosenblatt, who published a major work on reader response sixty years ago, *Literature as Exploration* (1938; 5th ed., New York: Modern Language Association, 1995). Rosenblatt has been a tremendous influence on the teaching of literature in the schools and is cited everywhere by reading specialists in colleges of education; she has only recently begun to be noticed in university English departments. Her most important work relevant to the present essay is *The Reader, the Text, the Poem: The Transactional Theory of the Literary Work* (Carbondale: Southern Illinois University Press, 1978).

14. *The Poems of John Keats,* ed. Jack Stillinger (Cambridge, Mass.: Harvard University Press, Belknap Press, 1978). All quotations of Keats's poetry are from this edition; line numbers are given in text.

15. Some of this is recorded in *John Keats, 1795–1995, with a Catalogue of the Harvard Keats Collection* (Cambridge, Mass.: Houghton Library, 1995); *John Keats: Bicentennial Exhibition, September 19–November 22, 1995* (New York: Grolier Club, 1995); and Robert Woof and Stephen Hebron, *John Keats* (Grasmere, England: Wordsworth Trust, 1995).

16. See especially Nicholas Roe's *John Keats and the Culture of Dissent* (Oxford: Clarendon Press, 1997).

17. Elizabeth Jones, "The Suburban School: Snobbery and Fear in the Attacks on Keats," *Times Literary Supplement,* October 27, 1995, 14–15; "Keats in the Suburbs," *Keats-Shelley Journal* 45 (1996): 23–43 (and see Jones's essay in the present volume).

18. Susan J. Wolfson, "Feminizing Keats," in *Critical Essays on John Keats,* ed. Hermione de Almeida (Boston: G. K. Hall, 1990), 317–56; Wolfson, "Keats and the Manhood of the Poet," *European Romantic Review* 6 (1995): 1–37; Marjorie Levinson, *Keats's Life of Allegory: The Origins of a Style* (Oxford: Basil Blackwell, 1988).

19. The most useful criticism on this topic is Martin Halpern's "Keats and the 'Spirit that Laughest,'" *Keats-Shelley Journal* 15 (1966): 69–86.

20. Georgia S. Dunbar, "The Significance of the Humor in 'Lamia,'" *Keats-Shelley Journal* 8 (1959): 19.

21. Kenneth Burke, "Symbolic Action in a Poem by Keats," *Accent* 4 (1943): 30–42, reprinted in Burke's *A Grammar of Motives* (New York: Prentice-Hall, 1945), 447–63; Wasserman, *The Finer Tone*, 13–62.

22. See, for example, Murray Gell-Mann, *The Quark and the Jaguar: Adventures in the Simple and the Complex* (New York: W. H. Freeman, 1994).

Keats's Poems

The Material Dimensions

———◆———

M. H. ABRAMS

THE CHIEF CONCERN of modern critics of Keats has been with the semantic dimension of his poems—their component meanings; their thematic structures; and what, in a well-known essay, Douglas Vincent Bush called "Keats and His Ideas."[1] This was the primary issue for the New Critics of the midcentury, who read Keats's poems with the predisposition to find coherence, unity, and ironies; it is no less the issue for poststructural theorists, who read the poems with the predisposition to find incoherence, ruptures, and aporias. The concern with semantics is understandable, for Keats was a remarkably intelligent poet, almost without parallel in the rapidity with which he grasped, elaborated, and deployed philosophical and critical concepts. To deal with Keats's poems exclusively on the ideational level, however, is to disembody them and so to delete what is most characteristic about them. My aim in this essay is to put first things first: What is the immediate impact of reading a passage by Keats? And by what features do we identify the passage as distinctively Keatsian?

I

Consider the following lines from Keats's poems:

> My heart aches, and a drowsy numbness pains
> My sense, as though of hemlock I had drunk.

> From silken Samarcand to cedar'd Lebanon.

36

Singest of summer in full-throated ease.

> whose strenuous tongue
> Can burst Joy's grape against his palate fine.

Thy hair soft-lifted by the winnowing wind.

'Mid hushed, cool-rooted flowers, fragrant-eyed.[2]

The passages differ in what they signify, but we can say about all of them, as about hundreds of other lines, that if we were to meet them running wild in the deserts of Arabia, we would instantly cry out, "Keats!" On what features does this recognition depend?

Robert Frost used the word "sound" to describe the perceived aspect of a poem that is distinctive for each poet: "And the sound rises from the page, you know, a Wordsworthian sound, or a Keatsian sound, or a Shelleyan sound. . . . The various sounds that they make rise to you from the page."[3] The term is helpful, but it needs to be unpacked. In the current era of semiotics and Derrida's warnings against "phonocentrism," we commonly refer to literary works as "*écriture*" and to poems as "texts." The material medium of poetry, however, is not the printed word. To think so is a fallacy—a post-Gutenberg fallacy of misplaced concreteness. Yet neither is the poetic medium a purely auditory sound as such. The material medium (in current parlance, "the material signifier") of a poem is speech, and speech consists of enunciated words, so that the sound of a poem is constituted by speech-sounds. And we don't—we can't—hear speech-sounds purely as sounds. Instead what we hear (to use Derrida's apt phrase) is "always already," and inseparably, invested with two nonauditory features. One of these is the significance of the words, phrases, and sentences into which the speech-sounds are conjoined. The other is the physical sensation of producing the speech-sounds that we hear or read. For when we read a poem slowly and with close attention, even if we read it silently to ourselves, the act involves—often below the level of distinct awareness—the feel of enunciating the words of the poem by remembered, imagined, or incipient movements and tactile sensations in the organs of speech, that is, in the lungs, throat, mouth, tongue, and lips. Because this feature, although essential to the full experience of a poem, has been neglected in literary criticism, I want to dwell for a while on the material, articulative aspect of Keats's language.

In taking pains, as Keats once said, to make a poem read "the more richly,"[4] he characteristically manages his language in such a way as to bring up to, or over, the verge of an attentive reader's consciousness what it is to form and enunciate the component speech-sounds. He makes us sense, for example, the changing size and shape of our mouth and the configuration of our lips as we articulate a vowel; the forceful expulsion of breath that we apprehend as syllabic stress; the vibration or stillness of our vocal chords in voiced or unvoiced consonants; the tactile difference between a continuant consonant and a stopped (or "plosive") consonant; and in the pronunciation of the various consonants, the movements of our lips and gestures of our tongue. Keats also makes us aware, as we pronounce consonants, of the touch of our tongue to the roof of the mouth or upper gum, and the touch of our lower lip to the teeth or (in labial consonants) of our lower lip on the upper lip. It is not possible to extricate with any precision the role of enunciation from those of sound and significance in the overall experience of a poem. It is evident, however, that Keats, by using long vowels, continuant consonants, and consecutive strong stresses to slow the pace at which we read, heightens our attention to the palpability of his material signifiers, and makes their articulation, juxtaposition, repetition, and variation into a richly sensuous oral activity. Consider the beginning of *Ode to a Nightingale:*

> My heart aches, and a drowsy numbness pains
> My sense, as though of hemlock I had drunk. (1–2)

In such passages, Keats enforces the realization that a poem, like other works of art, is a material as well as a significant thing; its significance is apprehended only by being bodied forth, and the poem's body is enunciated speech, which has a complex kinetic and tactile as well as auditory physicality. Of all the forms of art, furthermore, the material base of poetry, whether spoken or sung, is the most intimately human, because it is constituted solely by our bodily actions, and because its vehicle is the breath of our life.

When discussing poems, we tend to attribute to the sound—the purely auditory qualities—of the words what are in much greater part the effects of enunciating the words conjointly with understanding the reference of the words. For example, in the line from *The Eve of St. Agnes,*

> From silken Samarcand to cedar'd Lebanon (270),

we say that the words are euphonious—that is, they sound good. But they sound good to the ear only because, meaning what they do, they feel good in the mouth; their pleasantness, as a result, is much more oral than auditory. It is a leisurely pleasure to negotiate the sequence of consonants in "cedar'd Lebanon": the oral move from *r* to *d* to *l*, concluding in the duplicated *n*s, feels like honey on the tongue. And it is only because we articulate the phrase while understanding its references that we seem to hear in this line the susurrus of the silks from Samarcand.

All poets more or less consciously make use of the enunciative dimension of language, but Keats exceeds his predecessors, including his masters Spenser, Shakespeare (the Shakespeare of the sonnets), and Milton, in the degree and constancy with which he foregrounds the materiality of his phonic medium. In this aspect he also exceeds his successors, except perhaps Gerard Manley Hopkins, who stylized features he had found in Keats to stress the artifice of his coined compounds, repetitions and gradations of speech-sounds, and sequential strong stresses:

> Though worlds of wanwood leafmeal lie.[5]

Keats's awareness of the orality of his medium seems clearly connected to his sensitivity to the tactile and textural, as well as gustatory, qualities of what he ate or drank. For example, in a letter to his friend Charles Wentworth Dilke, he suddenly breaks off to say:

> Talking of Pleasure, this moment I was writing with one hand, and with the other holding to my Mouth a Nectarine—good god how fine—It went down soft pulpy, slushy, oozy—all its delicious embonpoint melted down my throat like a large, beatified Strawberry. I shall certainly breed. (*L*2:179)[6]

In our cultural moment of trickle-down Freudianism, Keats's orality of course invites charges of regression to the infantile stage of psychosexual development. Such speculations, I think, in no way derogate from his poetic achievement. A thing is what it is, and not another thing to which it may be theoretically reduced. Keats's remarkable sensible organization generated distinctive qualities of a great and original poetry, for which we should be grateful, whatever our opinion of its psychological genesis.

Keats's exploitation of the component features of a speech-utterance (oral shape, gesture, directionality, pace, and tactile sensations) helps account for another prominent aspect of his poetic language: its iconic quality. By "iconic" I mean the impression we often get, when reading Keats's poems, that his verbal medium is intrinsically appropriate to its referents, as though the material signifier shared an attribute with what it signifies. Alexander Pope, in a noted passage in *Essay on Criticism,* said that in poetry "the sound must seem an echo to the sense."[7] As Pope's own examples show, this echoism is by no means limited to ono-matopeia. Keats's iconicity is sometimes such a seeming mimicry of sound by sound: "The murmurous haunt of flies on summer eves" (*Ode to a Nightingale* [50]) and "The silver, snarling trumpets 'gan to chide" (*The Eve of St. Agnes* [31]), for example. But sound mimicry is only one of many types of utterance mimicry in Keats. Take, for example, his notorious description, in his early poem *Endymion,* of what it feels like to kiss

Those lips, O slippery blisses. (II.758)

Even after Christopher Ricks's acute and often convincing casuistry with respect to the morality and psychology of embarassment in Keats's poetry,[8] many of us continue to find this line off-putting. This is not, I think, because Keats's phrase, in what Ricks aptly calls his "unmisgiv-ing" way, signifies the moist physicality of an erotic kiss, but because the act of enunciating the line is too blatantly a simulation of the act it signifies, in the lip-smacking repetitions, amid sustained sibilants, of its double-labial stops. The blatancy is magnified by the effect of mor-pheme symbolism, that is, frequently recurrent combinations of speech-sounds in words that overlap in what they signify. In this instance, the iconicity of the *sl* combinations, heightened by the internal rhyme in "those lips" and "O slippery," is accentuated to the point of caricature by the underpresence of related sound-and-sense units such as "slither" and "slide," even, one must admit, "slobber" and "slurp."

But Keats is always Keatsian, and the oral gesture and sensation mimicry in his early and less successful passages remains the condition, subdued and controlled, of his later writing at its best. In the line "Singest of summer in full-throated ease" (10) from *Ode to a Nightin-gale,* the unhurried ease of articulating the open back vowels and the voiced liquids *r* and *l* in the spondaic "full-throated" is sensed, fully and deeply, within the resonant cavity of the throat to which the words refer. In Keats's description (in *Ode on Melancholy*) of one

> whose strenuous tongue
> Can burst Joy's grape against his palate fine,

the plosive onset and muscular thrust of the tongue in uttering the heavily stressed "burst" duplicates the action of the tongue in crushing a grape, while, in enunciating the phrase "his palate fine," the touch of the blade of the tongue, in forming the consonants *l* and *n*, is felt on the palate that the words designate. In the line "as though of hemlock I had drunk" from *Ode to a Nightingale,* to articulate the word "drunk" is to move with the vowel *u* from the frontal consonant *d* back and down through the mouth and throat, by way of the intermediate *r* and *n*, to close in the glottal stop *k*, in an act that simulates the act of swallowing that the word denotes. The effect is heightened by the anticipation of this oral gesture in the second syllable of "hemlock" and by its repetition in the following rhyme word, "sunk": "and Lethe-wards had sunk."

An instance that is subtler and more complex is Keats's description in *Ode to Autumn* of a personified Autumn sitting careless on a granary floor,

> Thy hair soft-lifted by the winnowing wind. (15)

The exquisite aptness of this utterance to what it signifies is in part the effect of its changing pace and rhythm: the slow sequential stresses in "háir sóft-liftĕd" give way to fast-moving anapests—"sóft liftĕd bў thĕ wínnŏwĭng wínd"—in a way that accords with the desultory movement of the wind itself, as this is described in the next stanza of the poem. But the iconicity is to a greater degree the effect of the pressure and sensation of the inner airstream, the breath, that is sensed first in the throat in the aspirated (i.e., air produced) *h* in "hair," then between the tongue and hard palate in the aspirated *s*, and on to the upper teeth and lower lip in the aspirated *f*s of "soft-lifted," to become most tangible when the air is expelled through the tensed lips to form the *w* that occurs no fewer than three times—each time initiating the puff of air that forms the syllable *win*—in the two words that denote the outer airstream, "winnowing wind."

II

The conspicuous materiality of Keats's linguistic medium accords with the dense materiality of the world that his poems typically represent. In the line about bursting Joy's grape, for example, Keats converts an abstract psychological observation—only someone capable of the most intense joy can experience the deepest melancholy—into the specifics of eating a grape. And in this line from *Ode to Psyche,*

'Mid hushed, cool-rooted flowers, fragrant-eyed. (13)

the references of the seven words, themselves so richly sensuous to utter, run the gamut of the senses of hearing, sight, odor, and touch (a touch involving both temperature and kinetic thrust in the spondaic compound "cool-rooted"). The materiality of Keats's representations, however, seems to run counter to his frequent practice, when referring to poetry in his letters, of applying to the imaginative process and its products such terms as "ethereal," "spirit," "spiritual," "empyreal," and "essence." In the traditional vocabulary of criticism, such terms have commonly been indicators of a Platonic philosophy of art, and this fact has led some commentators to claim that Keats—at least through the time when he wrote *Endymion*—was a Platonist in his theory about poetry, which he conceived as aspiring to transcend the material world of sense experience.

Platonic and Neoplatonic idealism is a philosophy of two worlds. One is the material world perceived by the human senses—a world of space, time, and contingency that is regarded as radically deficient because subject to change, loss, corruption, and mortality. To this the Platonist opposes a transcendent otherworld, accessible only to the spiritual vision. The otherworld is the locus of ultimate human desire because, since it consists of immaterial essences that are outside of time and space, it is unchanging, incorruptible, and eternal.

In an enlightening discovery, Stuart Sperry, followed by other scholars, showed that Keats imported "essence," "spirit," "spiritual," "ethereal," and related terms not from Platonizing literary theorists, but from a very different linguistic domain. In Keats's time, they were standard terms in a natural science, chemistry, in which Keats had taken two courses of lectures during his medical studies at Guy's Hospital in the years 1815 and 1816.[9] In the chemical experiments of the early nineteenth century, the terms were applied to various phenomena, and especially to the basic procedures of evaporation and distillation. When a substance was subjected to increasing degrees of heat (for which the technical term was "intensity"), it was "etherealized," or refined; in this process, it released volatile substances called "spirits" and was purified into its "essences," or chemical components. The crucial fact, however, is that the products at the end of this process remain, no less than the substance at its beginning, entirely material things, except that they have been refined into what Keats called the "material sublime" (*To J. H. Reynolds, Esq:* [69]). ("Sublime" and "sublimation," as Sperry points out, were the terms for "a dry distillation.")[10] The technical vocabulary of chemistry, that is, provided for Keats's quick intelligence unprecedented metaphors for poetry—metaphors that made it possible to represent what he called the "silent Working" (*L*1:185) of the poet's imagination as a process of refining, purifying, etherealizing, spiritualizing, and essentializing the actual into the ideal without transcending the limits and conditions of the material world.

In the opening lines of his early poem *Endymion,* Keats says that he intended the work to be "A flowery band to bind us to the earth" (I.7), that is, to this material world. When copying out the poem, Keats inserted the famed passage (I.777ff) that he described, in a letter to his publisher, as setting out "the gradations of Happiness even like a kind of Pleasure Thermometer"; the writing of these lines, he added, "will perhaps be of the greatest Service to me of any thing I ever did" (*L*1:218). In these crucial but obscure lines, the gradations of happiness that culminate in what Keats calls "A fellowship with essence" have often been interpreted as a Platonic ascent to a supraterrestrial realm. Despite some coincidence of terminology, however, Keats's gradations are entirely opposed to the dematerializing process of philosophical meditation that Plato describes in the *Symposium.* In that dialogue, one climbs "as by a stair" from the beauty of a single material body up "to all fair forms," and then to "the beauty of the mind," in order to reach the goal of ultimate desire, the idea of "beauty, absolute, separate, simple, and everlasting." Keats's "Pleasure Thermometer," on the other hand (as the word "thermometer" implies) measures what he calls the "intensity" (the degree of heat applied to a retort in a chemical experiment)[11] in an imaginative ascent that is metaphorically equated with the stages of refinement in a process of evaporation and distillation. The ascent begins with the pleasurable sensations of physical things; these pleasures are successively refined and purified from all self-concern, until one achieves the selfless stage of "love and friendship." At the application of a final ("chief") degree of "intensity," the grosser (the "more ponderous and bulky") element of friendship is in turn separated out, leaving only, "full alchemiz'd," the purified "essence" that is love. Thus, at the end of the psychochemical procedure,

> at the tip-top,
> There hangs by unseen film, an orbéd drop
> Of light, and that is love. (I.805–7)

As Donald Goellnicht acutely noted, this "orbéd drop" is "an exact description of a drop of pure distillate condensing on the lip of a retort to drip into a beaker."[12]

The point is important, because to Platonize Keats—just as to intellectualize or to textualize him—is to disembody him and thereby eliminate what is most Keatsian in his poems. To read him rightly, we need to recognize that he is preeminently a poet of one world, however painful his awareness of the shortcomings of that world when measured against the reach of human desire. And Keats's one world is the material world of this earth, this life, and this body—this sexual body with all its avidities and its full complement of the senses, internal as well as external, and what traditionally are called the "lower" no less than the "higher" senses. (Remember Keats's relish of a nectarine and of "Joy's grape.") His term for the goal of profoundest desire is "happiness," which he envisions as a plenitude of the physical and intellectual satisfactions in this earthly life, except that they have been purified from what he calls their "disagreeables." And in a "favorite Speculation," he imagines the possibility of enjoyments in a life "here after" as simply a repetition of "what we called happiness on Earth," except (this time Keats resorts to a musical instead of a chemical analogue) that it is "repeated in a finer tone and so repeated" (L1:185).

III

Lest I give the impression that I share the nineteenth-century view that Keats is a poet of sensations rather than of thoughts, I want to comment on the way that, at his mature best, he deals with matters of profound human concern but assimilates the conceptual import of his poems with the material qualities of his spoken language and the material particulars that his language represents.

I concur with the readers for whom Keats's short ode *To Autumn* is his highest achievement. The poem is about a season of the year, but as in his other odes, the ostensible subject (a nightingale, a work of Grecian art, the goddess Melancholia) turns out to be the occasion for engaging with the multiple dilemmas of being human in the material world, in which nothing can stay. In *To Autumn*, however, more completely than in the other odes, Keats leaves the concepts implicit in the choice and rendering of the things, events, and actions that the verbal medium bodies forth. My onetime teacher Douglas Vincent Bush was an acute, as well as learned, reader of poetry, but I think he was mistaken when he described Keats's *To Autumn* as "less a resolution of the perplexities of life and poetic ambition than an escape into the luxury of pure—though now sober—sensation."[13] On the contrary, Keats's poem is a creative triumph because, instead of explicitly treating a perplexity of life, he identifies and resolves a perplexity by incorporating it in a work that presents itself as nothing more than a poem of pure sensation.

A knowledgeable contemporary of Keats no doubt recognized what a modern reader is apt to miss, that *To Autumn* was composed in strict accord with an odd lyric model whose origins go back to classical times but which enjoyed a special vogue from the 1740s through Keats's own lifetime. This is the short ode (sometimes it was labeled a hymn) on a general or abstract topic. The topic is named in the title and formally invoked in the opening lines, where it is personified, given a bodily form, and accorded the status of a quasi divinity, usually female. The poem proceeds to praise, describe, and expatiate on the chosen subject, but it does this, strangely, in the grammatical mode of a second-person address to the personified topic itself. In this genre the direct precursors of Keats's *To Autumn* were the odes addressed to a time of year or a time of day, described by reference to scenes in nature; this subclass includes William Blake's short poems on each of the four seasons, written in the 1770s, in which Blake gives the standard matter and manner of the ode a prominently biblical cast and compacts them into the compass of sixteen to nineteen lines. Within this latter type, it seems to me likely that Keats's particular antecedent was William Collins's *Ode to Evening*, published in 1746.[14] But whether or not Keats remembered Collins while composing *To Autumn*, it is useful to note the similarities between the two poems—in their use of the linguistic medium, their subject matter, and their poetic procedures—in order better to isolate what is distinctively Keatsian in this most formulaic of Keats's odes and to identify the innovations by which he brought what was by his time a stale convention to vibrant life.

Collins's *Ode to Evening* is unrhymed; in place of the standard recurrences of terminal speech-sounds, his invocation exploits the enunciative changes in the procession of the speech-sounds inside the verse line:

> If aught of oaten stop, or pastoral song,
> May hope, chaste Eve, to soothe thy modest ear. (1–2)

That is, Collins foregrounds the oral feel of producing the succession of vowels in the first line and of effecting the transition from the open back vowels (in "hope" and "soothe") to the closed front vowel (in "Eve" and "ear") in the second line.[15] He makes us all but aware, in enunciating these lines, that we produce the different vowels, even though the vibration of the larynx remains constant, by altering the configuration of our mouth and lips and by moving our tongue forward or back. He also brings to the edge of our awareness that the stopped consonants that punctuate these lines are effected by interrupting, with our tongue or lips, the sounding of the vowels: "If aught of oaten stop . . . ."

Collins goes on, always in the mode of an address to the personified evening, to detail selected scenes and events in the declining day, including prominently (as in *To Autumn*) the sounds of insects. Later in the poem he holds constant the time of day and describes the change in a typical evening during each of the four seasons. By an inverse procedure, Keats holds the season constant and describes the changes during the course of a typical day, from the mists of the autumnal morning in the opening line to the setting of the sun in the closing stanza.

These and other parallels however only highlight the differences between the two poems. Collins's linguistic medium is only subduedly physical, and his descriptions are exclusively visual, intangible, and expressly represented as generic items in a conventional eighteenth-century landscape modeled on the paintings of Claude Lorraine. He asks to be led, for example,

> where some sheety lake
> Cheers the lone heath, or some time-hallow'd pile,

Or up-land fallows grey
Reflect its last cool gleam. (29–32)

Keats, on the other hand, makes us feel, in the act of enunciating his words, the very weight, pressure, and fullness that he ascribes not just to the physical processes by which autumn conspires (an interesting word!) with her "close bosom-friend," the virile sun, to "load," "bend," "fill," "swell," and "plump" the vines and trees, but also to their conspicuously edible products. Collins's Eve is young and virginal; she is "chaste," a "Maid compos'd," a "calm Vot'ress" from whom the male sun is segregated "in yon western tent." She is attended by an allegorical retinue of hours, elves, and "Pensive Pleasures sweet" but remains elusively diaphanous, emerging only to merge again into the visibilia of the landscape. "Be mine the hut" that

marks o'er all
Thy dewy fingers draw
The gradual dusky veil. (34–40)

But when Keats's autumn makes a personal appearance in his second stanza, it is as a mature woman who, far from dissolving into the outer scene, remains a full-bodied person who supervises, and sometimes herself engages in, the physical labors of the seasonal harvest.

This leads me to the important observation that whereas the setting of Collins's ode is the natural landscape, the setting of Keats's ode is not nature but culture or, more precisely, the union of natural process and human labor that we call agriculture. Keats's poem was in fact inspired by the sight of a cultivated field just after it had been reaped. "Somehow a stubble plain looks warm," Keats wrote to his friend John Hamilton Reynolds. "This struck me so much in my sunday's walk that I composed upon it" (*L2:167*). In fact, in *Ode to Autumn*, what Keats's descriptions denote or suggest allows us to reconstruct the concrete particulars of a working farm. Before us there is a cottage with a thatched roof around which grapevines have been trained. In the vicinity are the other plantings that provide what Keats calls the "store" of farm products—a grove of apple trees, a garden producing gourds and other vegetables, hazelnut trees, and a partly reaped grainfield. There are also a granary with a threshing floor, beehives, and on a near hillside a flock of sheep with their full-grown lambs.[16] In this Keatsian

version of a georgic poem, two plants are mentioned that are not products of human cultivation, but both are explicity related to the activities
of farming: the autumn flowers (9–11) that are harvested by the bees to
fill the "clammy cells" of the farmer's beehive and the poppies (17–18)
that are cut by the reaper in mowing the stalks of grain that they en-
twine. In the first stanza, even the natural process of ripening is con-
verted, figuratively, into a product of the joint labors of autumn and
the sun, and in the second stanza, the four functions attributed to the
personified autumn all have to do with the workings of a cottage farm
during the harvest: autumn sits on the granary floor where the grain is
winnowed; watches the oozings from the cyder-press; sleeps on a fur-
row that, tired by her labor, she has left only half-reaped; and carries
on her head the basket of grain that has been gleaned in the cornfield.

Most important, finally, is the difference in the overall purport of the
two poems. Collins's *Ode to Evening* is a fine period poem of the Age
of Sensibility that is content to praise, with established odic ceremonial,
the time and natural scenes favored by the lyric speaker, represented in
the first person, who wanders through the poem as a typical penseroso
figure and connoisseur of picturesque and sublime landscapes. He seeks
out not only the "sheety lake" and "time-hallowed pile," but also, in
stormy weather, the hut

> That from the mountain's side,
> Views wilds, and swelling floods,
> And hamlets brown, and dim-discover'd spires. (35–37)

In Keats's *To Autumn*, the lyric speaker never intrudes as a first-person
participant or even by specifying his responses to what he describes.
The descriptions, however, are represented not simply for their sensuous selves, but in such a way as to communicate what is never expressly
said. Keats, that is, concretizes the conceptual dimension of his poem,
which declares itself only by the cumulative suggestions of the phenomena that he describes, the constructions of his syntax, the qualities and
interrelations of the speech-sounds in which he couches his descriptions, and the increasingly insistent implications of the metaphors he
applies to these phenomena in the course of the autumn day.

It is notable, for example, that *To Autumn* ends not in a decisive
closure, but on a triple suspension—in syntax, meaning, and meter:

And gathering swallows twitter in the skies.

The suspension is syntactic, in that the line (set off from what precedes it by a semicolon)[17] concludes a sentence that lists the varied contributors to the music of autumn, in which the only connective is a noncommittal *and;* Keats enumerates the sounds made by gnats *and* lambs, hedge-crickets *and* red-breast; *and* gathering swallows . . . with which the series simply breaks off. The suspension is also semantic, in that "gathering," a present participle used adjectivally, signifies a continuing activity still to be completed.[18] Lastly, the suspension is metrical. The line can be read, according to the metric pattern established in the ode, with five iambic stresses:

And gáthering swállows twítter ín the skíes.

An expressive reading, however, does not stress the inconsequential preposition "in," but renders the line with only four strong stresses:

And gáthering swállows twítter in the skíes.

The result is that the poem closes with an empty fifth beat that we experience as portending something yet to come. The effect, although less conspicuous, is like that of the truncated last line in each stanza of Keats's *La Belle Dame sans Merci:*

> O what can ail thee, knight at arms,
> Alone and palely loitering?
> The sedge has wither'd from the lake,
> And no birds sing.

The multiple suspension, coming so unexpectedly as the conclusion to *Autumn,* is inherently suggestive, and also heightens our retrospective awareness of earlier features of the poem. For example, there is the repeated use of present participles that indicate an ongoing, unfinished process, from "conspiring" in the third line to "gathering" in the last. We become more sensitive to the illusoriness of the bees' belief that "warm days will never cease" (10); to the emblematic associations, in stanza 2, with the scythe of a reaper only momentarily suspended; and to the portent in "the last oozings" of the cyder-press. The ending also sharpens our realization that in the last stanza the sunlit day of the preceding stanzas has lapsed into evening, and that although autumn, as the lyric speaker reassures her,[19] has her music, its mode, unlike that of "the songs of spring," is elegiac, in a tonality established by the gnats (27) who "mourn" in a "wailful choir" (the suggestion is of a church choir singing a requiem) even as the swallows are gathering for their imminent flight south. We come to realize that the poem is from beginning to end steeped in the sense of process and temporality. Critics have often noted the static quality of Keats's descriptions, especially in the second stanza, but the seeming stasis, as the closing line both suggests and exemplifies, is in fact only a suspension on the reluctant verge of drastic change and loss. The precise moment of poise on the verge is denoted by the "now" in line 31. I must have read the poem a score of times before I realized the full poignancy of that word, coming at the end of a sequence of temporal adverbs beginning at line 25: "While," "Then," "and now" . . . the swallows are gathering. *Sunt lacrimae rerum.* What Keats expresses without saying, even as he celebrates the season of fruition, is awareness that in this world such fulfillment is only a phase in a process that goes on "hours by hours"; he expresses also his quiet acceptance of the necessity that this rich day must turn into night and this bountiful season into winter.

To return to the material base with which we began: Throughout the poem the interplay of the enunciated speech-sounds helps to effect—in fact, greatly enlarges—this conceptual reach beyond assertion. The final word of the last line, "skies," is itself experienced as a suspension, in that we need to go no less than four lines back for the word whose speech-sound, in the elaborate odic rhyme scheme, it replicates.[20] That word is "dies"—

> Or sinking as the light wind lives or dies.

Collins applies the same metaphor to the wind in his opening invocation to evening,

> Like thy own solemn springs,
> Thy springs and dying gales,

but "dying gales" was a stock phrase in the poetic diction of Collins's time, and its function in his poem is simply to comport with the pervasive mood of "the Pensive Pleasures sweet." In Keats's *To Autumn,* on the other hand, the wind that lives or dies resonates with a number of earlier elements in the poem; most markedly, it reiterates the metaphor in the phrase "the soft-dying day." These two allusions, reserved for the stanza that ends with the premonitory flocking of the swallows, widens the reach of reference from the processes of the natural world to the human speaker of the poem, for whom living and dying are not, as for the wind, the day, and the season, merely metaphors. The initial allusion to death, however, is oblique and is mitigated by its embodiment in a sequence of speech-sounds that are a delight to utter: "While barred cloúds blóom the sóft-dýing day." The procession is slowed for our closer apprehension by the two sets of successive strong stresses; as we enunciate the line, our awareness of the evolving changes in the seven long vowels (no vowel occurs twice) is enhanced by the slight impediments to be overcome in negotiating the junctures between adjacent consonants; while in the last two words the first syllable of "dying," by a vowel shift forward and up, modulates into "day," even as we realize that although the sunset can color ("bloom"), it cannot impede the death of the day.

Repetition cannot dull the sense of ever-renewing discovery in attending to the interrelations of material medium, metrical pace, syntax, tone of voice, and spoken and unspoken meanings in this marvelous stanza:

> Where are the songs of spring? Ay, where are they?
>   Think not of them, thou hast thy music too,—
> While barred clouds bloom the soft-dying day,
>   And touch the stubble-plains with rosy hue;
> Then in a wailful choir the small gnats mourn
>   Among the river sallows, borne aloft
>   Or sinking as the light wind lives or dies;
> And full-grown lambs loud bleat from hilly bourn;
>   Hedge-crickets sing; and now with treble soft
>   The red-breast whistles from a garden-croft;
>   And gathering swallows twitter in the skies.

Since we are celebrating the two-hundredth birthday of Keats, it seems appropriate to end this essay by situating his poem in the context of his life. *To Autumn* was the last work of artistic consequence that

Keats completed. His letters and verses show that he achieved this celebratory poem, with its calm acquiescence to time, transience, and mortality, at a time when he was possessed by a premonition, little short of a conviction, that he had himself less than two years to live.[21] As it turned out, Keats died of tuberculosis only a year and five months after he composed his terminal ode. He was twenty-five years old. His career as a poet between his first successful poem, *On First Looking into Chapman's Homer,* October 1816, and *To Autumn,* September 1819, was limited to a span of thirty-five months.

NOTES

1. Douglas Vincent Bush, "Keats and His Ideas," *English Romantic Poets: Modern Essays in Criticism,* ed. M. H. Abrams (New York: Oxford University Press, 1960).

2. All quotations of Keats's poetry are from *The Poems of John Keats,* ed. Jack Stillinger (Cambridge, Mass.: Harvard University Press, Belknap Press, 1978).

3. Robert Frost, lecture on the bicentennial of Wordsworth's death (April 1950); transcribed from the tape recording in *The Cornell Library Journal* 11 (spring 1970): 97–98.

4. *The Letters of John Keats:1814–1821,* ed. Hyder E. Rollins (Cambridge, Mass.: Harvard University Press, 1958), 2:106. Quotations of Keats's letters are from this edition, abbreviated *L* in text; volume and page numbers are given in parentheses in text.

5. Gerard Manley Hopkins, *Spring and Fall,* in *Poems of Gerard Manley Hopkins,* ed. Robert Bridges and W. H. Gardner, 3d ed. (Oxford: Oxford University Press, 1948), 8.

6. I take "I shall certainly breed" to signify Keats's awareness that this kind of sense experience was effective in the poetry he composed.

7. Pope, *An Essay on Criticism,* 2.365.

8. Christopher Ricks, *Keats and Embarrassment* (Oxford: Clarendon Press, 1974), 104–5.

9. Stuart M. Sperry, *Keats the Poet* (Princeton: Princeton University Press, 1973), chap. 2. For a detailed treatment of Keats's medical training and its role in his poetry, see Donald C. Goellnicht, *The Poet-Physician: Keats and Medical Science* (Pittsburgh: University of Pittsburgh Press, 1984).

10. Sperry, *Keats the Poet,* 45.

11. Keats's use of "intensity" as the measure of the degree of heat in a process of evaporation is especially clear in his oft-quoted statement that "the excellence of every Art is its intensity, capable of making all disagreeables evaporate" (*L*1:192).

12. Donald C. Goellnicht, "Keats's Chemical Composition," in *Critical Essays on John Keats,* ed. Hermione de Almeida (Boston: G. K. Hall, 1990), 155.

13. Bush, "Keats and His Ideas," 337.
14. *The Norton Anthology of English Literature*, ed. M. H. Abrams et al., 6th ed. (New York, 1993), 2:2465–66.
15. Collins's vowel play brings to mind Benjamin Bailey's testimony that one of Keats's "favorite topics of discourse was the principle of melody in Verse . . . particularly in the management of open and close vowels. . . . Keats's theory was that the vowels . . . should be interchanged, like differing notes of music to prevent monotony" (*The Keats Circle*, ed. Hyder E. Rollins [Cambridge, Mass.: Harvard University Press, 1948], 2:277). For an analysis of some of Keats's elaborate vowel patternings, see Walter Jackson Bate, *John Keats* (Cambridge, Mass.: Harvard University Press, 1963), 413–17.
16. In Keats's draft of *To Autumn*, a canceled line adds a barn to the cottage setting, after line 15: "While bright the Sun slants through the husky barn" (Stillinger, *The Poems of John Keats*, 477). The sacramental aura with which Keats invests the rich yields of the harvest season is suggestive of the rural scenes that Samuel Palmer was to paint some six years later, in the mid-1820s.
17. Although the punctuation varies in the various manuscripts of *To Autumn*, the preceding line ends with a semicolon in the printed text of 1820, which Keats oversaw and for which he may have written out a printer's copy-manuscript. (For this matter, and for the variations between "gathered" and "gathering swallows" below, I am indebted to Jack Stillinger's annotations in *The Poems of John Keats* and to his analysis of the facts in a letter to me dated May 19, 1997.)
18. In this passage Keats very probably recalled the lines in James Thomson's *Seasons*: "Warned of approaching Winter, gathered, play / The swallow-people. . . . / They twitter cheerful" (*Autumn* [836–38, 846], see *The Poems of John Keats*, ed. Miriam Allott [London: Longman, 1970], 654–55). Keats, after some vacillation between "gathered" and "gathering," fixed on the latter form in the printing of 1820. It is notable that Thomson makes explicit the "approaching Winter," whereas Keats, although he names the spring, summer, and autumn, only implies the coming of the fourth season.
19. The quick sympathy with which Keats consoles autumn for her lack of the songs of spring—"Think not of them, thou hast thy music too" (24)—parallels the poignant moment in *Ode on a Grecian Urn* when Keats interrupts himself to console the young lover, frozen in marble: "never, never canst thou kiss,"

> —yet, do not grieve;
> . . . .
> For ever with thou love, and she be fair! (18–21)

20. In *Autumn* Keats added an eleventh line to the ten-line stanzas of four odes he had written in spring 1819 (*Nightingale, Grecian Urn, Melancholy,* and *Indolence*). In these poems, the rhyme in the concluding line is suspended over only three lines. In *Autumn*, the extra line suspends the recurrence of the final rhyme word over four lines.
21. Aileen Ward, *John Keats: The Making of a Poet*, rev. ed. (New York: Farrar, Straus, Giroux, 1986), 185 and 431 n. 4; 199–200 and 432 n. 13b.

The Endurance of Keats

WALTER JACKSON BATE

I TOOK THE PANEL'S assigned topic, "The Endurance of Keats," in its direct sense of meaning: What is there about Keats that has made him endure as both a great poet and a great human being? Trying to explain this in the space of a few pages is like trying to pick up water, from a large barrel, with a fork. It seemed to me that I had only two alternatives. I could, in a series of abstractions, list some of his virtues that have continued to appeal to readers, with everyone here already more than prepared to recite or chant them in unison. Or else I could be briefly anecdotal. I thought you'd forgive me if I did the latter, followed by a brief attempt at the former.

When I entered high school, at fourteen, I encountered Keats in a school reader that contained five or six of his poems. I was especially captivated by *Ode to a Nightingale* and felt I'd never read a poem so wonderful. Looking through a children's encyclopedia that included articles about great writers, I was struck by a remark about Keats: that he was a "poet's poet" and that most poets since his time were drawn to him. That article had been written back in the early 1920s, before the advent of what David Perkins, in a now famous phrase, called "the High Modernist Mode," in the first volume of his authōritative *History of Modern Poetry*. And I later, in college, discovered how true this was of most English and American poets of the nineteenth century, many of whom refined or continued some one aspect of Keats. Later I found that this was especially true of the parents of the "High Modernist Mode." T. S. Eliot in his *early* years was rather severe on the Romantics and yet spared Keats, whom he viewed as unique, as did I. A. Richards,

Eliot's cofounder of the "New Criticism," and as other poets and critics since Eliot and Richards have done.

Also, while still in high school, I picked up a book my father had brought home from the town library—John Dewey's *Art as Experience*. A dry, old, pragmatic Yankee and the guiding spirit of Columbia Teachers College before and after World War I, Dewey thought Keats unique for his insight into art. He cited a mysterious phrase of Keats's about Shakespeare, "Negative Capability," that so interested me that, as a college freshman, I wrote a paper, and later, as a senior I wrote a small thesis with that title, which they liked well enough to publish in 1939 in a series of college theses. In time, I learned that college literature, philosophy, and history teachers were as much drawn to Keats as adolescent freshmen. Why is this so?

Aristotle said that everything has four causes, and I can think of four causes of Keats's endurance, which coalesce into a condensed unity of appeal.

Of course, the first, and what Aristotle would call the final, cause, is the quality of Keats's poetry after he hit his stride at the age of twenty-three. His verse is almost Shakespearean in its felicity and mastery of phrase and presents an astonishing concreteness of image that captures simultaneously the intellectual and emotional imaginations. At the same time, starting with *Hyperion* (when he was twenty-three) Keats showed his sudden brilliance and power in the art of prosody and versification; we must go back to Milton, or at least Pope, to find his superior.

The second cause of Keats's endurance is what is given in the magnificent letters—"certainly," as T. S. Eliot said, "the most notable and the most important ever written by an English poet." Eliot went on to say, "There is hardly one statement of Keats about poetry, which, when considered carefully . . . will not be found to be true; and what is more, true for greater and more mature poetry than anything that Keats ever wrote." Upon considering the letters in addition to the poems, Eliot joined the ranks of those who believed, he said, that "the kind of greatness" possessed by Keats "seems . . . to be much more the kind of Shakespeare," in "contrast to the kinds we have been reviewing" from Sir Philip Sidney to the 1900s. It is interesting to note the diversity of writers who have said similar things about Keats. We can go back further than Matthew Arnold to Walter Savage Landor's clairvoyant remark: "What a poet would poor Keats have been, if he had lived: He had something of Shakespeare in him, and (what nobody else ever had) much, very much of Chaucer."

A third cause is the haunting story of Keat's life itself, and what he was able to do. Samuel Johnson rightly said that the value of biography is what "*comes home to us; what we can put to use.*" We wonder how Keats ever managed to do what he did, starting when he did (for he was not unusually precocious), and not only with all the personal disadvantages he started with, but also with his clairvoyant, even profound, understanding of the dilemma that the modern poet faces, with the intimidating example before us of great poets of the past: a subject I later tried to discuss in a small book on the eighteenth century and the Romantics called *The Burden of the Past.* How did Keats manage to do it?

So that, ever since, whatever the changes in poetic taste, poets and critics have dropped the usual querulousness over poetic idiom and looked with fascination at Keats's career, his experience, his reading, his courage, and his apprehensions—and looked with a kind of suspended hope: the hope of finding out how he ever managed to do what he did. This is indeed what Johnson said is the special value of biography: what *comes home* to us," he said; and "what can be put to use" in this strange adventure we call life.

As if all this were not enough, there is something else that has captured the imagination of so many readers, from the most to the least sophisticated. Keats's youth parallels the folktale of the orphan forced to seek his own fortune more closely than does that of any other major writer in any language. Thus an archetypal familiarity haunts the story of Keats's early years. It is the stuff of Charles Dickens's novels, right down to the law courts of Chancery, where the will of Keats's grandfather was tangled up and not completely settled until more than sixty years after Keats's death. There is even a villain—Richard Abbey, who held the purse-strings on what would have meant so much to the orphaned Keats children. There is also Keats's famous love affair with Fanny Brawne, severed by the virtual exile of the dying young Keats. Finally, the subject of this story from folklore is one of the permanent heroes of literature, courageous, high-minded, and not only deeply but broadly human. To conclude with Keats's own phrase about Shakespeare—which we all know by heart—this is indeed a "Life of Allegory."

The combination of all these things, though he died at twenty-five, has made Keats almost unique among the world's great writers, and therefore of perennial fascination and perennial endurance.

Keats and Endurance

AILEEN WARD

KEATS ONCE HOPED that his friends would honor his memory by drinking "a dozen of claret" on his tomb.[1] The two-hundredth anniversary of his birth may call for a slightly more sober commemoration. We are moved as we note the steady growth of his reputation and the endurance of his poetry through shifting critical tastes; we are also drawn by the attraction of his personality—applauding, for instance, the bravura of his dismissal of the Quarterly Review's attack on *Endymion* with the assertion, "I think I shall be among the English Poets after my death" (*L*1:394). Indeed, the lasting appeal of his work seems to derive from a personal quality almost as much as from a purely poetic one. We are reminded of Milton's insistence that to write enduring poetry, the poet must in some sense be a great poem. If approaching the question of Keats's greatness from a moral rather than simply a critical perspective seems a retrograde maneuver, it is validated by the response of many readers today—especially younger or nonacademic readers—to a dimension of his work not easy to describe but unmistakably felt. One can argue that among the Romantic poets, or even among all English poets up to our own time, Keats is regarded as an exemplar to a unique degree. Poets turning the fateful age of twenty-five often measure their own production against Keats's final achievement: students find in his work, especially when they discover his letters, a character, a living presence, a response to experience with which they can identify, often for the first time in their reading of poetry. Philip Levine recently paid tribute to this exemplary quality when he referred to Keats as "a moral Titan."[2]

It hardly needs remarking that this was not always the case. The prevailing critical estimate of Keats in the 1820s was not as a moral Titan but as either a moral renegade, "a radically presumptuous profligate," or a poetic weakling—one whose works were writ in milk and water, to repeat the quip of Joseph Severn's acquaintances in Rome. Keats paid dearly for his early allegiance to Leigh Hunt, from the slashing reviews of the 1817 *Poems* and *Endymion* to John Wilson's summation of the charges leveled by *Blackwood's Edinburgh Magazine* in 1826: "out-hunt[ing] Hunt in . . . emasculated pruriency," "encrusted with conceit," "flatter[ed] into bad citizenship, and wheedl[ed] out of his Christian faith." The legend of Keats's vulnerability to the Tory reviewers that Shelley launched in *Adonais* did little to redeem him among more sympathetic readers: William Hazlitt and even Hunt lamented his "effeminacy" after his death. These two myths, of "Johnny Keats" the upstart anarchist in poetry and morals and of the pale flower withered by blasts of criticism, posed the challenge that Richard Monckton Milnes met in his 1848 biography with such admirable effect. Perhaps he leaned too far backward in defending Keats's character by stressing his middle-class respectability and his upper-middle-class connections, a view somewhat deflated by Harry Buxton Forman's publication of Keats's letters to Fanny Brawne in 1878. The revelation of this love affair aroused the disgust of Arnold and Swinburne, who denounced Keats as a "sensuous man of a badly bred and badly trained sort," "a vapid and effeminate rhymester" with the epistolary style of a surgeon's apprentice cited in a divorce case, and "the most exclusively aesthetic and absolutely non-moral of all serious writers on record," an "intellectual opium-eater."[3]

This scathing appraisal undercut the Pre-Raphaelites' extravagant admiration of Keats for his sensuous richness and romantic "magic," but Arnold, to his credit, softened his indictment almost at once by praising the spiritual insight of Keats's best poetry; in fact, he ended up by comparing him to Shakespeare. The outpouring of tributes in 1921, the hundredth anniversary of Keats's death, showed he had found his place at last at the forefront of the Romantic poets. A long series of critical studies followed—discussions of Keats's range of mind, his religion, his craftsmanship, and his re-creation of the great tradition of English poetry. In this light, it seemed to matter little that the new poets of the 1930s had no use for him. ("Let's kick out anyone who writes like Keats," Auden is said to have remarked to Spender in discussing plans to start a poetry magazine at Oxford.) The New Critics of the 1940s made an exception of Keats in their general downgrading of the poetics of Romanticism, acclaiming his sense of form and command of imagery. Despite the considerable critical attention paid to his work, however, it was not until 1951, with Lionel Trilling's essay "The Poet as Hero," that a critic raised again the question of Keats's moral character that had so vexed his nineteenth-century commentators.[4]

Ideas of morality have changed greatly since the 1870s, of course, and Trilling's post-Freudian approval of Keats's appetitiveness contrasts dramatically with the Victorians' distress at his cayenne pepper-and-claret extravagances. Trilling's emphasis on Keats's "geniality," along with other critics' commendations of his "Negative Capability," his sympathetic imagination, his capacity for what he called self-annihilation, all point to traits we value highly today, what might be summed up as the liberal imagination in a quasi-political sense. One thinks of Keats's hope that by abjuring disputation and self-assertion "every human might become great" and society itself become "a grand democracy of Forest Trees" (*L*1:232). But this laudable stress on Keats's openness to ideas and tolerance for ambiguity tends to obscure something more tough-minded in his nature—what might be called "achieved identity," the end-product of soul-making.

Trilling implied this steadfast and assertive aspect of Keats's character in viewing him as "Hero," and "endurance" seems as good a word to describe it as any other, with its connotation of firmness in contrast to his more often noted flexibility of mind. So with a shift in emphasis, the idea of the persistence or endurance of Keats may be refocused from the critical question of the enduring qualities of his work to a moral question of the quality of character it reveals. It should be stated at the start, however, that Keats rarely used the word "endurance" or "endure,"[5] preferring "bear" or "bear up" as the occasion demanded (*L*1: 139; *L*2:186, 351). It is curious that the most memorable of all occurrences of the word in English literature—"Men must endure / Their going hence, even as their coming hither: / Ripeness is all"—went unmarked in his copy of *King Lear*.[6] Perhaps it is too bald a statement for a young poet who looked on fine phrases as a lover: indeed, it is an old man's wisdom, a gnomic perception of the kind that would appeal to Arnold or Eliot but hardly to a twenty-two-year-old. Yet in the early years of his life Keats had encountered much to endure, in the sense of suffer: the deaths, in a close-knit family, of his infant brother, his father, his grandfather, his mother after a disastrous remarriage and prolonged illness, his much-admired uncle, and his much-loved grandmother. These early misfortunes, as he once cryptically referred to them, left him with a precocious sense that no happiness could endure "beyond the present hour" (*L*1:293, 186). The fallibility of duration and the necessity of endurance are the poles on which the poems of his maturity turn, and the instances of endurance scattered through his poems and letters provide significant markers of his development.

To begin, Keats's notion of endurance in the rudimentary sense of staying power, the ability to hold out to the end in a trial of strength, appears in his admiration of the athlete—young Leander toiling in the waves, or the bare-fisted boxer going to thirty-four rounds.[7] Physical stamina in pursuit of a prize became creative endurance in the test of his powers of imagination that he set himself in *Endymion*, the "glorious great intent" (*L*1:134) of writing a poem four thousand lines long in six months' time and persevering through discouragement and self-doubt toward the goal of poetic fame. Keats's image for this task as he started out was mountain-climbing, struggling up "the Cliff of poesy" as it towered above him, or "continual uphill Journeying" (*L*1:141, 169, 139). In the poem Endymion undergoes a long drawn-out trial of perseverance in the quest of his goddess through "wild uncertainty and shadows grim," in which he comes to identify with the endurance of Leander, Orpheus, and Pluto in their "strange journeyings" (II.273; III.93–99). More striking is the author's identification with his hero as the tale unfolds: Keats learned, like Endymion, to endure the anxiety of isolation—the loneliness of the long-distance runner—and, toward the end, the possibility of failure, as he completed the poem in November 1817 with a premonition that he would be attacked by the Cockney-baiters of *Blackwood's*.

Keats's trust that enduring effort would be rewarded by fame, which had obsessed him in the *Poems* of 1817 and sustained him through the long labor of *Endymion*, was severely shaken in the months that followed. The lukewarm response of his friends and ominous rumblings from the Tory reviews in the spring of 1818 contributed to his own growing dissatisfaction with the poem, which erupted in the rejected draft of the preface. He began to suspect that the only reward for the "agonie ennuiyeuse" of composition (*L*2:32) was the poem itself. "Life must be undergone," he wrote to Benjamin Bailey in a dark moment in June 1818, with his only consolation the thought of "writing one or two more Poems before it ceases" (*L*1:293)—a remark which might be read as an unwitting paraphrase of Edgar's admonition to Gloucester. He met the onslaught of the *Quarterly's* attack the following autumn by disavowing all hope of immediate fame, declaring himself content to write from his "mere yearning and fondness for the Beautiful," unafraid of failure for "I would sooner fail than not be among the greatest" (*L*1:388, 374).

This retreat into solitary indifference to praise or blame could defend him against the sneers of the reviewers, but the spectacle of his brother Tom's illness proved a sterner test of what must be called spiritual endurance, the strength to share and thus relieve the suffering of others. In the spring of 1818, in the verse epistle *To J. H. Reynolds Esq.* ("Dear Reynolds, as last night I lay in bed"), Keats confronted the possibility that suffering might have no redeeming end, not even the award of philosophical insight, "the lore of good and ill" (75). But this vision of mere purposeless endurance, in the face of "eternal fierce destruction" without meaning, was a temptation to despair, and he turned his back on it after one "look too far into the sea" (94–97). As Tom grew worse, Keats wrote to George that one can "bear up against any Calamity" if only for the sake of helping others to bear it (*L*1:391).

In *Hyperion* the intellectual despair of the verse epistle to Reynolds is echoed in Hyperion's lament, with its repeated questionings of "darkness, death and darkness" (I.242). However, Oceanus's stoic counsel "to bear all naked truths" (II.203) foreshadows the insight into the meaning of suffering that Keats had attained by the spring of 1819 after a long struggle. In his description of the "Vale of Soul-making," suffering is a positive force, not so much an obstacle in the hero's path as the necessary means by which a mere intelligence or individual consciousness is schooled and formed into a soul or identity (*L*2:102–3). The reward of endurance is now completely internalized or spiritualized as the achievement of identity; so endurance itself has been transformed from a kind of stamina, or holding out against an external pressure, into a form of insight, the psychic ability to ingest and assimilate painful experience, just as intelligence "sucks its identity" (*L*2:103) from the teat of the heart. So Oceanus concludes, "Receive the truth, and let it be your balm" (*Hyp.* II.243).

Keats seems to have intended the deification of Apollo at the end of *Hyperion* to illustrate this process, but the imperfect nature of Apollo's endurance may be one reason for his abandoning the poem. Like Hyperion, Apollo suffers from "aching ignorance" (III.107)—the "Agony of ignorance" of which Keats complained in March 1819 (L2:81); yet he bears this "painful vile oblivion" (III.187) with a premonition of enlightenment to come, whereas Hyperion foresees only his own over-throw. But Mnemosyne's "wondrous lesson" is imparted "all at once" too suddenly for Apollo to have fully endured it (III.112–16). "Nothing ever becomes real till it is experienced" (L2:81), Keats noted in March 1819: Apollo's "knowledge enormous" seems to come not so much from his own anguished experience as from without, by report, in the form of "Names, deeds, gray legends, dire events" (III.113–14). So the introduction of the dreamer-poet into *The Fall of Hyperion: A Dream* recasts the experience of enlightenment into the long, increasingly pain-ful process that soul-making had become for Keats as he realized more and more clearly the certainty of his own illness. The dreamer endures not only the doubt that Moneta casts on the value of his poetic enter-prise and his terror at the cost of endurance visible in her face, "death-wards progressing / To no death" (I.260–61), but also his despair in contemplating and then identifying with the Titans in their overthrow:

> Without stay or prop
> But my own weak mortality, I bore
> The load of this eternal quietude,
> The unchanging gloom, and the three fixed shapes
> Ponderous upon my senses a whole moon.
> For by my burning brain I measured sure
> Her silver seasons shedded on the night,
> And every day by day methought I grew
> More gaunt and ghostly. Oftentimes I pray'd
> Intense, that death would take me from the vale
> And all its burthens. Gasping with despair
> Of change, hour after hour I curs'd myself. (I.388–99)

The price of the "power of enormous ken, To see as a God sees" (I.303–4) is to endure that "immortal sickness which kills not" (I.258), which has brought the indescribable pallor to Moneta's face: the con-sciousness of human suffering past, present, and future.

Keats's foreknowledge of what he was finally required to endure pre-dates the composition of *The Fall of Hyperion* by more than a year. He had foreseen his approaching death since the spring of 1818, and in July 1818 he predicted its date with uncanny accuracy: the opening line of the sonnet *This mortal body of a thousand days* overshot the mark by only a few weeks.[8] The record of his final agon, after giving up *The Fall of Hyperion* in the late autumn of 1819,[9] belongs not to his poetry but to his letters. What makes the letters of 1820 almost unbearable to read is his growing belief that his illness was indeed a struggle not merely without an ultimate reward, but even without meaning—endurance for its own sake alone. Twice he described his sensation in facing the voyage to Italy as the controlled despair of a soldier marching up to a battery (L2:315, 322). Grasping for some explanation, he exclaimed to John Taylor, "I am convinced that this sort of thing does not continue for nothing" and to Charles Brown, "Is there another Life? . . . There must be we cannot be created for this sort of suffering" (L2:315,346). "I long to believe in immortality," he wrote in agony to Fanny Brawne. "I wish to live with you for ever" (L2:293). As Severn recorded, however, this longing for the reassurance of faith was not fulfilled.[10] Death remained "the great divorcer for ever," at best only a release from physical and mental pain (L2:315, 346). The anguish of his separation from Fanny was matched only by his bleak conviction that he had failed to win the place among the English poets for which he had striven so long. Yet even as he lost hope he endured. In his dying words to Severn—"Don't be frightened"[11]—he summoned up the central strengths of his character: soldierly courage, the doctor's selfless solicitude, and the poet's imaginative ability to take part in the existence of others. It was a heroic assertion of identity at the moment of annihilation.[12]

The question inevitably arises, What is the relevance of this moral achievement to Keats's achievement as a poet? Clearly it casts a retrospective light on the poetry of his peak. The last stanza of *To Autumn*, for instance, acquires particular resonance from the knowledge of what Keats knew of what lay ahead: "Ripeness is all." To put it another way, his *annus mirabilis* was fueled not only by his knowledge of how little time was left, but still more by his resolve to make the most of it, to hold out to the end. For this a hardening of purpose, or endurance in the sense of indurance or induration, became necessary: his admiration for the imperturbability of the sailors in an accident at sea that he witnessed in August 1819 reflected the "iron" discipline he laid on himself that summer (L2:142, 141, 146). More significantly, this achievement illuminates what poetry came to mean to Keats in his deepening identification with the great poets as exemplars of human experience as well

as practitioners of the poetic art. Wordsworth's genius, as Keats defined
it in the spring of 1818, was to explore the "dark Passages" of human
life and "make discoveries, and shed a light in them" for others to follow (*L1:281*). In 1819 Shakespeare, who once had been to Keats a
treasure-house "full of fine things" that left his young admirer "nothing
to say about nothing or any thing" (*L1:189*), became "a miserable and
mighty Poet of the human Heart" (*L2:115*), whom he read with increasing and exclusive intensity throughout 1820. Even Milton, tem-
peramentally so different from Keats, stood by him during his illness.
In a letter to Fanny Brawne he recalled from *Lycidas* the indispensable
phrase for his effort to become "as good a Philosopher as possible" and
surmount the longing for poetic fame—"that last infirmity of noble
mind" (*L2:263*). "May *I* say it?" he added, in half-ironic apology. This
paradoxical modesty reveals the nobility of mind Keats had learned
from his exemplars that finally secures his place among the greatest.

NOTES

1. *The Letters of John Keats: 1814–1821,* ed. Hyder E. Rollins (Cambridge,
   Mass.: Harvard University Press, 1958). L2:139. Quotations from Keats's
   letters are from this edition, abbreviated *L* in text; volume and page numbers
   are given in parentheses in text.
2. Philip Levine, citing the poet Mary Karr, in "Beauty and/or Truth," *The
   Threepenny Review* 15 (winter 1994): 11. More recently, Ellen Voigt recom-
   mended that her fellow poets read Keats's life as "an antidote to self-pity"
   (*Poets' Readings* [Ann Arbor, Mich.: Borders, 1997], 18).
3. James Robertson MacGillivray, *Keats: A Bibliography and Reference Guide*
   (Toronto: University of Toronto Press, 1949), xlii–xliii, lxvi–lxviii; and G. M.
   Matthews, *Keats: The Critical Heritage* (London: Routledge and Kegan Paul,
   1971), 245, 248, 251–52.
4. In *The Selected Letters of John Keats,* ed. Lionel Trilling (New York: Farrar,
   Straus and Young, 1951), reprinted as "The Poet as Hero: Keats in His Letters," Trilling, *The Opposing Self* (New York: Viking Press, 1959), 3–49.
5. He used "endure" only three times, all in *Endymion* (I.854: II.591: IV.801),
   with no special emphasis except perhaps when he describes Endymion in the
   first phase of his journey as "assured / Of happy times, when all he had
   endur'd / Would seem a feather to the mighty prize" (II.590–92). Quotations
   of Keats's poetry are from *The Poems of John Keats,* ed. Jack Stillinger (Cambridge, Mass.: Harvard University Press, Belknap Press, 1978); line numbers
   are given in parentheses in text.
6. Edgar to Gloucester, *King Lear,* V.ii.9–11. See Caroline Spurgeon, *Keats's
   Shakespeare* (London: University Press, 1928), 5, for markings of *Lear* in vol.
   7 of Keats's duodecimo edition; for his Folio edition markings, see R. S.

White, *Keats as a Reader of Shakespeare* (Norman: University of Oklahoma Press, 1987), 23–30, 168–94, 213–19.

7. Aileen Ward, *John Keats: The Making of a Poet*, rev. ed. (New York: Farrar, Straus & Giroux, 1986), 231 and 433 n. 21; for Keats's use of boxing slang, see L2:272–73.

8. Ward, *John Keats*, 185, 431 n. 4; 199–200, 432 n. 13b.

9. On the date, see Ward, *John Keats*, 439–40 n. 15.

10. *The Keats Circle: Letters and Papers 1816–1878*, ed. Hyder Edward Rollins (Cambridge, Mass.: Harvard University Press, 1948), 1:181, 196–97.

11. Joseph Severn, in an unsent letter to Charles Brown, no date (February 24?, 1821), in William Sharp, *The Life and Letters of Joseph Severn* (New York: Charles Scribner's Sons, 1892), 94.

12. Ward, *John Keats*, 395: Trilling, *Selected Letters*, 48.

Keats and Friendship

◆

RONALD A. SHARP

T HE "SCRAP OF PAPER" that Keats asked his publisher, John Taylor, to take as his last will and testament concludes with a line of poetry, perhaps Keats's final line of poetry: "My Chest of Books divide among my friends."[1] Coming as it does after three sentences of prose, in a note written a month before Keats set sail for Italy, the line enacts a ceremonial gesture of closure, a sense of an ending whose formality is emphasized by inverted syntax and iambic pentameter. No one familiar with Keats's poetry, letters, or life should be surprised that the emphasis falls on friends, for to an extent virtually unparalleled, the story of his life and work is indeed a story of friendship.

From the magical night of reading with Cowden Clarke and returning home at dawn to write *On First Looking into Chapman's Homer* to the final hours in Rome, dying in the arms of Joseph Severn; from the long talks with Benjamin Bailey at Oxford, and the teasing with John Hamilton Reynolds, to the weeks roaming the northlands with Charles Brown; from the publication of his first poem by his new friend Leigh Hunt to the afternoon in 1820 when he broke down in Hunt's company and told him he was dying of a broken heart; from beginning to end, Keats's was a life densely crowded and textured with friendships and resonant with friends' voices. He was aware of the importance of friendship and profoundly reflective about its nature.

On the Monday that Keats sailed for Italy, Fanny Brawne wrote, in her first letter to Keats's sister: "I cannot tell you how much every one have exerted themselves for him, nor how much he is liked. . . . I am certain he has some spell that attaches them to him, or else he has fortunately met with a set of friends that I did not believe could be found in the world."[2] "She knew," as Robert Gittings suggests, "that the first part of this explanation was the real truth." That spell—"the power," as Gittings puts it, "to reflect everybody around him at their best"[3]—was felt even by strangers, such as John Aitken, a young Scotsman who in August 1820, upon hearing about Keats's ill health, wrote him an extraordinary letter inviting him to come to his house in Dunbar to recuperate. "There is nothing selfish in my request," said Aitken. "It is prompted as much by the amiable qualities of your heart, which are so abundantly apparent in your productions as by the e[min]ence which you have attained" (*L*2:325). That John Gibson Lockhart, in his patronizing "Letter from Z. to Leigh Hunt" (*Blackwood's Magazine*, May 1818), should have used the same word, *amiable*, in describing Keats as an "amiable but infatuated bardling" (*L*1:294*n*) is a bitter irony, but Aitken put his finger squarely on something that generations of readers have sensed in Keats: that one of the characteristics of his life and work was a certain friendliness, and that this quality undergirds and radiates from his poetry.

So fully did friendship pervade Keats's life and work that it can have the dulling force of the obvious. For this reason, we need to remind ourselves just how abiding a presence it was. For the same reason, it ought to strike us as surprising that though critics have from time to time remarked on the importance of friendship for Keats, no one has studied the place of friendship in Keats's life and work as a whole.[4]

There is, of course, a considerable body of commentary, especially from biographers, about Keats's *actual* friends and friendships. For example, in *The Everlasting Spell,* Joanna Richardson speculates at length about why Brown made Keats leave Wentworth Place when his health was still uncertain and why he did not accompany Keats to Italy.[5] My own concern lies not with the biographical details, but with Keats's conception of friendship, his understanding of it as a complex human phenomenon with crucial implications for his conception of spirituality as well as his ethics and aesthetics. Although Richardson's book is subtitled *A Study of Keats and His Friends*, she makes no attempt to explain Keats's larger conception of friendship, either in its own right or as it relates to other central aspects of his vision. The only other book-length study that pretends to deal with this subject is Warren Stevenson's *Poetic Friends: A Study of Literary Relations during the English Romantic Period*, but his brief chapters on Keats offer scarcely a word about our subject.[6]

Much has been written about love, sexuality, and desire in Keats, but, as has been the case with virtually every other writer studied in the twentieth century, friendship has been ignored. There are, to be sure, a few recent books and essays about friendship in general, and there are also a few recent works of literary criticism that deal with friendship. But with relatively few exceptions, friendship—which up through the nineteenth century remained a major issue for serious writers and philosophers—seems to have fallen into the hands of pop psychologists and self-help enthusiasts. As Wayne Booth observes, "After millennia during which friendship was one of the major philosophical topics, the subject of thousands of books and tens of thousands of essays, it has now so dwindled that our encyclopedias do not even mention it."[7]

To ask what friendship meant to Keats is to study him precisely at the intersection of his most fundamental concerns and from a perspective that illuminates many of those concerns in a new way. In this essay, I shall focus on two of these: first, the nature of beauty and its relation to suffering and mortality and, second, the nature of the self and its transactions with others, particularly in the context of gift exchange. Friendship was not simply one among many themes equally important to Keats. It was fundamental to him at a level he hinted at when he told Reynolds, "I could not live without the love of my friends" (*L*1:267).

Anyone reading Keats's letters with an eye to his view of friendship cannot but be struck by the magnitude of his concern with the subject: the sheer frequency of his discussions of it, the subtlety of his reflections on it, and the characteristic sensitivity to virtually the full range of its concerns. Keats's insights are invaluable in themselves; they constitute a body of wisdom worthy of our most serious attention. They also, I believe, inform his poetry in indirect but crucial ways. I do not claim that the poetry itself undertakes an elaborate consideration of friendship; the main source for Keats's conception of friendship is clearly the letters. However, I do suggest that understanding Keats's views of friendship provides a useful wedge into certain important aspects of his poetry.

In his early poetry, friendship does actually figure as a major subject. Poems like *O Solitude, To a Friend Who Sent Me Some Roses,* and the verse epistles to George Felton Mathew and Charles Cowden Clarke take up the subject directly. Think, for example, of the early sonnet that goes like this:

Keen, fitful gusts are whisp'ring here and there
   Among the bushes half leafless, and dry;
   The stars look very cold about the sky,
And I have many miles on foot to fare.
Yet feel I little of the cool bleak air,
   Or of the dead leaves rustling drearily,
   Or of those silver lamps that burn on high,
Or of the distance from home's pleasant lair:
For I am brimfull of the friendliness
   That in a little cottage I have found;
Of fair-hair'd Milton's eloquent distress,
   And all his love for gentle Lycid drown'd;
Of lovely Laura in her light green dress,
   And faithful Petrarch gloriously crown'd.[8]

In his most ambitious early poem, *Sleep and Poetry*, friendship stands at the center of Keats's conception of poetry. "The great end / Of Poesy," he writes, is "that it should be a friend / To sooth the cares, and lift the thoughts of man" (245–47). Like friendship, poetry is a consolation, a balm, "a friend to man," as *Ode on a Grecian Urn* (48) proclaims in a phrase whose striking similarity is not accidental.

How exactly is poetry a consolation? In what sense is it a friend? In *Sleep and Poetry*, Keats distinguishes two kinds of poetry: that of "Flora, and old Pan" (102) and that of "the agonies, the strife / Of human hearts" (124–5). The former refers to idealized poetry, portraying fanciful situations and enchanting landscapes, whereas the latter engages human suffering and the ravages of time. As a shorthand, let us call this a distinction between the pastoral and the tragic. In one sense, friendship functions as a consolation in the same way that pastoral poetry does: it soothes by providing a bower of pleasure apart from the pains of life.

Sleep and Poetry also takes up friendship's analogy with tragic poetry. If both friendship and poetry should "sooth the cares, and lift the thoughts of man" (247), the poem is quite explicit about which kinds of poetry are most effective in accomplishing that task: "And they shall be accounted poet kings / Who simply tell the most heart-easing things" (267–68). That is to say, the best poets will be those who are most consoling, and the most consoling poetry, paradoxically, will be the poetry of the agony and strife of human hearts, which Keats says is "nobler" (123) than the poetry of Flora and old Pan. Given the image of the poet king, the hierarchical image of "nobler" clearly implies that tragic poetry eases the heart more than pastoral poetry, presumably because it is based on a more comprehensive view of life.

It would follow, then, that one could distinguish two kinds of friends: those associated with Flora and old Pan and those associated with the agony and strife of human hearts. In *Ode on a Grecian Urn*, when Keats refers to the urn as "a friend to man," he has just three lines earlier chided it for being a "Cold Pastoral" (45), that is, a product of the world of Flora and old Pan. Even after recognizing its limitations, Keats praises the urn for its ability to console. In a world in which suffering is constant ("in midst of other woe / Than ours" [47–48]), art and friendship perform their vital function of consolation. But just as in the realm of art we recognize the difference between Flora and old Pan on one hand and the agonies of the human heart on the other— between the pastoral Grecian urn of antiquity and Keats's more tragic rendering of it in his poem—so in friendship there are pastoral friends and there are "tragic" friends, friends strong and close enough for the stuff of tragedy.

With pastoral friends we may not share our deepest life or our deepest pains; those we reserve for one or two friends, if we are lucky, with whom we relate at the most profound and inclusive level of our being. One thinks, for example, of Keats suffering through his early illness with Brown at his side, confiding in Brown about his love for Fanny Brawne, and later confessing his anguish as death closes in and trying, in his last letter, to say his farewells. "I am so weak," he wrote, "that I cannot bear the sight of any hand writing of a friend I love so much as I do you. . . . I can scarcely bid you good bye even in a letter" (*L*2:360).

Pastoral friendship is clearly limited compared with this sort of "tragic" friendship. Both pastoral poetry and pastoral friendship are attractive, however, precisely because they do *not* bring into their orbit the darker side of life. If their attraction is that they provide a respite from sorrow, their danger is that they can become an escape. We all know the appeal of a certain kind of pastoral art and of innocent, even frivolous friendships, and we also know that though they may not be superficial, they lack the comprehensiveness and depth of the most serious art or friendship. What is characteristic of Keats is that although he saw the superiority of the tragic in friendship and poetry, his vision was capacious enough to recognize the beauty and importance of the pastoral as well—which is why, I take it, he still calls the urn a friend after chiding it for being a "Cold Pastoral." Both as poet and as friend, the comic, sensual, light-hearted Keats was part and parcel of the young man confronting death and sorrow.

Although pastoral poetry or friendships may provide refuge from life's sorrows, tragic poetry and friendships are even more "heart-easing," to borrow the language of *Sleep and Poetry,* because they do more than provide a comforting alternative to suffering. Like *King Lear,* Keats's touchstone, they actually discover a paradoxical beauty and value in the extremity and depth of human suffering itself.

We confront here paradoxes of enormous spiritual import: what is the most sorrowful has the potential to be the most consoling; in suffering can be found the highest beauty. In an earlier book, I outlined Keats's radical skepticism about any sort of higher reality beyond this world, and I argued that the sources of his hope never violate that abiding skepticism and never blink the hard reality of suffering and transience.[9] This is emphatically true of Keats's conception of friendship as well. At the foundation of that conception—indeed, at the foundation of Keats's work—is the paradox that a sense of mortality increases one's sense of beauty, that life accrues value precisely to the extent that one experiences it as fragile and transitory.

The way in which these paradoxes play themselves out in relation to friendship is illustrated by a brief examination of the ode *To Autumn.* Though the theme of friendship is not as explicit in this poem as it is in the early poems, it informs *To Autumn,* as it does *Ode on a Grecian Urn,* in ways that seem to me vital.

Like Apollo in *Hyperion,* Keats in *To Autumn* does not merely register or admit "Knowledge enormous," but lets the experience of mortality "Pour into the wide hollows of [his] brain" (III.113, 117). Although in the poem the day is dying, its death is figured as a blossoming: "barred clouds bloom the soft-dying day" (25–26). Keats offers no fantasy of rebirth here. If autumn is beautiful, it is not because winter will be followed by spring. "Where are the songs of spring?" he asks. "Ay, where are they? / Think not of them, thou hast thy music too" (23–24). Keats addresses a personified autumn here in tones that characterize nothing so much as the comforting of a friend—a gesture that has been prepared for as early as the second line of the poem, where the poet calls autumn a "Close bosom-friend of the maturing sun" (2). Autumn's most beautiful music, Keats suggests, can be heard only when we cease regretting loss (the youthfulness of spring), shed fantasies of rebirth (a new spring), and accept the reality of death (the coming winter). When we do that, the ending of a day can be perceived as a fruition, a coming into itself. The fields may then be "stubble-plains," but, seen in this light, they will take on a "rosy hue" (26).

To put the matter in this way is to see how delicately the poem's central trope of cycles is interwoven with the trope of friendship. To the extent that autumn is personified, her impending death is figured as a coming to fruition, a coming into her own, and the poet comforts her in the tone one would use to comfort a dying friend. Biographically, of course, we know that it was Keats himself who was dying, but that fact is poetically engaged by projection. Just as in the "vale of Soul-making" letter Keats considered suffering necessary to making a soul, so here mortality is considered integral to the ripening of identity. In these terms, Keats's admonition to autumn that she not think about the songs of spring ("Ay, where are they?" [23]) first acknowledges the painful reality of winter and death and then offers the friend an alternative: "thou hast thy music too."

Notice the assumption behind that alternative. To say that autumn has her own music is to suggest that the poet knows his friend's identity and that it has a beauty of its own, which warrants calling it "music." Among the many reasons this passage is resonant is that in crucial respects its rhetoric is that of a friend helping to ease the pain of a dying friend. Keats brings to the task the fullness of his empathy, so that there is no sense at all here of offering a solution glibly or naively, without a genuine appreciation of the friend's pain. Having accepted the mortality of his friend, Keats finds her even more precious, more valuable, more beautiful. Having heard the music of mortality, he implores her to hear it too, knowing that only by coming to understand her mortality as music will his friend be able to come to grips with the finality of death. What he offers her is a gift from a friend: a gift of knowledge about herself and about the ways in which "Death," as Wallace Stevens would later put it in *Sunday Morning,* "is the mother of beauty." [10]

The courageous serenity of the speaker's voice in *To Autumn* stems from the poet's discovering not only that mortality has its own music, but that its music may be more beautiful than the youthful and innocent music of spring—the music, as it were, of Flora and old Pan. Keats embraces sorrow and transience, but he does so without rubbing our noses in them and without turning that embrace into an ideology of therapy. In the long journal letter to George and Georgiana, his brother and sister-in-law, which also includes the discussion of the "vale of Soul-making," Keats touched on this issue indirectly. "Very few men," he wrote,

> have ever arrived at a complete disinterestedness of Mind: very few have been influenced by a pure desire of the benefits of others—in the greater part of the Benefactors ⟨of⟩ & to Humanity some meretricious motive has sullied their greatness—some melodramatic scenery has fascinated them. (*L*2:79)

The conception of friendship that underlies *To Autumn*, I contend, has absolutely nothing meretricious about it. It is the furthest thing imaginable from the "crisis insurance" model of friendship that seems to be common today (at least in America), in which one invests, as it were, in a "relationship" in order to protect oneself against some future crisis or to fulfill one's needs. Keats would have abhorred such a concept, partly because it stages itself amidst "melodramatic scenery," making a self-congratulatory show of its supportiveness. In such a relationship, one gives not so much because one cares about one's friend or wants to help that friend, but because one wants partly to ensure that one is later a recipient and partly to feel good about giving. That is, one gives in order to get something in return: both the immediate gratification of being considered generous and the delayed satisfaction of being paid back. In the California joke, one does not change a light bulb; one has the *experience* of changing it. Keats would have appreciated the difference between helping or caring about a friend and having the *experience* of being helpful or caring.

Though Keats regarded sorrow as inherent in the best friendships, he was able to give it its due without reducing friendship to an implicit agreement to provide mutual therapy. Certainly, for Keats, a kind of therapy was vitally important to friendship, but if it was the only—or even the most important—function, then friendship was relegated to the position it holds in the old English proverb: "A true friend shall be like a privy, open in necessity."[11] The question of whether and how to share one's sorrow with a friend raises important issues about the nature of privacy and intimacy, including the possibility that there may be some natural tension between those two ideals. For if it is true that good friends will want to aid each other in distress, it is also true that they will want to spare each other pain. And while sincerity is crucial to friendship, there are instances in which the claims of privacy will press hard against it.

These issues are at the center of the literature of friendship, from Aristotle to Jane Austen, from Cicero and Montaigne to Hemingway and Adrienne Rich. For a poet like Keats, who was concerned with the omnipresence of sorrow but was also sensitive to matters of sincerity, privacy, and intimacy, these issues focused many of his larger concerns in friendship, and we see them played out, often with dazzling finesse, throughout his letters. What we call the art of friendship often involves negotiating precisely these tensions. Keats's success in that art stemmed partly from his legendary sympathetic imagination and partly from his "Negative Capability," both of which figured hugely in virtually every dimension of his conception of and genius for friendship.

For example, Keats began an early letter to Bailey by wondering how a particular "unfortunate Family" (not identified in the letter) "lived through the [last] twelve" days:

> One saying of your's I shall never forget ... "*Why should Woman suffer?*" Aye. Why should she? ... These things are, and he who feels how incompetent the most skyey Knight errantry to heal this bruised fairness is like a sensitive leaf on the hot hand of thought. (*L*1:209)

Letters like the "vale of Soul-making" letter and poems like *The Fall of Hyperion* or even *Ode on Melancholy* and *Ode to a Nightingale* are often cited as examples of Keasts's mature confrontation with darkness. But we do well to remember that, as we saw in *Sleep and Poetry,* with its famous reference to "the agonies, the strife / Of human hearts" (124–25), Keats was keenly aware that the highest poetry is that which comes to terms with tragic realities. We should also recall that his early work is filled with statements along the lines of "we live . . . in a continual struggle against the suffocation of accidents" (*L*1:179). In the preceding letter to Bailey as well, which was written in January 1818, Keats was concerned with the ineffectiveness of otherworldly and overly idealistic attempts "to heal this bruised fairness." The "skyey Knight errantry" that he indicted in this regard is closely associated with that of the enthralled hero in Book I of *Endymion,* which Keats had completed just a week before.

It is in just this context of hardheaded facing up to suffering that Keats proceeded, in the next sentence of this letter to Bailey, to thank and praise his friend for enacting what Keats was later to call his ideal of "disinterestedness" (L2:79): "Your tearing, my dear friend, a spiritless and gloomy Letter up to rewrite to me is what I shall never forget— it was to me *a real thing*" (L1:209, emphasis added). Keats was expressing gratitude to Bailey for not burdening him with his sorrow. In one sense, this is simply consistent with the classical idea, best expressed by Aristotle (whom Keats probably never read but whose ideas about friendship provide a useful contrast with Keats's), that while "it is perhaps fitting for a man to go unasked and eagerly to a friend in misfortune," we should "be reluctant to ask our friend to share our misfortunes."[12] The more important point, though, is that Keats felt the poignancy of Bailey's tact in direct proportion to the intensity of his own sense of the pervasiveness of misfortune and suffering, and it was precisely that intensity he addressed.

Keats valued this gesture of generosity on Bailey's part all the more because he knew how rare it is. "Upon the whole," he wrote Georgiana, "I dislike Mankind: whatever people on the other side of the question may advance they cannot deny that they are always surprised at hearing of a good action and never of a bad one" (L2:243). Keats began this letter with the most unsentimental recognition of the persistence of self interest, which he developed with a blazing insight: "The worst of Men are those whose self interests are their passion—the next those whose passions are their self interest" (L2:243). The latter are motivated entirely by their passions, by which Keats presumably meant such traditional passions as lust, pride, and envy. The former, however, are even more despicable, because, through a wretched perversion, they have no passions at all except one: their own self-interest. These bleak realities did not lead Keats to despair, however. "The more I know of Men," he wrote,

> the more I know how to value entire liberality in any of them. Thank God there are a great many who will sacrifice their worldly interest for a friend: I wish there were more who would sacrifice their passions. (L2:243)

Clearly, there are limitations: some degree of self-interest appears to be the norm of human motivation. Complete disinterestedness—utterly selfless motivation—is as rare as "a pearl in rubbish," to quote Keats, and that, he says, is a "pity" (*L*2:80). Still, from time to time, we enact a kind of heroism, in which we transcend self interest, perhaps not escaping it altogether but acting in a way that is at least relatively pure. That, for Keats, was the central territory of friendship. "To say that an act is altruistic," says Lawrence Blum in *Friendship, Altruism and Morality,* "is only to say that it involves and is motivated by a genuine regard for another's welfare; it is not to say that in performing it the agent neglects his own interests and desires."[13]

I raise these complex philosophical issues about the nature of generosity and self interest not to suggest that Keats worked out an elaborate philosophical position on them, but to suggest that he made sense of them in much the same way he comprehended other such issues: within a conceptual structure of limitation and possibility. Given that we suffer, given that we die, how do we find meaning? On what grounds do we affirm life? Likewise, given that self interest dominates our behavior, how can we be generous, how can we be friendly? There are, plainly, limitations, but they are not claustrophobic: the space for significant human action remains expansive. For Keats, just as suffering and mortality can intensify beauty, a norm of self interest makes acts of friendship and generosity even more valuable. One need not deny the existence of self-interest in order to affirm the presence of generosity or friendship.

It is in gift exchange, which always has a principle of self-interest built into it, that Keats found his deepest model for friendship: "Give and ye shall receive." At the foundation of gift exchange is the idea of reciprocity. We know from the anthropologists that in economies based on gift exchange, if there is no reciprocity, the system breaks down. The same is true in friendship: if the giving is all on one side, the friendship fails. But the dynamics of both gift exchange and friendship are very delicate in this regard. For if one gives with the *intent* of receiving, one is involved in a version of commodity exchange, investing, as it were, with the expectation of a future return. If I am generous to my friend because it may be to my advantage later, I am acting out of the kind of self-interest that is inimical to friendship. "For we do not exercise kindness and generosity," wrote Cicero, "in order that we may put in a claim for gratitude; we do not make our feelings of affection into a business proposition."[14] Still, if I am generous to my friend because I care about him and want to help him, I may well find that I get something back later.

The fact that the giver gets a gift in return does not, then, mean that the giver's motives are selfish, but neither does it mean that gift exchange takes place in an atmosphere so rarified as to be foreign to actual experience. I make this point to underscore the unique combination of tough-minded realism and high idealism that we find, characteristically, in Keats's view of friendship. Keats recognized that he was no Socrates or Jesus, but that recognition did not make him despair of human imperfection so much as make him grapple with its implications.

When you give a gift, says Lewis Hyde in his wonderful book *The Gift,* "it is as if you give a part of your substance to your gift partner and then wait in silence until he gives you a part of his." [15] The dynamics are similar in friendship, and we can see them paradigmatically in the example of the exchange of letters, in which the letter writer assumes but is not guaranteed a letter in return and thus with each letter is making him- or herself vulnerable, risking a silence that may grow loud with denial or rejection. Keats was attuned to these issues when he began a letter to Bailey in the autumn of 1817. While he was writing the letter, which was apparently overdue, another letter arrived from Bailey, and Keats responded immediately:

> I am glad that I have been neglectful . . . therefrom I have received a proof of your utmost kindness which at this present I feel very much—and I wish I had a heart always open to such sensations—but there is no altering a Man's nature and mine must be radically wrong for it will lie dormant a whole Month. (*L*1:173)

By explaining his neglect as the result of his unalterable inclination to indolence, Keats invited Bailey not to take the neglect personally. But Keats's acceptance of responsibility did not prevent him from taking delight in a completely unanticipated bonus that arose from his neglect, namely, the reassurance of Bailey's generosity and friendship toward him. Keats did not *intend* to give Bailey the opportunity to forgive Keats's silence, thus reassuring Keats of his friendship, but that is what happened, and "at this present," Keats wrote, he "feel[s] it very much."

Although Keats understood that in friendship, as in gift exchange, there must be an underlying principle of equilibrium and reciprocity, he also understood that the accounting in gift exchange and friendship is not strict. If we pay too much attention to keeping score and evening the balance, we risk, through a deadening self-consciousness, losing the spirit of the gift.

Keats's understanding of these subtleties and his ability to enact that understanding in his friendships seem to me unrivaled. I suggest that for Keats, gift giving, in its widest metaphorical sense, was the quintessential act of friendship. Friendship for Keats was a relationship or an act conducted in the spirit of gift exchange.

But because the gift is fragile, the equilibrium of gift exchange is always delicate. Samuel Johnson understood the implications of this fact for friendship, arguing in one of his *Rambler* essays that "benefits that cannot be repaid and obligations which cannot be discharged, are not commonly found to increase affection; they excite gratitude . . . but commonly take away that easy freedom, and familiarity of intercourse, without which . . . there cannot be friendship." [16] Johnson is concerned here with acts of extreme generosity having the same effect on friends as, to take an example of my own, God's love of Satan has on the latter in *Paradise Lost:* a feeling of the burden of the debt, "the debt immense of endless gratitude." [17] "Thus imperfect," says Johnson, "are all earthly blessings; the great effect of friendship is beneficence, yet by the first act of uncommon kindness it is endangered." [18]

Lest one imagine that the gift model simply yields a new version of Keats as sentimentalist, I want to argue that Keats fully understood the issues that Johnson explored. He knew that generosity, especially in friendship, is rarely an uncomplicated phenomenon, and he was always alert to nuances of imbalance and reciprocity. In September 1819, for example, Keats told Brown that he, Brown, had been so generous to him that he had become overly dependent on him and it was therefore Brown's duty to even up the balance. The subtlety with which Keats played competing notions of obligation and generosity against each other is dazzling:

> And here I will take an opportunity of making a remark or two on our friendship, and all your good offices to me. I have a natural timidity of mind in these matters: liking better to take the feeling . . . between us for granted, than to speak it. But, good God! . . . You have been living for others more than any man I know. This is a vexation to me; because it has been depriving

you, in the very prime of your life, of pleasures which it was your duty to procure. . . . I speculate upon it frequently; and believe me, the end of my speculations is always an anxiety for your happiness. . . . I had got into a habit of mind of looking towards you as a help in all difficulties. This very habit would be the parent of idleness and difficulties. You will see it is a duty I owe myself to break the neck of it. (*L*2:176–77)

Brown, Keats asserted, had a duty to procure happiness, and Keats, a duty to avoid dependence. Even more important is their duty to their friendship, and it is for that reason that Keats wanted to restore balance. The wonderfully disingenuous argument Keats deployed for restoring that reciprocity was that he would be hurt by the continuation of this generosity. What this did was release Brown from the burden of being generous at the same time it released Keats from the burden of receiving that generosity. Both giving and receiving gifts can in certain circumstances become a burden. Of course, Keats's gesture was itself a great act of generosity and friendship, in which Keats kept Brown's gift moving. The gift now went back to Brown, recompensing him, as it were, for his own generosity, but only—and this is crucial—because he gave his gifts without the expectation of return.

It is because true gifts are not given with the intent of getting something in return that the "crisis insurance" model of friendship, to which I referred earlier, is inadequate for Keats. For that model is based on commodity exchange: I will "invest" in my relationship with you in order to protect myself against some future crisis. I'll be there for you *because* I want you to be there for me. In friendship based on the gift model, on the other hand, I will be there for you because I want to help you, because I care about you. This does not mean that when one acts on the gift model one has absolutely no sense of a possible return. We are not dealing here with motivation of that order of tidiness or purity. Even when one is truly giving, there may well be some consciousness of an eventual return. But the distinction remains crucial between giving mainly in order to get something back and giving mainly in order to help your friend.

Though I have focused on Keats's concern with sorrows and mortality in friendship, his concern with suffering was balanced by an abiding attention to the joys of his friends, which he celebrated fully. His letters are filled with the delight he took in the happiness of his friends and expressions of his own joy. I will leave that for another essay, however. What I want to emphasize here is that Keats's ability to accept the sorrow inherent in friendship without reducing friendship to therapy accounts in large measure for the authenticity—the lack of meretriciousness—of both his empathy and his delight. In a world of inevitable pain, Keats turned to friendship not just because it was a source of consolation, but also because, to quote from *Hyperion*, there is a "sorrow more beautiful than Beauty's self" (I–36). A sense of mortality heightened rather than diminished his sense of the importance and beauty of friendship. "Your third Chamber of Life," Keats told Reynolds, "shall be a lucky and a gentle one—stored with the wine of love—and the Bread of Friendship" (*L*1:282–3). Like every other aspect of the human situation, friendship for Keats yielded its fullest measure when it was understood and experienced in the context of transience and mortality. Only within that context, only when he had passed through the chamber in which the world appeared "full of Misery and Heartbreak" (*L*1:281) could friendship leaven into the secular sacrament, the gift, that it so clearly became for Keats.

NOTES

This chapter appeared in the *Kenyon Review*, n. s. 21, no. 1 (winter 1999).

1. *The Letters of John Keats: 1814–1821*, ed. Hyder E. Rollins (Cambridge, Mass.: Harvard University Press, 1958), 2:319. Quotations of Keats's letters are from this edition, abbreviated *L* in text; volume and page numbers are given in text. Unless otherwise noted, quotations appear without alteration of Keats's frequently erratic spelling, punctuation, and syntax.

2. *Letters of Fanny Brawne to Fanny Keats: 1820–1824*, ed. Fred Edgcumbe (New York: Oxford University Press, 1937), 4.

3. Robert Gittings, *John Keats* (Boston: Little, Brown, 1968), 410.

4. Aside from John Middleton Murry's brief essay, "Keats and Friendship," in *Keats*, 4th ed. (New York: Noonday, 1955), 305–11, the fullest discussion of the subject appears here and there in the pages of Christopher Ricks's fine book, *Keats and Embarrassment* (1974; reprint, London: Oxford University Press, 1976).

5. Joanna Richardson, *The Everlasting Spell: A Study of Keats and His Friends* (London: Jonathan Cape, 1963).

6. Warren Stevenson, *Poetic Friends: A Study of Literary Relations during the English Romantic Period* (New York: Peter Lang, 1990).

7. Wayne C. Booth, *The Company We Keep: An Ethics of Fiction* (Berkeley: University of California Press, 1988), 170.

8. *The Poems of John Keats*, ed. Jack Stillinger (Cambridge, Mass.: Harvard

University Press, Belknap Press, 1978), 75. Quotations from Keats's poetry are from this edition. Line numbers are given in text.

9. Ronald A. Sharp, *Keats, Skepticism, and the Religion of Beauty* (Athens: University of Georgia Press, 1979).

10. Wallace Stevens, *The Collected Poems of Wallace Stevens* (New York: Knopf, 1954), 68–69.

11. *A Dictionary of the Proverbs in England in the Sixteenth and Seventeenth Centuries* (Ann Arbor: University of Michigan Press, 1950), 245.

12. Aristotle, *Nicomachean Ethics,* trans. Martin Oswald (Indianapolis, Ind.: Bobbs-Merrill, 1962), 270.

13. Lawrence A. Blum, *Friendship, Altruism and Morality* (London: Routledge and Kegan Paul, 1980), 10.

14. Cicero, "On Friendship," in *On Old Age and on Friendship,* trans. Frank O. Copley (1967; reprint, Ann Arbor: University of Michigan Press, 1971), 60.

15. Lewis Hyde, *The Gift: Imagination and the Erotic Life of Property* (New York: Random, 1983), 15.

16. Samuel Johnson, "Rambler 64," in *The Yale Edition of the Works of Samuel Johnson,* vol. 3, *The Rambler,* ed. W. J. Bate and Albrecht B. Strauss (New Haven, Conn.: Yale University Press, 1969), 344.

17. John Milton, *Paradise Lost,* ed. Merritt Y. Hughes. (Indianapolis, Ind.: Odyssey/Bobbs-Merrill, 1962), 85.

18. Johnson, "Rambler 64," 344.

The Limits of
the Imagination

Eavan Boland

D ESPITE THE PIETIES of tradition, the contact between one poet and another from a distant age is always fragile: history and heritage can as easily divide them as bring them together. According to these circumstances, I should never have found John Keats. I was born, after all, in Ireland. The tradition of poetry I came to know and be part of was formed against, rather than with, the defining elements of his poetic inheritance. What is more, the Irish poetic world was essentially Bardic. Its roots were deep in the eighteenth century but a very different eighteenth century to any that John Keats knew or contested. Come to that, it has often seemed to me that more poets are divided from one another by which eighteenth century they inherit—which eighteenth century they learned to think with as a poet—than by almost any other factor. Certainly, the eighteenth century I inherited as an Irish poet— although it has taken me many years to know this—was radically different from John Keats's. The coffeehouses and the civil music of Augustan England are a world away from the Ireland of broken treaties and heartbroken bards. But at the very time when the English eighteenth century was sponsoring the couplets and cadences of a high moment of civilization, which became, ironically, the diagrams of an orderly world of a different music, Ireland was caught in the death struggle of the Bardic order.

Nevertheless, one unforeseen circumstance gave me a chance to cross those boundaries of history and find this utterly essential poet. Because of my family background, I spent six years of my childhood in England.

And so, reluctantly, I learned the language of his place, rather than mine. Like all exiles, I resisted doing so. But it came to me nevertheless—a slow erosion of my lingua franca of place and a gradual instruction in his: I learned the difference between meadows and fields. I made the distinction between an orchard and a plain garden. I saw the big shadows that came before the fog on winter mornings in London. I stayed for a week when I was eleven in the cathedral city of Winchester. And, therefore, without having any idea that I was doing so, I traveled without papers in John Keats's world.

For all that, the Keats I learned in school was the Keats of caricature. He was represented as the poet of the sensual phrase and the immediate response. He was considered in the context of his great Romantic contemporaries and forbears as more eloquent and less responsible: a poet of gorgeous phrase and irresistible music. The title of this panel is "The Art of Poetry." And there is a great temptation because of it, and because this conference honors the poet, to confuse honor with reverence. For that reason alone, it seems to me important to isolate that caricature of Keats—those customary platitudes about his language and imagery which exempt us from a more demanding critique—and remove it from the poet who changed the art of poetry in his time. Certainly, John Keats was a dedicated, headstrong craftsman; he was also variable and erratic. His relationship to language was rigorous and ambitious; it was also escapist. And it was not always completely assured. He is one of those central poets whose contribution to the craft of poetry is far less than his defining role in shaping the art of poetry. It is his relation to the art of poetry which happens to be the subject here. And I want to speak not just about Keats's gifts of definition to that art, but also to try, even in so brief a space, to question what it is, in any generation of poets, that adds to and amplifies the art of poetry—whether it is the poet's sense of history, or the conscious enactment of a tradition. Or whether it is these two and something more again: an heroic act of cartography: a mapping of the imagination which makes the terrain safer for those who come after.

I have no doubt John Keats changed the map. He changed the art of poetry. And I want to briefly state here my sense—as a poet from another time, place, and tradition—of how he did that, and how in doing it, he dissolved every boundary of nation and tribe and time. That in turn involves me in sketching two landscapes which Keats inhabits, only one of which is the world I glimpsed as a child. That landscape of nineteenth-century England with its great, green oak trees and airy distances, its pre-imperial confidence and its peerless moment of poetic revision—what a temptation there is, in talking about Keats, to leave him in that magical and misleading distance! To fix him, in other words, in the world he came from, without recognizing that he belongs also in the world he made. And that world is our fractured, volatile landscape of contemporary poetry—where there is no peaceful cathedral close, no single and measurable field of oceanic corn, no unified and coherent space of time or tradition. Where everything is changing, and dissolving; where the corridor between tradition and the past and the poet is now filled with quarrelling voices; whose quarrels may be fruitful but are also painful. Where the future is no longer a clear and linear continuation of the poetry which is being written now. I have no doubt—if the continuance of poetry means anything—that John Keats belongs here in this landscape, just as certainly as in Hampstead or Wentworth Place. He belongs here precisely because it is not a safe place nor a static one. And because, most importantly, we owe to those who made poetry their exact place in the continual making of it.

And so my sense of Keats's relation to the art of poetry begins with the August of 1819 when he took up residence in the cathedral city of Winchester. Here in Hampshire, over the valley of the Itchen and right under the chalky hills, lies the peace of a legendary England. Here is the city I saw for a moment as a child, with its settled light and its cathedral and its storied high street. *We removed to Winchester for the convenience of a library* he wrote to Benjamin Bailey *and find it an exceeding pleasant town, enriched with a beautiful cathedral and surrounded by fresh-looking country.* When he came to Winchester Keats had already finished most of his great work and was in the process of putting the final touches to *Lamia*. Here, in this brisk narrative, in the exchanges between a serpent and a philosopher and a poet, he enacts not just a parable of the imagination; not just a poem which speculates on the values of expression; but a revisiting and re-stating of poetic history as well. He goes back to the fast couplets of that eighteenth century which he had disowned. He takes Dryden's lively music and uses it respectfully. And with it he embarks on a consideration of poetry, which is enabled by the eighteenth century, but not confined by it. At the end of *Lamia*, the weak poet and the powerful serpent and the stubborn philosopher face one another. Each drains and undermines the others' powers. The charms of the serpent are defeated. The strength of the poet is confused. The clarity of philosophy is called into question. By the end of the poem, the differing elements of enchantment, reason and expression are at each other' throats.

> What wreath for Lamia? What for Lycius?
> What for the sage, old Apollonius.
> Upon her aching forehead be there hung
> The leaves of willow and of adder's tongue;
> And for the youth, quick, let us strip for him
> The thyrsus, that his watching eyes may swim
> Into forgetfulness; and for the sage
> Let spear grass and the spiteful thistle wage
> War on his temples. Do not all charms fly
> At the mere touch of cold philosophy?
> There was an awful rainbow once in heaven:
> We know her woof and texture; she is given
> In the dull catalogue of common things.
> Philosophy will clip an angel's wings,
> Conquer all mysteries by rule and line,
> Empty the haunted air and gnomed mine—
> Unweave a rainbow.

Eliot said of Tennyson that he was great because of the quality of his doubt rather than that of his certainty. The doubts which Keats may have entertained in the last stage of his working life are also apparent in the first Canto of *The Fall of Hyperion*, composed and revised after *Lamia*. When the speaker in the poem, after many ordeals, encounters Moneta, a goddess both of memory and warning, he is suddenly confronted with harsh and unexpected questions about poetry itself. *Thou art a dreaming thing / A fever of thy self*, says Moneta accusingly. And the speaker replies with a recognizable search for reassurance:

> Majestic shadow tell me: sure not all
> Those melodies sung in the world's ear
> Are useless; sure a poet is a sage;
> A humanist, physician to all men.

But Moneta answers that the poet and the dreamer are distinct. That one pours out a balm upon the world and the other vexes it. The speaker, now turned listener, is left comfortless. The fragment ends and John Keats, having left Winchester, returns to London and begins the painful approach to his own mortality. And the questions were never answered.

But they were asked. And that is what endures. In his last poems— to which I've only been able to make the very briefest reference—John Keats confronted the single issue which is most crucial, it seems to me, to the contemporary poet: not the powers of the imagination, but its limits. Not the hubris of language but its responsibilities. Not the destiny of poetry but its ambiguity. The heroes of his final poems, those distraught and anxious voices in *The Fall of Hyperion,* are fictions of the weakened certainties and strengthened purposes of the poet. They do not press the claims of poetry. They do not assert the inherent value of expression. Instead, these poems cast a dark and beautiful color over the whole art of poetry. They suggest that the poet should not so much rejoice in the strength of the imagination as suffer its infirmity with courage. They argue for the humane purposes of art rather than its ornamental glory. This lack of certainty in a poet who, by grace and ordeal, took on the glory of the art when he was young and renounced that glory when he was still hardly more than a boy, remains to me one of the most powerful examples we have that poetry is a humane art.

If I may return to the two landscapes which I spoke about at the beginning, then, hopefully, I may have a chance to bring them together at the end. That first landscape is the city of Winchester:no more and no less than the usual local place where poetry is written and endured. On the twenty-first of September Keats wrote to John Hamilton Reynolds a letter which is a reminder that poetry is always famished for the local and the temporal, that it needs to be among black doors and brass keyholes, that it requires the ordinariness of a time and a place if it is to go beyond them. *The doors here* he wrote *are most part black with a little brass handle just above the keyhole so that In Winchester a man may very quietly shut himself out of his own house. How beautiful the season is now — How fine the air. A temperate sharpness about it. I never liked stubble fields so well as now — Aye better than the chilly green of the spring. Somehow a stubble plain looks warm — in the same way that some pictures look warm. This struck me so much in my Sunday's walk that I composed on it.* The poem he composed is the ode *To Autumn.* It is full of the beautiful peace of acceptance. There is no search for the dazzle of language in it. Above all, it does something which many poets have found just too hard. It creates, by the sheer power of its reality, a place where experience can be taken from the erosions of time and space and made safe. But having created that exemption for experience, Keats does not try to avail of it himself. He uses the necessary powers of language, without seeking their protection. He creates the paradox which is the true art of poetry: he creates a world where the sufferings of time are set aside, but only by taking the full penalties of those sufferings on himself.

It may very well be that we live in an age when the poem and the act of poetry will be harshly tested. Neither in this University, nor outside it, nor in my own country of Ireland, nor in North America or Britain, can anyone guarantee that the historic consensus as to what is a poem, who writes it, and how it is to be valued will continue without challenge. If that consensus breaks down then poetry will enter an age of unrest, where the reader and the advocate become one and the same; and the poet may be isolated by faction. But neither can there be a false consensus. There are so many new voices, so many new values, and the act of poetry has historically and traditionally been strong enough to include them. And must continue to be so. The continuation of poetry and the consensus that gives power and strength and peace to each new poet has to come from somewhere. It comes from within, of course. But it also comes in those fragile connections I mentioned between poet and poet, from age to age. It is confirmed when the new poet sees that the poets of the past made a humane art of poetry; an art which values the human above the ornamental and the experience above the expression. No poet I can think of encountered that art more humanely than John Keats. No poet left it more ready for the testing times which are ahead of it.

Keats and Gender Criticism

SUSAN J. WOLFSON

KEATSIAN SLIPS

BOTH AS A WRITER and as a subject of writing, Keats vexes the question of gender, especially when it is negotiated at unstable boundaries between masculine and feminine. This essay concerns the relation between Keats as the agent of thinking (not always critically) about gender, and the situation of Keats himself in gender criticism. A review of the general terrain shall set the stage for a more detailed reading of the inscriptions of a subject that preoccupied Keats and has divided his readers: the gender of that famously Keatsian character, "Indolence."[1]

From his debut, Keats attracted, even courted, judgments in the language of gender. To review the outline. The favorable reviews of his work, mostly from friends, gave an inadvertently feminizing emphasis to his stylistic beauties, and/or celebrated a budding masculine power of intellect, evident, say, in the sonnet on Chapman's Homer and the scrappy assault on Augustan poetics in *Sleep and Poetry*. More divided notices spoke of promising talent, but also of unripe judgment. The hostile judgments, motivated by political and class antipathy, mobilized Keats's youth to ridicule unmanly, adolescent affectation. This last Keats—inept, puerile, pretentious—was the infamous abject hero of the anti-Cockney reviews of the 1817 *Poems* and *Endymion*.[2] The obituaries—unwittingly, Shelley's *Adonais* and, wittily, Byron's soon-to-be-famous stanza in *Don Juan* ("John Keats . . . killed off by one critique"; "Poor fellow! . . . snuffed out by an Article")[3]—whipped this abjection alternatively into pathos or farce, with the result that by midcentury,

Keats was culturally installed as a sensitive and vulnerable boy, a creature of too-feminine delicacy.

The first biographers (Leigh Hunt, Richard Monckton Milnes, Sidney Colvin) tried to resurrect Keats-the-man, but seemed to protest too much, belaboring his boyhood pugnacity, his terrier courage, his drubbing a butcher, and the manliness (sometimes called precocious) of the sonnet on Chapman's Homer and the Preface to *Endymion*. Or, on another tack, they advocated more liberal borders of the "manly," to include gentleness, tenderness, and sensitivity.[4] Oscar Wilde complicated things further when his rhapsodic romance of martyred Keats amplified the homoerotic aura of the Keats circle.[5] The question of gender was still demanding spin control from twentieth-century editors and biographers, including Amy Lowell, Douglas Bush, Walter Jackson Bate, Lionel Trilling, and Aileen Ward.[6] Jack Stillinger's (in)famous essay, "The Hoodwinking of Madeline," then produced a seismic shift in the trials of Keats's manliness, not just entering the defense, but prosecuting the alliance of Porphyro (at least) with aggressive, even Satanic seducers and summoning the salaciously male-tuned passages of *The Eve of St. Agnes* that Keats's publishers demanded he revise, to his annoyance ("He says he does not want ladies to read his poetry: that he writes for men," reported Richard Woodhouse, the publishers' advisor [L2:163]).[7] Meanwhile, Christopher Ricks was reviewing the nineteenth-century diagnosis of "effeminate" Keats—that regressive sensuous imagination, those habitual swoons—with an eye to revaluation. Ricks wanted to praise a poet unembarrassed by such embarrassments, and so able to indulge audacious expression of them: this was a decidedly mature, if not conventionally manly, performance.[8]

Then, in the 1970s, Keats was embraced by feminist criticism. His limited education, economic insecurity, and class status—the "Cockney" targets of Regency disdain—seemed akin to the marginality of women, while his poetics of "Negative Capability" and "no self" / "no identity" were recruited for a "feminist" poetics and ego ideal, an enabling alternative to the strong ego boundaries and egotism taken to characterize "masculine" practices. Within a decade, however, this adoption was contested by another turn of reading that restored Keats to the patriarchy, not only marking his commitment to male heroes, "brother Poets" (*To George Felton Mathew*), and to fame in the patrilinear canon, but also pointing to the sexism, sometimes misogyny, informing his figures of women and the feminine.

These various descriptions, a virtual polymorphism of Keats's gender, are the epiphenomenon of the provocation, and problem, of its referent. More than any other male poet of the Romantic era, Keats writes from a confluence of poetic genius, penetrating critical insight, and adolescent uncertainty. In this entanglement of adolescence and genius, and in its nexus of intellectual, psychological, and social pressures, Keats shows divided, often contradictory investments—by turns, speculative, anxious, risky—in a variety of masculinities and their proximity to a "feminine" differential. About women, he is (also by turns) adoring, sympathetic, defensive, and hostile, especially about their claims as readers, writers, and arbiters of his personal and professional self-definition. His overall syntax of gender is more zigzag than linear, and the total story more indeterminate than definitive.

Consider one of Keats's most famous formulations, "Negative Capability," that capacity for being in "uncertainties, Mysteries, doubts, without any irritable reaching after fact & reason" (*L*1:193). I shall return to the problematic denotation in our century of this capability as "feminine," even "feminist," but I want to suggest briefly why I think the claim for Keatsian sponsorship must admit impediments. For one, the path to this idea was mapped through masculine terrain. A few weeks before, in November 1817, Keats was thinking about two chief forms of male self-definition: "Men of Power," who "have a proper self," and "Men of Genius," who "have not any individuality, any determined Character" (*L*1:184). Evoking Alexander Pope's notorious barb (authorized by "a Lady") that "Most women have no Characters at all,"[9] Keats rearranges the gender binary into genres that discriminate male Genius. Within a year, he would be advertising his own "poetical Character" as one of "no self . . . no character . . . no identity" (*L*1:387) and, contra Pope, affiliating the negatives with a positive value, a creative capability of "speculation."

Keats elides the feminine and refers his formulations to men only: the different ways "Men" orient their thinking, social conduct and writing. His ideal is Shakespeare (not Katherine Philips, Ann Radcliffe, or Mary Tighe, all of whom he read and admired in varying degrees). So, too, his famous simile of life as a "Mansion of Many Apartments" is not just a genetic fable, but a gendered one. Its "Chamber of Maiden-Thought" matures by becoming masculine in both agency and subject matter: among the effects that thinking is "father of," Keats says, "is that tremendous one of sharpening one's vision into the heart and nature of Man" (*L*1:280–81).

This gendering of maturity affects Keats's vision of the social "reality" of "Woman" outside of his own Maiden-Thought, the "soft nest" of "Boyish imagination" (as he describes this stage a few months later to his friend Benjamin Bailey [*L*1:341]). The transition from the maiden in the nest of the boy's mind to "Women" in social perception is a transition from reverence to disdain. Arnold discerned this antipathy. Even as he lamented the want of "character and self-control" in Keats's letters to Fanny Brawne, he found a "curious" "coldness" in Keats's comments about "love and women,"[10] noting both his description of the "generallity of women" as "children to whom I would rather give a Sugar Plum than my time" (*L*1:404) and his edginess over reports of "the offence the ladies take" at his poetry (*L*2:327). Keats understood the involution of personal feeling and social determinants. In an early (1814) ritual, he took a line from "Terence's *Eunuch,* Act 2, Sc. 4" ("What wondrous beauty! From this moment I efface from my mind all women") for the epigraph of his petition for "some drug design'd / To banish Woman from my mind" (*Fill for me a brimming Bowl* 3–4). This is less manly bravado than a plea for relief from sexual anxiety ("I want not the Stream inspiring, / That heats the Sense with lewd desiring" [5–6]), which is soon confessed futile: "'Tis vain—away I cannot chace / The melting softness of that face" (13–14), "melting" covering both categorical Woman and her effect on the poet. No wonder Keats concedes in his letter to Bailey, "I am certain I have not a right feeling towards Women," and goes on to complain,

> I must absolutely get over this—but how? The only way is to find the root of evil, and so cure it "with backward mutters of dissevering Power" That is a difficult thing; an obstinate Prejudice can seldom be produced but from a gordian complication of feelings, which must take time to unravell{ed} and care to keep unravelled—I could say a good deal about this.
> (*L*1:341–42)

The two narratives he weaves into this dilemma are revealing, if not unraveling. Keats "among Women" (*L*1:341) feels himself like the imprisoned Lady in Milton's *Comus,* her "stony fetters fixt and motionless," indissoluble without her enchanter's wand "revers't, / And backward mutters of dissevering power" (816–19).[11] Perhaps no mere wand is sufficient, implies Keats's second allusion: confronting the famously intricate Gordian knot, Alexander the Great does not try to unravel it; he boldly severs it, thus claiming the prophesy of imperial conquest, a masculine fame par excellence.

Part of Keats's unheroic ravel is his self-reading, and not just through those intellectual forms at odds with Regency "Men of Power," such as Negative Capability and "camelionism." It also involves social displays, such as being "smokeable"—Regency slang for naive, and hence vulnerable to ridicule, and an implicitly gendered slur. "Women with few exceptions—the Dress Maker, the blue Stocking and the most charming sentimentalist differ but in a Slight degree" in this "inadequacy"; they "are equally smokeable" (L2:19). But if this is so, this equation extends to his own character as a writer of romance, the genre he describes as feminine in the sonnet on rereading *King Lear*. Keats's contempt for Bailey's inconstancy as a lover reflects a self-recognition: "that the man who rediculus romance is the most romantic of Men— that he who abuses women and slights them—loves them the most" (L2:67). The fault of *Isabella* and, less glaringly, "Sᵗ Agnes Eve," he reflects to Woodhouse, is that they are "mawkish," "too smokeable," exposing "too much inexperience of li[f]e, and simplicity of knowledge" (L2:174, 162).[12] Francis Jeffrey famously derided Wordsworth's poetry for its "maukish affectations of childish simplicity,"[13] and Keats tunes the implied charge of unmanly simplicity to read his own mawkish poems as figurative women, their arts penetrable by a superior male reader, and their innocence of this effect synonymous with deficiency: "Women must want Imagination" (L1:293).

Although he exempts *Lamia* from this "objection" (L2:174), the extremity of its antidote, rendering everyone, everything, every attitude smokeable, looks more like a smoke screen around a gordian complication still raveled up in the shifty "brilliance feminine" (I.92) of its eponym—by turns seductive, demonic, and fragile—and in the strange and strained shifts in the representations of her mortal lover. The counterpart in the anecdote of Burton's *Anatomy of Melancholy,* "one Menippus Lycius, a young man twenty-five years of age," declares the Keatsian transparency. Keats's Lycius changes from a romantic Keatsian swooner in Part I into a "cruel" and "perverse" figure of "tyranny" in Part II (69–81)—a policy with which Keats was complicit ("Women love to be forced . . . by a fine fellow—*such as this,*" he assures Woodhouse [L2:164])—and finally into a fatally disillusioned bridegroom.

The extremes of *Lamia* seem generated not only by this double-mindedness but also against another gendered imprint on Keats's disdain for his "too smokeable" poems, that of female success in gothic romance, an idiom to which he was ambivalently attracted. "I shall send you the Pot of Basil, Sᵗ Agnes eve, and if I should have finished it a little thing call'd the 'eve of Sᵗ Mark,'" he tells George and Georgiana early in 1819, adding, "you see what fine mother Radcliff names I have—it is not my fault—I did not search for them—I have not gone on with Hyperion" (*L*2:62). He disclaims his possession of Radcliffe names as inadvertency, a joke about a merely commercial venture that he half-disowns as a chance matriarchal affiliation, not a serious patriarchal venture. But he is clearly raiding the source he affects to mock.[14] Across Keats's inventory, moreover, falls the shadow of one particularly potent man of achievement in literature, marked even in the Spenserian stanzas deployed for *The Eve of St. Agnes* and the ottava rima used for *Isabella.* Just before he gives his list of romances, Keats writes, "I was surprised to hear from Taylor the amount of Murray the Booksellers last sale—what think you of £25,000? He sold 4000 coppies of Lord Byron"—that is, Canto IV of *Childe Harold's Pilgrimage,* a romance with a difference.[15] Having this news of Byron's commercial potency from his own publisher must have been difficult, especially because it came at a time when Keats was giving up on his proposed antidote to romance, *Hyperion,* a work in the genre that his prospectus of late 1816, *Sleep and Poetry,* projected as the "nobler life" (123) that would prove "strength of manhood" (163).

What Keats wrestled with in his reading and in his social experience, what he expressed over the course of his writing, and what others would read in him, was Negative Capability with a vengeance when it came to the question of what quality went to form a man of achievement, in literature or in life. In our century, this negative has been given a liberal, even deconstructive positive spin as mental "androgyny." Thus Virginia Woolf, citing Coleridge's claim that "a great mind must be androgynous," included Keats in the canon of such writers.[16] Trilling's reading of Keats in *The Opposing Self* took this androgyny into a binary of self and culture. Identifying the "distinguishing characteristic" of self as an "intense and adverse imagination" of the "culture in which it has its being," especially the "unconscious portion of culture," he admired Keats for his bold identification of "passivity" as a "female principle" that "he does not shrink from experiencing," believing it "to be half of his power of creation."[17]

A few decades later, this half-female Keats was promoted to a fully "feminist" Keats, its definition sharpened against "masculinist" poetics. In 1983, with an unconscious echo of Keats's remark that "axioms in philosophy" need to be "proved upon our pulses" (*L*1:279), Elaine Showalter described "feminist" (as opposed to male-authored) "theories of women's writing" as "theories proved on our own pulses," infusing essentialist biological authority with Keatsian epistemology.[18] A few years before, in some incidental remarks in *Women Writers and Poetic Identity*, Margaret Homans proposed that Keats's class origins and lack of classical education shared "certain aspects of women's experience as outsiders relative to the major literary tradition" and its "masculine" practices, and she noted with interest Adrienne Rich's designation of Negative Capability as a female aesthetic.[19] Rich was thinking about Nancy Chodorow's work on woman's "so-called 'weak ego boundaries'" and suggested that this might "be a negative way of describing the fact that women have tremendous powers of intuitive identification and sympathy with other people." Her conversant, Barbara Gelpi, then remarked, "John Keats had weak ego boundaries," and Rich took the cue: "Negative capability. Exactly. Any artist has to have it."[20] Soon after, Erica Jong, writing on Rich, made Keats's phrase a badge of feminist sensibility: "feminism *means* empathy. And empathy is akin to the quality Keats called 'negative capability'—that unique gift for projecting oneself into other states of consciousness."[21] In this discourse, Keats is doubly feminized: as mediator between women, his role is the traditional feminine position as mediator "between men," and his ideological sign is his promotion to "an honorary woman," as Homans remarked in a later reading of this interview.[22]

This honor has a decidedly retro tinge. For all Rich's and Jong's claims of "radical" resistance to patriarchy,[23] their feminism harkens back to nineteenth-century stereotypes. It was, after all, the conservative conduct advisor "Mrs. Sandford" who named the distinctly female charm of "forgetting one's self, and sympathising with others" and who cautioned that "to be agreeable, a woman must avoid egotism."[24] Ironically, too, Rich and Jong seem to have forgotten, or not to have known, that Keats coined Negative Capability to define a "Man of Achievement" and that his attitude toward women of genius, and views, and achievement,—I mean that sort of which Woolf, Rich, Gelpi, and Jong are members, writers and intellectuals—was patently hostile.[25] He longed for "some real feminine Modesty in these things" (problematically citing the homoerotic passion of "the matchless

Orinda") and was eager to be the scourge of this modern "set of Devils" (*L*1:163).

The partiality of "feminist" Keats was redressed by Homans in a provocative lecture at the English Institute in 1986 (published in 1990) in which she reworked Keats through his "resentment of [women's] real and imagined power over him and his compensatory wish to assert his own masculine authority."[26] Macho Keats received an even stronger articulation in another essay published in 1990, by Marlon Ross, who argued that *Hyperion*—the poem whose hero even Keats's loyal defender Leigh Hunt thought "effeminate"—bears Keats's desire "to assert not just [his] coming into *manhood* but also his coming into discursive power": his ability to perform the "rituals which define poetic maturity in terms of patriarchal culture." Whereas earlier defenders admired the manly/manful/masculine manner of Keats's bravely self-critical Preface to *Endymion*, Ross saw this as an audition for patriarchal culture and ably identified the power plays of its "patrilineal discourse."[27]

More recently, Anne Mellor and Grant Scott charted a middle ground. Mellor's is a bipartisan Keats, an "ideological cross-dresser" on the scene of gender, "occupying the position of the woman in life [as caretaker] or in discourse, or by blurring the distinction between genders."[28] Although her Keats is entangled in sexism and misogyny, his ultimate evolution, capped for Mellor in *The Fall of Hyperion*, is toward female self-identification, as a jealous honorer of female creativity. Approaching a maternal Moneta, "ach[ing] to see what things the hollow brain / Behind enwombed" (I.276–77), Mellor's Keats finds his poetic power in her "pregnant tragic consciousness":

> the male poet discovers what is ultimately for Keats the appropriate relationship between female and male in poetic discourse: that of goddess/mother/muse to human/son/poet, a relationship that sustains the role of humble submission and dependency Keats has everywhere adopted in relation to feminine creative power.[29]

In effect, Mellor seeks to recuperate, in a finer feminist tone, the tenor of Z.'s sneering advertisements of Keats as "The Muses' son of promise; and what feats / He may yet do."[30] Scott is less decided about a less decided Keats, nodding to both the feminists and the skeptics when he describes Keats as a poet in "uneasy alliance with femininity."[31]

SLIPPERY KEATS

How has Keats managed to inform and fill so many different, even contradictory perspectives? Although I've just used his language for his self-effacing "camelion" poetics (L1:387), this is a misleading key insofar as it suggests a deliberate strategy, aesthetically controlled. A more accurate measure would be Keats's sense, in the same letter, of the correlation of his aesthetic preference with, and emergence from, a related existential sensation:

> When I am in a room with People if I ever am free from speculating on creations of my own brain, then not myself goes home to myself: but the identity of every one in the room begins to press up me that, I am in a very little time an[ni]hilated . . . among Men; . . . I know not whether I make myself wholly understood. (L1:387)

At the end of his twenty-third year, Keats recognizes his social identity as still unsettled, still not fully legible, still susceptible of varying impressions and self-readings in the contradictory pressures of self-definition: he is a young, untitled man choosing a career in "Poetry" that seems a manly and heroic romance ("I will assay to reach to as high a summit in Poetry as the nerve bestowed upon me will suffer"), but not as manly as "doing the world some good" ("If I should be spared that may be the work of maturer years"), and perhaps even "feminine" in its sensuous, swooning enthusiasm ("The faint conceptions I have of Poems to come brings the blood frequently into my forehead . . . I should write from the mere yearning and fondness I have for the Beautiful"), or stoically "masculine" ("even if my night's labours should be burnt every morning and no eye ever shine upon them"). To these different auditions "among Men," Keats's final impulse, on this occasion at least, is a retreat into "camelion" aesthetics: "But even now I am perhaps not speaking from myself; but from some character in whose soul I now live" (L1:387–88).

Retreat is no solution, but neither is it a default. Keats's amused, aggrieved confessions mark an intelligently ironic, nervously alert ideological irresolution, generated by a provisional, untheorized sensation of difference, dislocation, and sometimes critical alienation from the cultural stage of manhood and the sorts of performances it requires.

This pleomorphic array of gender forms and the contradictions between them are part of Keats's historical meaning, both as these varying
positions reflect ideological divisions in his own age and as they are
transmitted through his captivating example.

One compelling structure in this irresolution is Keats's gordian complication of indolence, ambition, and poetry, which besides being a
critical perplexity for him has proven a revealing challenge to gender
criticism. The knot is tied through a train in Keats's writing that was
only privately communicated or drafted as poetry left unpublished.
Irresolution is a Keatsian enough temper in his published work, but its
unpublished forms suggest intensities that may have resisted successful
aesthetic management. The strands are his speculations, to a trusted
circle of friends and family, on male postures of passivity and receptiv-
ity—the ones that Trilling admired for their exploration of the "feminine" principle and that Scott saw as "anxious flexing of half dubious
muscles." Trilling felt compelled to note that Keats "must still assert
the virtue of a specifically 'masculine' energy" by affirming "the active
principle" in his "conscious . . . surrender to the passive, unconscious
life," and he offered friendly support in referring to Keats's project as
a concern with "the *power* of passivity." Homans then shifted the
stakes, observing in Keats both a defensiveness in his "feminine" self-
identifications and a tendency to counter this with an "assertion
of masculinity." And Scott tracked Keats's "fears of feminine influence."[32]

I find the overall bearing elusive, not just because Keats's texts toil
and spin, but because they do so with parodic, even self-parodic, energy. The key text is his elaborate meditation in a letter to his friend
John Hamilton Reynolds, February 19, 1818, on "diligent Indolence."
He first describes this oxymoron with a double-sexed figure:

> Now it appears to me that almost any Man may like the Spider
> spin from his own inwards his own airy Citadel—the points of
> leaves and twigs on which the Spider begins her work are few
> and she fills the Air with a beautiful circuiting: man should be
> content with as few points to tip with the fine Webb of his Soul
> and weave a tapestry empyrean— (*L*1:231–32)

Mellor, with an echo of Trilling and indebtedness to Scott, sees Keats
aligning himself with the traditionally female occupation of weaving.[33]

Yet what is remarkable about this circuitry of speculation is its swift counterchange of gender: a "Man" thinking the way a she-Spider spins; the Citadel, the defense-building of men, transforming into a tapestry-making, the labor of women; then the resorption of this female art as the metaphor for Man's soul.

From his double-sexed spider figure of diligent work and play Keats moves into double-gendered figures of delicious, if not exactly diligent, indolence, ones that playfully unsettle the gender map:

> It has been an old Comparison for our urging on—the Bee hive—however it seems to me that we should rather be the flower than the Bee—for it is a false notion that more is gained by receiving than giving—no the receiver and the giver are equal in their benefits—The f[l]ower I doubt not receives a fair guerdon from the Bee—its leaves blush deeper in the next spring—and who shall say between Man and Woman which is the most delighted? (L1:232)

As he perplexes the dynamics of giving and receiving, Keats complicates gendered lore about passivity and activity. The syntactic alignment of the question that brings "Man and Woman" into the equation challenges the "old Comparison": resisting the chiasmus that upholds the alignment of Man with the active, giving Bee, Keats deploys a parallel in which Man mirrors flower, and in such passive delights radiates super-manly self-possession:

> Now it is more noble to sit like Jove tha[n] to fly like Mercury—let us not therefore go hurrying about and collecting honey-bee like, buzzing here and there impatiently from a knowledge of what is to be arrived at: but let us open our leaves like a flower and be passive and receptive—budding patiently under the eye of Apollo and taking hints from eve[r]y noble insect that favors us with a visit. (L1:232)

Nobly, divinely "passive and receptive," even in the "female" position of being gazed upon by Apollo (who himself is imaged as maternally doting), male passivity is floral and Jovian at once.

We can see why Homans argues that Keats thus appropriates the "passive female position" for "masculine power and pleasure."[34] But despite Keats's insistently inclusive plural pronouns, his identification is ultimately not with this Jovian power. It is with a suspect indolence whose only remedy may be this Mercurial boy-buzziness:

> Now I am sensible all this is a mere sophistication, however it may neighbour to any truths, to excuse my own indolence—so I will not deceive myself that Man should be equal with jove— but think himself very well off as a sort of scullion-Mercury or even a humble Bee— (*L*1:233)

Homans notes this sentence only in a parenthetical coda and Mellor not at all.

In early 1818 the she-spider's spinning is beautiful work, but in the more bitter mood about his professional work that was Keats's in late summer 1819, the spider and indolence are both demeaned, and the gendering gets nasty. Resolving to remedy a life he thinks is becoming viciously "idle minded"—"I have not known yet what it is to be diligent," he tells his friend Charles Brown—he determines to write "for whoever will pay me" (*L*2:176). The same day, he writes to another friend, Charles Wentworth Dilke:

> Even if I am swept away like a Spider from a drawing room I am determined to spin—home spun any thing for sale. Yea I will traffic. Any thing but Mortgage my Brain to Blackwood. . . . It is fortunate I have not before this been tempted to venture on the common. . . . I . . . am confident I shall be able to cheat as well as any literary Jew of the Market and shine up an article on any thing. (*L*2:179)

This spider is now confederate with marginalized and patently despised workers: woman as whore, a trafficker and a commoner, and a fancy cheat who earns a dose of anti-Semitism. Its world is not empyrean, but a repetition in a darker tone of the more often quoted remark in this trope, from March 1818, in which Keats, in a "very sceptical" temper, describes "Poetry itself" as a market commodity with no use value: "As Tradesmen say every thing is worth what it will fetch . . . being in itself nothing" (*L*1:242). This proto-marxist analysis is still weighted in favor of imaginative desire, here called a creatively "ardent pursuit." But by late 1819, the ardor has become a cynical shining of whatever one can spin for sale in a value determined by the desire of the purchaser. The prostitute and the Jew spell this degradation, and if these figures do nothing for Keats's hopes, the sordid boon at least is to ally him with a dominant (Byronic) discourse of contempt.[35]

Between these extremes, in spring 1819, an ode "on Indolence" and a letter about its inspiration by a "temper indolent and supremely careless" (March 19, 1819; L2:78–79) reveal a more flexibly constrained gender play. In his letter, Keats calls his indolence "a state of effeminacy," but not carelessly. It is a morning-after story, of nursing a black eye from a vigorous cricket game with the guys the day before, and he camps up the gender codes of this hangover with some mocking melodramatic scenery: "if I had teeth of pearl and the breath of lillies I should call it langour— but as I am I must call it Laziness." His footnote, "especially as I have a black eye," may be a necessary assertion of masculinity (Homans), but if so, its sign of potency is not dominant, either in this scene or in the ode it inspired. Keats goes on to describe a happy relaxation of his usual urgencies about "Poetry," "Ambition," and "Love"—which he genders as "a Man and two women" (even as he says that "no one but myself could distinguish [them] in their disguisement).

The ode is only half-indolent, however, caught between the unstable "difference between an easy and uneasy indolence" that he defined for George and Georgiana the day before the cricket game (March 17; L2:77). There is a tone of urbane disdain of "the voice of busy common-sense" (40), the bee-buzzing of the mind. At the same time, the "three figures" of habitual desire do not yield to effeminate indolence, as they do in the letter, but appear as challengers to it, and with new gendering:[36]

> to follow them I burn'd
> And ached for wings, because I knew the three:
> The first was a fair Maid, and Love her name;
> The second was Ambition, pale of cheek,
> And ever watchful with fatigued eye;
> The last, whom I love more, the more of blame
> Is heap'd upon her, Maiden most unmeek,—
> I knew to be my demon Poesy. (23–30)

In the letter of March 19, "Poetry" is male, a summons to work; in the ode, poetry is the alluring she-demon Poesy. Effeminacy is challenged not with a masculine opposite, but by a "Maiden most unmeek." In normal codes, this boldness courts censure (in the effusion of *Woman!* [1817], Keats loves "Woman ... modest ... meek, and kind, and

tender"), but here it is a thing he acknowledges his own.[37] Simultaneously, the most likely antidote to indolence, alienated in the letter as a
female sign, appears here as a male "Ambition." This gender acknowledges the cultural command (Brown's busy writing "affronts my indolence and Luxury," Keats says [*L*1:344]), but the figure is also entirely
enervated. "Ambition" is a pale visionary like the Knight-at-arms in *La
Belle Dame sans Merci*, as if Keats were speculating about the price of
this devotion against a difference that was so alien that it had to be cast
into demonic feminine gendering. Although in the next spin of the ode,
all three subjects fade away from desire, it is telling that Ambition does
not so much retreat as it is banished by degradation. Love is left a folly
or a mystery, Poesy holds no joy, but Ambition is utterly diminished:
"poor Ambition—it springs / From a man's little heart's short fever-fit"
(33–34).

Now all this belittling may be mere sophistication. When Keats tells
a female friend in June 1819, "the thing I have most enjoyed this year
has been writing an ode to Indolence," he confesses not only a healthy
disenchantment, but a damning defeat: "I have been very idle lately,
very averse to writing; both from the overpowering idea of our dead
poets and from abatement of my love of fame" (*L*2:116). If indolence,
as he says, is "a rare instance of advantage in the body overpowering
the Mind" (*L*2:79), the other advantage, clearly, is overpowering the
overpowering idea of other men's (and probably other women's)
achievements. Yet this mood is also an opportunity to review the master
desire that joins poesy, ambition, and love, namely, his "love of fame."
The letter on "diligent Indolence" involved two references to Milton's
famous meditation on "Fame" in *Lycidas*:

> Fame is the spur that the clear spirit doth raise
> (That last infirmity of Noble mind)
> To scorn delights, and live laborious days. (70–72)

Milton goes on to lament that "the fair Guerdon we hope to find" is
thwarted by a feminine-gendered fate, the scissors-wielding "blind
Fury" who cuts life short (73–76), but he takes comfort in redemption
by male deities: the assurance of Phoebus himself that immortal fame
will be pronounced by the "perfect witness of all-judging Jove" (82).
This mediation is in the background of Keats's defense of indolence—
which is, seemingly, but only seemingly, a refusal of fame-devoted labor

from the start. In the Keatsian scene, the flower "receives a fair guerdon from the Bee," with the phrase from Lycidas unlinked from the labors for worldly fame, attached to momentary pleasure, and then aligned with the noble mind of one able "to sit like Jove" (L1:232), the guarantor of ultimate rewards. But the patent echoes expose the defensiveness.

Such defense is also the spur of two sonnets on fame written at about the time of *Ode on Indolence*—not for publication, just self-sobering (L2:104–5). In both, Keats addresses a fraternity of fellow suitors of worldly fame, urging a divorce from the degraded fame that is ultimately only, in Milton's words, "glistering foil / Set off to th' world" (79–80). "On Fame" begins, "How fever'd is that ⟨Man misled⟩," diagnosing the fever for public attention as a self-advertising that is more truly a self-molestation, whereby one robs one's "fair name of its maidenhood," in effect, soliciting regard as prostituted commodity. The pressure of gender is intensified by Keats's imagery of self-violation, the way a ripe plum might "finger its misty bloom," for this evokes the degradation of being reviewed, of making oneself "fingerable over by *Men*," as he describes it to Benjamin Haydon (December 22, 1818; L1:415), perhaps recalling Woodhouse's rage, two months earlier, about the *Quarterly*'s reviewer having "laid his finger of contempt upon [*Endymion's*] passages of . . . beauty" (L1:379).[38] This trope of public peril as a molested female body recalls the self-imaging that, with nervous wit, Keats addressed to his new publishers in June 1817. He was asking for an advance, in effect a self-selling: "I must endeavour to lose my Maidenhead with respect to money Matters . . . I am a little maidenish or so—and I feel my virginity come strong upon me—the while I request the loan" (L1:147–48). In the second sonnet of April 1819 ("Another on Fame"), Keats splits this self-commodifying into a heterosexed scenario, with the degraded object now cast as a female-gendered fame fetish that self-respecting men might well disdain. The call of she-Fame is reduced to the flirtations of a promiscuous girl who is by turns "coy," doting, teasing, jilting, maddening, and responsive, but in sum not worth any man's suits of woe. In a pose of jaded sophistication, his sonneteer plays out a self-possessed countercourtship.[39]

Keats weans himself with the further reminder that a fair guerdon, even if won, may not make the man but may yield him renown only as "a versifying Pet-lamb" (L2:116), a pretty creature for a little maiden's doting. He may be remembering Wordsworth's *The Pet-Lamb*, which he ridiculed to George and Georgiana (21 April 1819; *L*2:94).[40] The poet of *Ode on Indolence* casts this pet as the result of any appetite for fame: "I would not be dieted with praise, / A pet-lamb in a sentimental farce" (53–54)—a figure not only subject to feminine doting, but also itself female (a "milk-white lamb that bleats / For man's protection" in *Woman!*).[41] The counterpart is public judgment lapsed into effeminate indolence: "the Reviews have enervated and made indolent mens minds—few think for themselves," Keats complains (February 19, 1819; *L*2:65).

These rejections of ambition for worldly fame are accompanied by no retrenchment of masculine self-identification, however, nor even the promise of better, more manly work that Keats gave in his self-lacerating Preface to *Endymion* the year before. With this poem's "every error denoting a feverish attempt," Keats could only hope its "mawkishness" would be confined to "a space of life between" boy and man, "in which the soul is in a ferment, the character undecided, the way of life uncertain, the ambition thick-sighted" (Preface), and its failures chastened by devotion to "the Memory of great Men" and disdain of "a Mawkish Popularity" (April 9, 1818; *L*1:266–67). Although Keats's devotion to this cultural memory "of great Men" did not abate, it continued to have feminine rivals. In February 1820, in desperately ill health and doubting recovery, he tells Fanny Brawne of a dialogue of the mind with itself:

> "If I should die," said I to myself, "I have left no immortal work behind me—nothing to make my friends proud of my memory." . . . Thoughts like these came very feebly whilst I was in health and every pulse beat for you—now you divide with this (may *I* say it?) "last infirmity of noble minds" all my reflection. (*L*2:263)

The rueful allusion to Milton's anthem tugs at the whole gordian complication: Keats both recognizes the romance of immortal work as a last infirmity of manhood and feels it as the life-pulse of young ambition; it is a sign of a man's aspiring noble mind and a rival to the heart in love. Whether in agonized self reflection or in playful speculation, Keats lets himself experience and "say" these divisions, keeping us aware of the multiple and often conflicting interests that shape the languages of gender, in his cultural moment and in ours. This is why Keats continues to matter in gender criticism, and why, in turn, it is invariably enriched and challenged by his writing.

NOTES

This chapter has benefited from the advice of Ronald Sharp, Robert Ryan, and Ronald Levao. Some of its ideas were formulated in "Feminizing Keats," in *Critical Essays on John Keats*, ed. Hermione de Almeida (Boston: G. K. Hall, 1990), 317–56; "Keats and the Manhood of the Poet," in *European Romantic Review* 6 (1995):1–37; and "Keats Enters History: Autopsy, *Adonais,* and the Fame of Keats," in *Keats and History,* ed. Nicholas Roe (Cambridge: Cambridge University Press, 1995), 17–45.

1. Quotations of Keats's poetry published in his lifetime are from *Poems, by John Keats* (London: C. & J. Ollier, 1817) and *Lamia, Isabella, The Eve of St. Agnes, and Other Poems* (London: Taylor and Hessey, 1820), otherwise from *John Keats,* ed. Elizabeth Cook (Oxford and New York: Oxford University Press, 1990). Line numbers are given in the text. Quotations of the letters are from *The Letters of John Keats: 1814–1821,* ed. Hyder E. Rollins (Cambridge, Mass.: Harvard University Press, 1958), abbreviated *L* in text, with volume and page numbers.

2. For the celebrations of a "young" modern genius, see: Leigh Hunt, "Young Poets," *Examiner* no. 466 (1 December 1816):761–62, and his unsigned serial review of Keats's 1817 *Poems* in *Examiner* no. 492 (1 June 1817):345, no. 497 (6 July 1817):428–29, no. 498 (13 July 1817):443–44; and John Hamilton Reynolds's unsigned review of *Poems* in *Champion* (9 March 1817):78. For equivocal remarks on Keats's youth, see G. F. M. [George Felton Mathew], *European Magazine* 71 (May 1817), who finds him "promising" but also short on "maturity" and prone to "pretty . . . childishness," "puerility" and "feeble thoughts" (435–36); and *(Scots) Edinburgh Magazine* 2d ser. 1 (October 1817):255–57: Keats is "a very young man" of promising talent but also of "considerable affectation." Josiah Conder punctuates his unsigned review in *Eclectic,* 2d ser. 8 (September 1817):267–75, with words such as "immature," "childishness," "ridiculous excess" (270); attribution by Donald H. Reiman, ed., *The Romantics Reviewed: Contemporary Reviews of British Romantic Writers* (New York and London: Garland Press, 1972), Part C, *Shelley, Keats, and London Radical Writers,* 1:329.

For *Blackwood's Edinburgh Magazine's* Z.'s sheer ridicule of "Johnny Keats," see the key review, August 1818 (3:519–24), the anticipations in October and November 1817 (2:38, 2:194), May 1818 (3:197), and the echoes in 1819: January (4:482), April (5:97), September (5:640), and, repeatedly in the lead article, December (6:236–39). As J. R. MacGillivray remarks, any naming of "Johnny Keats" in the nineteenth century carried with it a winking agreement with Z.'s contempt (*Keats: A Bibliography and Reference Guide with an Essay on Keats' Reputation* [Toronto: University of Toronto Press,

1949], xxii). Many of the reviews are reprinted in Reiman (ibid.) and in *Keats: The Critical Heritage*, ed. G. M. Matthews (New York: Barnes and Noble, 1971).

3. *Don Juan* XI.60 (1823); in *Lord Byron: The Complete Poetical Works*, ed. Jerome J. McGann (Oxford: Clarendon Press, 1986).

4. Leigh Hunt, "Mr. Keats, With a Criticism of His Writings," in *Lord Byron and Some of His Contemporaries* (London: Henry Colburn; Philadelphia: Carey, Lea & Carey, 1828), 214–15; Richard Monckton Milnes (Lord Houghton), *Life, Letters, and Literary Remains, of John Keats* (1848; London: J. M. Dent & Sons / New York: Dutton, 1927), 9–12, 30, 50; Sidney Colvin, *John Keats* (New York: Harper, 1887), 6–9.

5. See *Glykypikros Eros*, in *The Writings of Oscar Wilde* (New York: Doubleday, Page, 1923), 1:243–46, and *The Tomb of Keats* (*Irish Monthly*, July 1887), *Writings*, 12:301–5.

6. For my fuller discussion of gender and the posthumous construction of "Keats," see "Feminizing Keats" and, with elaboration, "Keats Enters History"; bibliographical information is in the headnote to these notes.

7. Jack Stillinger, "The Hoodwinking of Madeline: Skepticism in *The Eve of St. Agnes*" (1961); reprinted in *The Hoodwinking of Madeline and Other Essays on Keats's Poems* (Urbana: University of Illinois Press, 1971), 67–93. Woodhouse is reporting a quarrel with Keats over some sexually explicit writing (*L*2:163).

8. Ricks, *Keats and Embarrassment* (London: Oxford University Press, 1976).

9. "To a Lady, of the Characters of Women" (2), in *Poems of Alexander Pope*, ed. John Butt (New Haven: Yale University Press, 1961); vol. 3, Part 2, ed. F. W. Bateson. Having said in his prefacing Argument that "the Characters of *Women* . . . as contradistinguished from the other Sex . . . are yet more inconsistent and incomprehensible," Pope still wanted this note to the line I quote: "their particular characters are not so strongly mark'd as those of Men, seldom so fixed, and still more inconsistent with themselves."

10. Matthew Arnold, "John Keats," preface to "Selections from Keats" in *English Poets*, vol. 4 (1880), ed. Thomas Humphry Ward; reprinted in *Essays and Criticism, Second Series* (1895). Quotations are from vol. 9, *The Complete Prose Works of Matthew Arnold*, ed. R. H. Super (Ann Arbor: University of Michigan Press, 1973), 205, 212.

11. Quotations of Milton here and following are from *John Milton: Complete Poems and Major Prose*, ed. Merritt Y. Hughes (New York: Odyssey, 1957).

12. Distinguishing Keats's sensibility from "that sugar & butter sentiment, that cloys & disgusts," Woodhouse reads Keats's self-judgment as an effect of his having read his work in a temper "more sobered" and "unpassionate" than the mood of writing, an effect "which comes upon us where any thing of great tenderness & excessive simplicity is met with when we are not in a sufficiently tender & simple frame of mind to bear it: when we experience a sort of revulsion, or resiliency . . . from the sentiment or expression" (letter to John Taylor, 19 September 1819; *L*2:162). Christopher Ricks shrewdly remarks that when Keats uses "mawkish," it is "usually the sign both that he is near to things that are urgent for him because his truest imaginings are

involved and also that he knows how necessarily open to ridicule is his refusal to ridicule" (*Keats and Embarrassment*, 146).

13. Jeffrey, *Edinburgh Review* 20 (November 1812): 438.

14. See Margaret Homans, "Keats Reading Women, Women Reading Keats," *Studies in Romanticism* 29 (1990): 360.

15. In February 1818, *Monthly Magazine* reported that 4000 copies of *Canto IV* "have been already bespoken" for the April publication (*L*2:62 n.4). At 12 shillings apiece, this would yield £2400, nearly a tenth of Murray's sale. Thanks to Jerome McGann and Peter Manning for help with these figures.

16. Woolf, *A Room of One's Own* (1929; New York: Harcourt, Brace, 1957), 102, 107. For Coleridge, see *Table Talk*, 1 September 1832; in *Table Talk*, ed. Carl Woodring (Princeton: Princeton University Press, 1990), 2:190–91. For male androgyny as a general ideal in Romantic poetics, see Diane Long Hoeveler, *Romantic Androgyny: The Women Within* (University Park: Pennsylvania State University Press, 1990).

17. Trilling, *The Opposing Self* (New York: Viking Press, 1955), x, 28–29.

18. Showalter, "Critical Cross-Dressing: Male Feminists and The Woman of The Year," *Raritan* 3.2 (1983): 147.

19. Homans, *Women Writers and Poetic Identity: Dorothy Wordsworth, Emily Brontë and Emily Dickinson* (Princeton: Princeton University Press, 1980), 240 n. 25, 251 n. 15.

20. "Three Conversations," in *Adrienne Rich's Poetry*, ed. Barbara Charlesworth Gelpi and Albert Gelpi (New York: Norton, 1975), 115. Chodorow, "Family Structure and Feminine Personality," in *Women, Culture, and Society*, ed. Michelle Zimbalist Rosaldo and Louise Lamphere (Stanford, Calif.: Stanford University Press, 1974), 44, 58–60. Elsewhere, Gelpi summons "Negative Capability" to gloss Dante Gabriel Rossetti's identification with the whore— "I have often said that to be an artist is just the same thing as to be a whore, as far as dependence on the whims and fancies of individuals is concerned" (*The Letters of Dante Gabriel Rossetti*, ed. Oswald Doughty and John Robert Wahl [Oxford: Clarendon Press, 1965–67], 3:1175; see also 2:849–50)— without noting Keats's own sense of writing for hire as "trafficking," a term he infuses with misogyny and anti-Semitism in a way remote from any negatively capable, sympathetic identification. "The Feminization of D. G. Rossetti," in *The Victorian Experience: The Poets*, ed. Richard A. Levine (Ohio: Ohio University Press, 1982), 105.

21. Jong, "Visionary Anger," *Ms.*, July 1973, 31–33; in *Adrienne Rich's Poetry*, 171–72.

22. See Luce Irigaray, "Des marchandises entre elles" (1975), trans. Catherine Porter and Carolyn Burke as "Commodities among Themselves," *This Sex Which is Not One* (Ithaca, N.Y.: Cornell University Press, 1985), 192–97; "The exchanges upon which patriarchal societies are based take place exclusively among men. Women, signs, commodities, and currency always pass from one man to another" (192). Homans, "Keats Reading Women," 343.

23. Rich, "Three Conversations," 114; Jong, "Visionary Anger," 172.

24. Mrs. [John] Sandford, *Woman, In Her Social and Domestic Character* (1831; 2d ed. London: Longman et al., 1832), 7, 9.

25. Woolf was aware that Coleridgean androgyny was for men only, and she did not mistake his theorizing for "any special sympathy with women" or "their cause"; similarly, her own canon of great androgynous minds was limited to men and she always gendered "writer" "he," saying that it would be fatal for her "in any way to speak as a woman" (*A Room*, 102–8).

26. Homans, "Keats Reading Women," 368.

27. Hunt, review of Keats's *Lamia* volume, *Indicator* 44 (9 August 1820): 350; Marlon B. Ross, "Beyond the Fragmented Word: Keats and the Limits of Patrilineal Language," in *Out of Bounds: Male Writers and Gender(ed) Criticism*, ed. Laura Claridge and Elizabeth Langland (Amherst: University of Massachusetts Press, 1990), 110, 122–23. Among the power plays Ross identifies are: a "will to power, the desire to overcome his foes and win their allegiance . . . schematizing compromise; performance, purposiveness, and spectatorship; and, perhaps most important, the establishment of territorial claims for the sake of engendering a lasting line of powerful discourse within culture" (122).

28. Mellor, *Romanticism & Gender* (New York: Routledge, 1992), 171. Mellor reargues Keats's position within the "realm of the feminine gender," endorsing the polarities by which Rich defined Negative Capability and empathic "camelion" poetics as "anti-masculine" (174–75), and adding a survey of Keats's metaphors of creation as maternal pregnancy and birth, female weaving, and tale-telling. She limned this figure to modify Homans's defensive misogynist into a Keats beset by "discomfort," "anxiety," and "ambivalence" about the feminine alliances of his sensibility, his attraction to subjects and genres associated with female writing, and his inability to succeed with more masculine genres of epic and tragedy (179–84).

29. Mellor, *Romanticism & Gender*, 185. Homans's reading of Moneta could not be more opposite: while Moneta is the poet's "most severe reader-critic," her power is diminished not only by her own status as victim and sufferer of that power, but chiefly by her transformation from a potentially threatening reader into a text that the poet reads and interprets in an act that looks like "extraordinary egotism, the appropriation of her memory and thoughts, or even a projection onto her" of his own first *Hyperion* ("Keats Reading Women," 356–58).

30. Lines from the epigraph to "On the Cockney School of Poetry, No. I," *Blackwood's Edinburgh Magazine* 2 (October 1817): 38; repeated in "No. II" (November 1817): 194.

31. Grant F. Scott, *The Sculpted Word: Keats, Ekphrasis, and the Visual Arts* (Hanover: University Press of New England, 1994), 112.

32. Scott, *Sculpted Word*, 112; Trilling, *Opposing Self*, 29, 28; Homans, "Keats Reading Women," 344–45; Scott, ibid., 113.

33. Scott, *Sculpted Word*, 110–11; Mellor, *Romanticism & Gender*, 177.

34. Homans, "Keats Reading Women," 345.

35. In *English Bards and Scotch Reviewers* (1809), Byron ascribed market-governed literary production to "prostituted muse and hireling bard" (182); the quotation is from *Lord Byron, Selected Poems*, ed. Susan J. Wolfson and Peter J. Manning (Harmondsworth, England: Penguin, 1996). Irigaray pro-

poses that "Marx's analysis of commodities" is also "an interpretation of the status of woman in so-called patriarchal societies" ("Le marché des femmes," 1978; trans. 1985 by Porter and Burke as "Woman on the Market," *This Sex*, 172).

36. For the ode's anti-indolent poetics (its "fitful rhythm of refusal"), see Helen Vendler on vacillation and recurrence (*The Odes of John Keats* [Cambridge, Mass.: Harvard University Press, 1983], 21–25, 38) and my *The Questioning Presence: Wordsworth, Keats, and the Interrogative Mode in Romantic Poetry* (Ithaca: Cornell University Press, 1986), 328–29. A month or so later, Keats tells George and Georgiana, "I am affraid more from indolence of mind than anything else" (*L*2:83).

37. Mellor suggests that this unmeek maiden is a figure for the bluestocking literary world with whose poetic subjects, Love and Poesy, Keats is in ambivalent sympathy (*Romanticism & Gender*, 182). Scott, by contrast, sees Keats's ultimate refusal of the ode's figures as disdain of the fame won by the tear-inducing, sentimental female writers of the day (*Sculpted Word*, 105).

38. *Quarterly Review* 19 (April 1818; publ. September): 204–8.

39. With a somewhat different emphasis, Sonia Hofkosh reads these sonnets as a staging of Keats's "desire for the recognition that both constitutes and subverts his authorship, both empowers him to write and undermines the singularity of his writing" ("The Writer's Ravishment: Women and the Romantic Author—The Example of Byron," in *Romanticism and Feminism*, ed. Anne K. Mellor [Bloomington: Indiana University Press, 1988], 97). With more emphasis on the empowerment/disempowerment ratio, Marjorie Levinson (not referring to these sonnets), sees the whole career of Keats's "literary / self-production" defining a "masturbatory dynamics (a taking of his subjectivity for an object), [that] renders him finally a thing dependent for its value upon the representation that will displace and derealize it" (*Keats's Life of Allegory: The Origins of a Style* [London: Basil Blackwell, 1988], 251–252).

40. "The Pet-Lamb, A Pastoral" (*Lyrical Ballads*, 1800) was classed in the 1815 *Poems* with "Poems of Childhood." Barbara Esthwaite, treating this pet as her baby, promises only a future of gentle thralldom: "I'll yoke thee to my cart . . . / My playmate thou shalt be" (46–47); quotation is from *"Lyrical Ballads" and Other Poems, 1797–1800, by William Wordsworth*, ed. James Butler and Karen Green (Ithaca: Cornell University Press, 1992). In December 1818, Keats confesses yet another, analogous self-image to Haydon, a reading in himself of "all the vices of a Poet, irritability, love of effect and admiration" and a tendency, when "influenced by such devils [to] say more rediculous things than I am aware of" (*L*1:414).

41. Woodhouse's note attests to the self-feminizing effects of this image on Keats: "When Keats had written these lines he burst into tears overpowered by the tenderness of his own imagination" (Stuart Sperry, "Richard Woodhouse's Interleaved and Annotated Edition of Keats's 1817 *Poems*," in *Literary Monographs*, ed. Eric Rothstein and Thomas Dunseath [Madison: University of Wisconsin Press, 1967], 1:145).

Keats and the Third Generation

DONALD H. REIMAN

M Y THESIS IS SIMPLE and not entirely new. I first glanced at it in some introductions in *The Romantics Reviewed* (1972), mentioned the possibility in introductions to various volumes of *The Romantic Context: Poetry* (1976–79), and explored the idea in more depth in the chapter on Keats in *Intervals of Inspiration: The Skeptical Tradition and the Psychology of Romanticism* (1988).[1] Here is the short form: *John Keats was not, as is usually thought, part of the second generation of English Romantic writers; he was simply the best poet in the third and final generation of English Romantics.* Among the implications of this conception is that some of the differences between Keats and the other "major Romantic poets" that have usually been ascribed to differences in social class may be, in part, generational instead.

By the time Keats turned to poetry, the first stage of the battle for pluralistic individualism in British society had been fought and won by the elder Romantics. Although Lord Byron and Percy Bysshe Shelley were driven into exile because of their alleged beliefs and behavior and though Leigh Hunt and William Hazlitt found it increasingly difficult to earn a living by their writing, these and other writers had inspired many younger men and women to follow their examples of independence and personal integrity in the face of societal pressures. The younger writers likewise refused to submerge the beliefs and values they had developed through first hand experience in deference to either social conventions or the dogmatic values of a hierarchical church and society.

As Elizabeth Jones has demonstrated, Keats's early poetry does exhibit affinities with a social class shift and the suburbanization of London.[2] The middle class from which Keats had sprung was on the verge of taking political control of Britain both because the power of merchants and industrialists grew as they expanded the nation's wealth and because during the Regency period the aristocrats' excesses had lost them all moral credibility. The diminution of the aristocracy ultimately displayed itself during the Punch-and-Judy "trial" of Queen Caroline in the late summer and fall of 1820, when the Duke of Wellington was taunted by unruly crowds as he rode daily to the proceedings at the House of Lords. But Keats and his contemporaries who formed the Third Generation of British Romantics had felt their superiority to Regency aristocrats and men of power much earlier, and Keats had clearly articulated these views in the first twenty-one lines of Book III of *Endymion*, beginning: "There are who lord it o'er their fellow-men / With most prevailing tinsel."[3]

Included in this often overlooked Third Generation of English Romantic writers were such poets and essayists as William Sidney Walker (1795–1846), John Hamilton Reynolds (1796–1852), John Chalk Claris ("Arthur Brooke," ?1796–1866), Charles Jeremiah Wells (1800–79), John Moultrie (1799–1874), and Winthrop Mackworth Praed (1802–39), as well as poets better known today, such as Felicia Hemans (1793–1835), John Clare (1793–1864), George Darley (1795–1846), Hartley Coleridge (1796–1849), Thomas Hood (1799–1845), Laetitia E. Landon ("L.E.L.," 1802–83), and Thomas Lovell Beddoes (1803–49). Bryan Waller Procter ("Barry Cornwall," 1787–1874), though older than these writers (he was a contemporary of Byron at Harrow), also belongs to this generation because of his class affinities with them, his delayed entry into the literary world, and his dedicated imitation of the second-generation poets. (Mary Wollstonecraft Shelley, on the other hand, although younger than some third-generation writers, shared the cultural psychology of the Second Generation because of her parentage and her close association with Percy Bysshe Shelley and Byron.)

A few writers in the first and second generations of British Romantics were, like Byron and Shelley, members of the landed aristocracy, and most of the others had fathers who either served as retainers to the upper classes (William Wordsworth and Charles Lamb), or belonged to the provincial clergy (Joanna Baillie, Samuel Taylor Coleridge, Hunt, Jane Austen, and Mathilda Betham), who as members of an established church also had close ties to the aristocracy. George Crabbe was a rural

clergyman, dependent upon the Duke of Rutland. William Godwin began as, and Hazlitt trained to be, a dissenting clergyman. Most of the
men in the first two groups attended either a university, a comparable
dissenting "academy," or at least a leading "public" school, including
such endowed charity schools as Christ's Hospital, which provided
Lamb and Hunt, as well as Coleridge, with a very sound classical education. Among the notable writers of these two earlier generations
whom we classify as Romantics, there were few native Londoners (William Blake, Lamb, and Hunt), and none whose family was "in trade."

Virtually all of the Third-Generation Romantics, on the contrary,
came from those "middling classes" or, in the case of John Clare, from
the peasantry. Some, as Hood testified about himself, had truly inferior
educations. Most of these men and women trained for, or earned a
livelihood in what were then regarded as the lower professions. Reynolds began working as a clerk in an insurance office and then became,
like Procter, Praed, and Moultrie, a solicitor. Claris, Darley, Hartley
Coleridge, Hemans, Hood, and L.E.L. earned their livings as journal-
ists or as men or women of letters, heretofore a lowly calling that was
just beginning to be made socially acceptable by the glorification of the
creative imagination by the elder Romantics and the income provided
by the growing reading public.

Keats tried to escape the competition between his poetic calling and
his medical training by living on his inheritance and writing poetry, for
he saw the trap that financial exigencies could close upon one's higher
aspirations. After John Hamilton Reynolds had become a solicitor,
Keats, upon finding that his friend and colleague, whom Hunt had
praised (along with Keats and Shelley) as one of the most promising
"Young Poets," actually enjoyed his new profession, wrote in dismay:
"Reynolds is completely limed in the law: he is not only reconcil'd to it
but hobby-horses upon it."[4] But before illness closed the doors on
Keats's choices, the legal tangle of the Jennings inheritance and the demands of his brother George, who emigrated to America to start a business, almost forced him to revert to his professional training as an
apothecary-surgeon.[5]

As scions of the mobile middle classes, in which social status depended upon individual success within a self-chosen field of endeavor,
rather than on family status or traditional hierarchical roles, the Third
Generation eagerly accepted the philosophical, social, and literary ideals embodied in poetry and critical prose of their Romantic predeces-

sors, who saw individual genius and imagination as the fountainheads of social values. On the other hand, The First Generation of British Romantics—including Blake, Godwin, Wollstonecraft, Helen Maria Williams, Wordsworth, Coleridge, Robert Southey, Walter Savage Landor, Walter Scott, Lamb, and Baillie—did not begin with any such enthusiasm for individualistic values. They placed their confidence in the universalist rationalism of the Enlightenment, which they saw as in tune with the English ideals developed during the seventeenth century that had been ratified politically by the Glorious Revolution of 1688 and codified by John Locke and his followers. Thus, when the sudden triumph of those Enlightenment ideals in France led to the Reign of Terror and ultimately to Napoleon's imperium, these early Romantics pulled back in horror from a rationality that transmuted too easily into a lust for power. Having, during their quasi-Jacobin periods, alienated themselves to some extent from a rearoused British nationalism, most of these writers recovered from their disillusionment by returning to varieties of Christian humanism that, they believed, were to be found in the writings of Dante, Spenser, Shakespeare, Bacon, and Milton. All of these Romantics to a substantial degree—and Blake in particular—became skeptical of the feasibility of embodying their ideals in the external sociopolitical world; they ultimately chose to maintain their hard-earned values as internalized ideals, rather than compromise them in struggles for power. Wordsworth, for example, after the loss of his early hopes, described as vain his youthful belief that men of goodwill, united, could

> exercise their skill
> Not in Utopia, subterraneous Fields,
> Or some secreted Island, heaven knows where!
> But in the very world, which is the world
> Of all of us,—the place where in the end
> We find our happiness, or not at all![6]

Ultimately, the elder Romantics chose to measure the value of the limited, compromised entities and events of that outside world against a beau ideal within the soul. With individual differences, each saw the war for salvation waged within the human psyche, of which the ideological and moral struggles of the social and political realms were merely external manifestations. With the failure of the French Revolution and the image of the American Eden tarnished by the slavery issue, these writers became willing to accept external imperfection and compromise in their daily lives, as long as they could retain an internal Palladium unsullied by the world.[7]

The Second Generation of English Romantics, including Hazlitt, Hunt, Thomas De Quincey, Byron, Thomas Moore, Austen, and the Shelleys, had been born late enough to miss both the older writers' early enthusiasm for the Revolution in France and their later disillusionment with its failure. Admiring the writings of the First Generation, they learned from them to honor the principles of human dignity embodied in the slogan "Liberty, Equality, and Fraternity," while withholding total commitment of their hopes from any particular sublunar social and political embodiment of these ideals. Yet they also saw dangers in what they sensed to be a retreat from reality by their disillusioned elders. In general—and even the best generalizations are but partial truths—this Second Generation believed that compromise, even if inevitable, was still likely to corrupt the soul. Because of this shift in perspective, however, they exhibited a greater sense of guilt than did their elders at their particular failures to maintain the initial purity of their ideals or to translate them into meaningful social action, and each of them adopted a mode of confronting this guilt. Some compensated for their sense of having betrayed their ideals by externalizing the guilt, as Hazlitt did by projecting his own shortcomings onto a fallen angel to whom he gave the name "Coleridge."[8] Austen projected her distaste for the necessity of social compromises involving love and money, prudence and romantic devotion, in ironic portraits of bumbling lovers and officious or irresponsible parents and patrons involved in plots that, against all odds, eventuate in the marriage of sense with sensibility, supported by the requisite number of pounds per annum, thus compensating the author (and her readers) for the failure of life to reward her moral intelligence as it should have.

Other second-generation Romantics confronted the discrepancy between their ideals and the outer world in which they had to operate by attempting to implement these values through symbolic actions that were intended to challenge morally, when they could not overthrow, the social order. These confrontations include Hunt's journalistic attacks on the Prince Regent; Shelley's youthful publication of radical poems and pamphlets and his early proselytizing expeditions to Ireland, Devonshire, and North Wales; Hazlitt's libel suit against *Blackwood's Mag-*

azine; and Byron's determined attacks upon the Duke of Wellington for contravening those ideals and Southey for pompously defending the establishment that his early work had excoriated. Byron, the great representative poet of the Romantic age and the creator of its master epic in *Don Juan,* felt most deeply the contradictions facing the literate people of the age, because his experience had given him divided perspectives on social, political, and sexual issues. His uninhibited creative genius was, therefore, able to transmit those feelings to the reading public with more resonance than any contemporary British writer. But he ended his career, not with additional words, but with practical expressions of solidarity with those fighting for self-determination in Italy and Greece. His most symbolic action was to give his life for a cause in which he deeply believed, in spite of the imperfections of its adherents.[9]

John Keats shares none of the touchstone qualities of the First and Second Generations of Romantics. He was not born early enough to be caught up in the ecstatic dawn of the French Revolution and then face disillusionment. Unlike Byron and Shelley, he did not grow up among the upper classes during the years of the anti-Jacobin reaction before the Peace of Amiens and find himself in direct opposition to that reactionary nationalistic temper. He did not have to struggle to work out for himself a progression from the ideal of feudally inherited noblesse oblige to a worldview that placed individualistic moral action at the center, with art as the means of transmitting the new moral values from one generation to the next. Having been trained in a practical profession dedicated to the relief of human suffering, but one that gave no promise of leaving a mark on the future, Keats gave up that avenue to human service because the elder Romantics had taught him and his contemporaries that not only did the poet find a place in a literary Valhalla,[10] but poetry and other unheard melodies had more power to soothe human misery than did the medicine of the day.

Keats was probably the first major British poet to begin his career believing that to be a Poet was the highest calling to which one could aspire. From the outset he subscribed to the idea that the poetic imagination was superior to other human faculties, adopting this ideology at nearly the time it was first fully articulated in Coleridge's *Biographia Literaria* (1816). Chaucer, Spenser, Milton, and Pope had used their pens in direct service of their political causes, patrons, or allies, and most other poets, up to and including Byron, began by considering poetry to be a personal outlet or recreation, unglamorized by any claim to extraordinary social significance. Most, including Donne, Herrick, Swift, Fielding, and Lamb, subordinated their vocations as creative writers to other duties and even other professions. Even Cowper, whose literary career was the only one he had, continued to believe that poets and artists were infinitely inferior to kings and men of the world.[11] Those who were forced by circumstance to earn their livings by the pen were thought to smell of Grub Street. And the best of them—even Shakespeare—submitted to the necessity of amusing or flattering their audiences, from courtiers to the groundlings at the Globe Theatre. Few, if any, poets before Keats had begun to write primarily with the idea of being "among the English Poets" after their deaths (*L*1:394).

What did it mean to Keats to be "among the English Poets"? At one level, he would have wished to have his poems anthologized or collected with those of other canonical poets, as had been done by various book-sellers since the mid-eighteenth century. In fact, despite his early death, Keats was very soon among the English poets, when in 1829 the Galig-nani brothers in Paris bound his collected poems in a volume with those of Coleridge and Shelley for the British and expatriate markets. But let me suggest a slightly higher goal that may have been in Keats's mind by 1820, when in two letters to Fanny Brawne he rephrased his forlorn hopes as "if I had time I would have made myself remember'd" (*L*2:263, 277). In *The Literary Pocket-Book for 1819* (published near the end of 1818), Hunt included not only two of Keats's sonnets, but also listed prominent living writers, artists, composers, and musicians; there Keats's name appears with a large number of the Romantic writ-ers, male and female, of all three generations; Keats remained in the lists of "Living Authors" in the *Literary Pocket-Books* for 1820 and 1821 (which appeared near the end of 1819 and 1820; Keats's early death caused his name to be removed from the list of "Living Authors" in the final two editions for 1822 and 1823).

But Hunt's annual diary also contained a more illustrious list, "A Chronological List of Eminent Persons in Letters, Philosophy, and the Arts, whose great original genius, individual character, or reputation with posterity, has had an influence in modifying the taste and opinions of the world." The first of these lists names just twenty-eight persons from all fields and nations who were born in the eighteenth century, Thomson, Johnson, Goldsmith, and Cowper being the only English po-ets included, and the 1820 edition added to those only the names of Gray, Collins, Chatterton, and Burns. The last persons entered in the chronological list of the noble dead were "Mary Wollstonecraft God-win, moral philosopher"; "Richard Porson, scholar and philologist"; "——Neckar, Baroness de Stael-Holstein, novelist, philosopher, and politician"; and "Kosciusko, the inflexible Polish patriot." This list of the great and good who had fostered civilization from its beginnings until Keats's day was, I believe, the company to which he aspired.

As Aileen Ward wrote in her sensitive essay, "Keats and the Idea of Fame," after starting out with a self-confessed "thirst for glory" and exulting at "What a thing it is to be in the mouth of Fame!", Keats finally concluded that "Not a great name, . . . but an enduring influence is what the poet should hope to achieve."[12] And Hunt's select list of early religious leaders and philosophers and later scientists, artists, and writers must have reminded Keats that the two goals were not incompatible. In such lists now appearing in almanacs and encyclopedias, Keats's name is always present.

Although the Third Generation of British Romantics numbered several writers of substantial talent (John Clare and Felicia Hemans being two who have gained prominence in the past thirty years), only Keats was recognized at once by his contemporaries as a major poet whose mature works merited comparison with the poetry of Wordsworth, Coleridge, Byron, and Shelley. By 1846, Landor, perhaps the best classicist among the Romantics, praised Keats in one of his *Imaginary Conversations* between himself and his friend Southey. At one point Landor's persona says, "When it was a matter of wonder how Keats, who was ignorant of Greek, could have written Hyperion, Shelley, whom envy never touched, gave as a reason, 'Because he *was* a Greek.'" Later in the same dialogue he adds, "Keats is the most imaginative of our poets, after Chaucer, Spenser, Shakespeare, and Milton." In the revised version of the conversation entitled *Florentine, English Visitor, and Landor,* he goes even further, saying that the only two poets who at all resemble Chaucer are Burns and Keats and praising Keats as "having surpassed" all his English "contemporaries . . . in the poet's most noble attributes."[13] Landor's testimonials to Keats's worth join the better known praise by Shelley and such younger men as the Cambridge Apostles, and they effectively refute a recent critical fashion, based on random comments in Byron's letters, that would have us think of Keats as a parvenu or interloper among the leading poets of his time. In the twentieth century, Keats's odes and other mature poems have not only lived, but they have achieved a kind of sanctity that has not been afforded to the work of any other English Romantic. I shall close by suggesting why this should be so.

The Third Generation of English Romantics consisted largely of individuals from the commercial classes who, like Horace, the son of a Roman freedman, found through literature a way to self-expression, social acceptability, and lasting fame. The same goals, at least, have motivated the great majority of poets and critics since Keats's day. His background, his education, his struggle to free himself from the trammels of bourgeois society through the exercise of the creative imagination that sees beyond its bourne, his egalitarian attitude, and his other ideals mark him not only as the most dedicated of the youngest group of English Romantics, but also as the closest model for most later English and, in particular, American creative writers.

Whereas it was once anomalous for the children of farmers or working-class families to aspire to a place in the world of letters, now the educational system affords, through the mastery of language, a pathway up from the slavery of limited knowledge and anonymity. In the Romantic tradition, which still prevails in our literature, self-expression remains central; poets, having jettisoned the formal boundaries of stanzaic patterns and even rhyme, so as to "play tennis with the net down," replace the craft of shaping and patterning language according to traditional forms with a record of their individual experience. John Keats, in spite of his mastery of some traditional forms, remains the best model for modern poets that the earlier period affords of one who overcame long odds and, through sheer talent and the will to succeed, escaped the surgery, the counting house, and the courtroom to win a place in the annals of our literary heritage. The example of his life and works thus helps to explain why many of us happen to have decided to write or teach or edit literature, instead of seeking careers on Main Street or Wall Street. John Keats's fame and influence have grown in our day because he was the nineteenth century's best twentieth-century poet.

Notes

1. *The Romantics Reviewed,* 9 vols. (New York: Garland, 1972); *The Romantic Context: Poetry,* 126 vols. (New York: Garland, 1976–79); *Intervals of Inspiration* (Greenwood, Fla.: Penkevill Publishing, 1988).
2. Elizabeth Jones's paper for the Keats Bicentennial Conference at Harvard was published in outline as "The Suburban School: Snobbery and fear in the at-

tacks on Keats" in the *Times Literary Supplement,* 27 October 1995, 14–15, and in its full scholarly panoply as "Keats in the Suburbs," *Keats-Shelley Journal* 45 (1996): 23–43.

3. *Endymion: A Poetic Romance* (London: Taylor and Hessey, 1818), 105.

4. Keats to George and Georgiana Keats, 17 March 1819, *The Letters of John Keats: 1814–1821,* ed. Hyder E. Rollins (Cambridge, Mass.: Harvard University Press, 1958), 2:78. Quotations of Keats's letters are from this edition, abbreviated *L* in text; volume and page numbers are given in the text. For Reynolds's background and early career, see *Letters from Lambeth: The Correspondence of the Reynolds Family with John Freeman Milward Dovaston,* ed. Joanna Richardson (London: Royal Society of Literature, 1981). See also my review of this edition in *Studies in Romanticism* 22 (1983): 470–74.

5. For the complexities of the inheritance due to John Keats and his siblings from their grandfather Jennings, see Robert Gittings, *The Keats Inheritance* (London: Heinemann, 1964), and the review by John Rutherford in *Keats-Shelley Journal* 15 (1966): 117–21.

6. "French Revolution, as it appeared to Enthusiasts at its Commencement" in *Poems* by William Wordsworth (London: Longman, Hurst, Rees, Orme, and Brown, 1815), 2:71.

7. Though the distilled expression of this perspective appeared later in Matthew Arnold's poem entitled "The Palladium," it is implicit in much of the thought of the initial generation of British Romantics, especially during the years 1802–20.

8. I have treated this phenomenon as it involved Hazlitt and Coleridge at some length in "Lamb and Hazlitt: The Convergence of the Twain," chapter 2 of my *Intervals of Inspiration,* esp. 91–106 and 366–69.

9. Again, I am asserting what my colleagues and I have been at pains to argue at length and support with substantial evidence in *Shelley and his Circle,* vols. 5–8 (Cambridge, Mass.: Harvard University Press, 1973, 1986), as well as in "Byron and the Other," chapter 7 of *Intervals of Inspiration,* esp. 307–49, 408–14 (partly reprinted in *Critical Essays on Byron,* ed. Robert F. Gleckner [New York: G. K. Hall, 1991], 249–65); "Byron in Italy: The Return of Augustus," in *Byron: Augustan and Romantic,* ed. Andrew Rutherford (New York: St. Martin's Press, 1990), 181–98; and "Byron and the Uses of Refamiliarization," in *Rereading Byron,* ed. Alice Levine and Robert N. Keane (New York and London: Garland Publishing, 1993), 101–17.

10. In Book XI of *The Prelude,* Wordsworth—addressing Coleridge—wrote of the "One great society" of "the noble Living and the noble Dead," implying not high birth in the feudal sense, but a new aristocracy created by the imaginations of moral individuals. In *Laon and Cythna (The Revolt of Islam),* Shelley mythologized a supernal destination for such people as the Temple of the Spirit, where, after their martyrdom, his hero and heroine join their peers, "The Great, who had departed from mankind, / A mighty Senate" (see Canto I, stanzas XLVIII-LX, and Canto XII, stanzas XVII-XLI.

11. Cowper makes this point more than once in his letters, but perhaps the most striking example occurs when he objects to celebrations marking the hundredth anniversary of Handel's birth, because he considered it sacrilegious to

celebrate a musician in a church, as one would a saint. See *The Letters and Prose Writings of William Cowper,* ed. James King and Charles Ryskamp (Oxford: Clarendon Press, 1981), 2:254, 264–65.

12. See Ward's essay in *The Evidence of the Imagination,* ed. Donald H. Reiman, Michael C. Jaye, and Betty T. Bennett (New York: New York University Press, 1978), 312–33.

13. *Imaginary Conversations of Walter Savage Landor,* ed. Charles G. Crump (London: J. M. Dent, 1891), 4:249, 274; 6:45.

The Cockney School of Poetry

Keats in the Suburbs

Elizabeth Jones

K EATS'S EARLY POETRY offers a literary parallel to a rapidly changing British urban landscape and allows us to see his being criticized for "vulgarity" in the light of a changing cultural consciousness that threatened some of the cherished values of Britain's established classes.[1] Besides the fact that Keats resided for the better part of his career at Hampstead, one of London's most popular suburbs, two aspects of Keats's poetry that led to his being branded "suburban" were the marked artifice and domesticity of his natural descriptions and his frequent presentation of these descriptions in enclosed and sheltered spaces, stylistic tendencies that inhibited an enlargement of vision leading to the philosophical expansiveness associated with Wordsworth. Yet the mixing of artificial with natural objects that struck Keats's reviewers as vulgar when compared with Wordsworth's rural purity became, in Victorian times, the ideal combination for suburban living.[2] The suburban lifestyle was a bourgeois creation, marked by a carefully constructed domesticity, cultivated in what was portrayed by Regency city planners as the unspoiled periphery of the urban centers. "The desire for a domestic life of privacy and seclusion," writes F. M. L. Thompson, "was a new experience for any sizeable section of the middle class, only gathering force for the first time around the beginning of the nineteenth century."[3] Thus, what was viewed as Keats's suburbanism reveals his association not with conventional Romanticism, but with an emerging Victorian and middle-class sensibility that sought domestic stability in the face of the political, social, and cultural up-heavals of the late eighteenth and early nineteenth centuries.[4] In keeping with the pre-Victorian domestication of nature, whereby the natural world was seen to offer leisure, recreation, and community in the face of an alienating industrial environment, Keats's early verse rehearses the social and cultural protocols of the suburban project; it reflects the bourgeois suburban ideal of the coexistence of nature and culture, within a carefully constructed domestic environment. Keats's suburban poetic has a place, therefore, in the history of the cultural domestication of nature that attained mass popularity with suburbanization and culminated in the wallpaperings of William Morris.[5]

The implications of Keats's suburban status for the readers of his time are best revealed in John Gibson Lockhart's critical reviews of Leigh Hunt and Keats and in several of Byron's letters to his publisher, John Murray.[6] In his series "On the Cockney School of Poetry," published in seven numbers in *Blackwood's Edinburgh Magazine* from October 1817 to December 1822, Lockhart juxtaposes the "purity" of the Lake school with what he viewed as the degraded artificiality of the poetry of Hunt and his follower Keats. For Lockhart to label a poet "suburban" was to make a direct attack on his or her social class, on poetry that "betray[s] the *Shibboleth* of low birth and low habits." Lockhart calls Hunt "the ideal of a Cockney Poet," who "raves" about nature "exactly as a Cheapside shop-keeper does about the beauties of his box on the Camberwell road." Lockhart's criticism of Hunt's nature as one seen in shop-window boxes, in the suburb of Highgate, or in Hyde Park directly attacks the poet's suburban lifestyle, whereby nature is seen "in the course of some Sunday dinner parties . . . in the neighbourhood of London."[7] Lockhart portrays Hunt's nature as one transplanted and cultivated, used for ornamentation and pleasure, rather than sought out in its habitat for the loftier purpose of moral or philosophical instruction. In his fourth essay on the Cockney school, Lockhart labels this propensity "Metromanie" and centers his attention on Keats, who, with Hunt, writes "laborious affected descriptions of flowers seen in window-pots, or cascades heard at Vauxhall."[8]

Byron had a similar, and no less vitriolic, reaction to the geographic characteristics of Hunt's and Keats's verse, referring more precisely to the Cockney school as the *"Suburban School."*[9] Byron makes his class bias clear in a letter to Murray in March 1821:

The grand distinction of the Under forms of the New School of poets—is their *Vulgarity*.—By this I do not mean that they are *Coarse*—but "shabby-genteel"—as it is termed.—A man may be *coarse* & yet not *vulgar*. . . . It is in their *finery* that the New-under School—are most vulgar;—and they may be known by this at once—as what we called at Harrow—"a Sunday Blood" might easily be distinguished from a Gentleman—[10]

Byron's attacks are consistent with the prejudices of English conservative society, who equated the suburban lifestyle with class pretension. To understand the connection between suburban living and "affected descriptions," and to clarify a culturally biased criticism that stayed with Keats for the whole of his writing career, it is useful to review the social history of English suburban life. What we now refer to as Keats's marginality, a concept that has been applied to his social class, lack of education, and economic insecurity, may also be applied geographically and culturally.

In its original form, a suburb was inhabited land that lay below hilltop walled towns, beneath the ramparts of classical and medieval cities. Always, it connoted inferiority, which helps explain Byron's reference to Hunt and his fellow suburbanites as belonging to an "under school" of poetry. In Chaucer's day, the suburbs were urban dumping grounds: they served as the location for leper hospitals; noxious trades such as butchering, tanning, and dyeing; and the activities of a criminal underworld that included, most lucratively, prostitution. In the early eighteenth century, both Daniel Defoe and John Macky were aware of the habit of London gentlemen to frequent suburban areas in order to take advantage of the wide variety of illicit activities available there.[11] Such a questionable cultural history may account for Lockhart's conflation, in his "Cockney School" articles, of the eroticism of Hunt's and Keats's verse with the vulgar heritage of suburban areas, and it explains the inability of Keats's more conservative critics to see the erotic content of his poetry as indicative of anything but the detestable suburban degradation that polite society had been battling against for centuries.[12] Despite the massive move to suburbanization around 1750 and the efforts of city planners and land developers to transform the suburbs into domestic havens, they never lost their culturally marginal associations.[13]

Hampstead, where Keats lived from 1817 to 1820 (between journeys away to write), was a fashionable resort and spa town as early as the late sixteenth century.[14] But by Keats's day all suburban areas were viewed as places that attracted social climbers, or what Byron called "Sunday Bloods"—people who aspired to living well in the country but who had neither land nor the security of a landowner's rents. The suburb had become, as Nicholas Taylor notes, "a fulcrum for social mobility . . . an expression of the distinctly English tradition of liberalism or Whiggery."[15] In his *Suburban Gardener and Villa Companion* (1838), John Claudius Loudon, the most widely read proponent of suburban living, promoted the green spaces surrounding England's industrial centers as spaces of possibility, remarking, "We have long seen that the poor, by cooperation and *self-cultivation,* may insure to themselves all that is worth having of the enjoyments of the wealthier classes" (italics mine).[16] Loudon's suburban propaganda gave the suburbs the power to turn a city-dwelling worker into an estate-owning member of the gentry; his rhetoric promised social advancement through geographical location that flew in the face of long-established notions of property and birthright. For Loudon, the main attraction to the suburbs was the domestic garden, which was not only a means of social advancement, but, through the notion of "self-cultivation," a metaphor for the nourishment of the industrial soul alienated from the romantic natural ideal.

The cultivation of the villa garden was one of the defining activities of the suburban resident; Loudon advocated the garden as a defense against the moral degradation of cities, a way for urbanites to ascend to the ethical heights of Horace's *beatus ille* without possessing large estates or traveling long distances to pursue the picturesque. But it was the act of garden cultivation, more than the mere possession of a garden, that Loudon promoted; his plan was to replace the picturesque aesthetic, which required the possession of large tracts of land, with the "gardenesque," a more private and personal aesthetic that was more appropriate to the suburban experience. Ann Bermingham notes that the project of the suburban gardener, who lacked huge tracts of land and extensive vistas, was "to impress not with land, but with plants."[17] Thus, although the suburbanites' properties were small, they could complete with estate owners in the arena of gardening, filling their small spaces with as many varieties of plants as they could fit into their yards. Loudon's gardenesque aesthetic, based on the ideals of individualism and privacy, made it possible for the professional classes to achieve a cultural (and aesthetic) status of their own, despite their lack of sizable property.

Hunt and Keats represented this professional class to those who, like Byron and Lockhart, disparaged their suburban poetic. They were seen as villa owners attempting to climb the cultural ladder by cultivating a nature in their poetry uncomfortably close to Loudon's gardenesque. As Alan Bewell points out, Lockhart saw Keats and Hunt as suburban pot-gardeners, betraying their social and cultural aspirations in the artifice and sheer abundance of their descriptions in the same way a middle-class professional and his wife aspired to gentrification by reading the gardening manuals of Loudon and Hunt's sister-in-law, Elizabeth Kent.[18] It is precisely this kind of domesticated nature that so appalled Lockhart; the liberalism inherent in the teachings of Loudon and Kent—the notion that nature's high morality could be taught in the dirty confines of London or in the closeness of its suburbs—did not agree with his conservative notions of natural purity. It was, as was the suburban ideal, a middling kind of poetry, both social and private, both rural and urban, and, like the pot-gardens that characterized suburban agriculture, both natural and artificial, imitating the suburbanite's attempt to strike that delicate balance required for a successful experience of *rus in urbe*.

The recreational, and particularly social, value that was attached to the experience of nature during the early nineteenth century was an important part of the suburban lifestyle, based as it was on a paradoxical combination of privacy and society. On an individual scale, suburban life offered domestic stability, privacy, and the satisfaction of possessing one's own bit of property; yet on a social scale, the city planners aimed to reconnect thousands of dispossessed people, both rural and urban, to their social roots and expected a renewed sense of community to arise from the garden-city model.[19] Both impulses—private and social—are evident throughout Keats's 1817 *Poems*. His bowers, intensely private spaces that he cultivated to reveal his own personal iconography in the same way suburbanites constructed their houses and gardens to reflect their tastes and habits, had as much to do with the suburban aesthetic as did the social tendency of these poems, wherein Keats balanced his private impulses with his need to see himself as part of the cultural and social revolution that was transforming domestic life.[20]

Keats's first published poem, *O Solitude!*, reveals a pre-Victorian experience of nature in its view of landscape as escape and spectacle.[21] Keats announces his suburban status not only in his expressed desire to escape the city's "jumbled heap / Of murky buildings" (2–3), but also in the phrase "Nature's observatory" (4), which indicates a Victorian interest in the scientific objectification of nature and recalls such domestications of nature as the terrarium, the vivarium, the Wardian case, and, on a larger scale, the museum of natural history. Similarly, in *To a Friend Who Sent Me Some Roses,* Keats values cut flowers over wild ones because of the former's social connection to "friendliness" (14) and reveals his suburban status in his esteem of social values over nature's: given the choice between favoring a natural flower in its habitat, and grown and cut ones given as an offering of friendship, Keats prefers those that speak of social affection "with tender plea" (13). In *To one who has been long in city pent,* Keats repeats the longing of the urban dweller, expressed in *O Solitude!,* to escape into nature. What marks this poem as suburban is the excursionary character of the escape. This is not the permanent retirement of a Horatian *beatus ille,* but the temporary escape of the harassed Londoner who seeks no more from nature than a change of scenery and some leisure. In this poem, poetry and nature indistinguishably deliver the same goods: they are both sought out with a dilettante's desire for recreation, and neither is appreciated purely for its own sake. The labor involved in what Lockhart would view as a true poet's experience of either nature or poetry is conspicuously absent here, as Keats uses both to produce an atmosphere of leisure, with the "pleasant lair" (5) of nature mirroring the "languishment" (7) of the poem. But the phrase "Returning home at evening" (9) would be the one to make Lockhart wince. To his mind, nature could be appreciated only by poets whose home was within it; to return home to the city from a day in the country would mark Keats as no better than the "dirty and debauched" working classes documented by Cornelius Webb—those who made an excursion to the suburbs part of their Sunday recreation.[22]

For Keats, what passes for nature often possesses distinctly social qualities; the natural world equals escape from urban pressures, and promises leisure, conviviality, and friendship. In much of the poetry in the 1817 volume, Keats instinctively associates the writing of poetry with close friendship and domestic ease, perhaps since much of his early associations with poetry came from the domestic-literary circles into which he was welcomed. His friendship with George Felton Mathew, a middle-class poet and leader of his own poetic circle, represented Keats's association with Hunt and his circle in embryo; eager to escape his working-class roots, Keats depended on the society of his professional friends. Mathew's large family provided an atmosphere of middle-class gentility, with their "little domestic concerts and dances," that offered Keats a glimpse into a life that combined artistic pursuits with domestic stability in a way he had never known.[23] The verse epistle *To George Felton Mathew* is particularly suburban in its odd combination of privacy and society and its seemingly unconscious association of poetry and poetic images with domestic and social convention.

In this epistle, after expressing his need to leave the "dark city" (33) in order to court the muse, Keats describes one of his first poetic bowers, the kind of private, erotically charged space that announced his Cockney status immediately to his critics. Not only the eroticism of this bower would have brought the charge of Cockneyism—there is also the sense that this place has been cultivated, designed with the eye of a landscape architect, in the lines "Where on one side are covert branches hung" (44) and "There must be too a ruin dark, and gloomy" (51). But what would have branded him as specifically suburban are the lines that follow these ones. The "place" conceived of is oddly domestic: the muse must be "greeted" as if she were a houseguest, humanitarian sentiments are "put on" like dinner jackets, and the stated desire to "sit, and rhyme and think on Chatterton" (53–56) reduces the poetic effort and the tragedy of Chatterton's life to the easy pleasure of a parlor game. Here, Keats imagines a place similar to those in which he must have spent countless hours with Mathew and his domestic-literary coterie. In Mathew's circle, poetry was soothing and recreational; under its influence, Keats reduces the potency of Shakespeare and Milton to a rather pathetic portrayal of each as "warm-hearted" and "blind," their poetry used "to flap away each sting / Thrown by the pitiless world" (64–65).

"They shall be accounted poet kings / Who simply tell the most heart-easing things" (267–68). So Keats writes in *Sleep and Poetry,* at the end of which he is relieved from the intensity of ambitious longing in the easy suburban atmosphere of Hunt's study. The "desperate turmoil" (308) of the poem's climactic, Daedalian suicide fantasy is immediately eased by a vision of a domesticated poetry. Just as Keats is comforted, in the sonnet *To My Brother George,* by "the social thought" (13) in the face of natural sublimity, so he is relieved in this poem by poetry's capacity to forge social bonds. Here, poetry is one with the "friendly aids" of "brotherhood" and "friendliness" (316–18), existing in a social and domestic sphere of sonnet-writing contests and book borrowing. A book of poetry is a social facilitator, bringing friends together "to cluster round it when we next shall meet" (326).

At the end of *Sleep and Poetry,* only a domestic fantasy—"a poet's house"—has the power to soothe Keats's ambitious ardor. It is Hunt, the art collector in his Hampstead villa, "who keeps the keys / Of pleasure's temple" (354–55). The library and the garden, integral parts of any middle-class residence, were the suburban substitutes for the cultural activities of the metropolis.[24] As families moved away from the city, they began cultivating the pleasures of nature and art entirely within the confines of their own homes, aided by gardening manuals like those of Loudon and Kent and by the rapidly expanding market for affordable reproductions of painting and sculpture. Hunt's study, as Ian Jack has documented, represented only one of many middle-class parlors that were being outfitted in the manner of domestic art galleries and libraries.[25] Finding ultimate solace in such a place would have seemed to Lockhart the essence of suburbanism. In Hampstead, lying "upon a couch at ease" (353), surrounded by plaster reproductions of classical sculpture and prints of Titian's paintings, Keats portrayed himself as a true suburbanite, aspiring to the ease and culture of English gentrified society.

While the lines at the end of *Sleep and Poetry* offer Keats's most explicit portrayal of suburban domestic life, there remain also his poetic bowers, which, in the abundance and variety of nature displayed in highly circumscribed spaces, anticipate the gardenesque aesthetic of Loudon and Kent, which was rapidly usurping the panoramic landscapes of the picturesque model. Bermingham notes that the suburban garden reflected a kind of "domestic narcissism," becoming "the repository of the owner's personal iconography."[26] This description suits Keats's bowers well; the number and variety of objects, both domestic and natural, that Keats can fit into what he describes as a "nest" or a "nook" are often remarkable.

A further explanation for the contemporary critical reaction to Keats's natural descriptions is found in the way they follow the protocol of Loudon's gardenesque aesthetic, which would have spoken to Lockhart of suburban pretension. The passage in *I stood tip-toe upon a little hill,* which clearly displays the artifice of Keats's nature, with its cut flowers that "spring from diamond vases" (134), also reveals a closeness, where flowers "brush against our faces" and "O'er head we see the jasmine and sweet briar, / And bloomy grapes laughing from green attire; / While at our feet, the voice of crystal bubbles / Charms us" (135–38). This is a place where the abundance and variety of nature can be taken in without climbing a hill and surveying a large tract of land; it reflects, as many of Keats's bowers do, the domestic economy that characterized the suburban ideal. Similarly, his description of Adonis's bower in book II of *Endymion* reveals a profusion of natural variety, densely contained within "A chamber, myrtle wall'd, embowered high" (387–427). As Adonis reclines upon a "silken couch" of roses (392), lilies above his head make a "coronal" under the bower's "woven roof" (426). Using the florist's name for bindweed, Keats invokes *Convolvulus,* a well-known garden annual, places it "in streaked vases" (415), and creates a literary garden that would suit perfectly any suburban villa, complete with "serene Cupids, watching silently" (419). In another bower later in book II, this time one made entirely of water, Keats conflates house and garden imagery in a potent example of this period's domestication of nature. He describes the streams of water as "delicatest lattices, / Cover'd with crystal vines" (614–15); as "watery gauze, . . ." / "Pour'd into shapes of curtain'd canopies, / Spangled, and rich with liquid broideries / Of flowers, peacocks, swans, and naiads fair" (618–20); and, finally, as looking like "the wrought oaken beams, / Pillars, and frieze, and high fantastic roof, / Of those dusk places in times far aloof / Cathedrals call'd" (623–26).

This remarkable passage combines nature, horticulture, textiles, and architecture in a paradigm for the suburban ideal of *rus in urbe,* the desire of the Regency bourgeoisie to have it all, within a carefully constructed domestic environment. It is also a potent reminder of Keats's contemporaneity: descriptions that jarred a Romantic sensibility were in fact reflecting a new cultural ethos that critics like Lockhart were unable to reconcile with their traditional—that is, Romantic—notions of the separation of nature and culture. The charge of vulgarity that reviewers leveled at Keats's suburbanism appears now to veil thinly a profound fear of the obscuring of distinctions between nature and culture, between country and city, and, ultimately, between classes in the cultural environment of a post-Romantic era.

NOTES

An abbreviated version of this chapter, "The Suburban School: Snobbery and Fear in the Attacks on Keats," appeared in the London *Times Literary Supplement.*

October 27, 1995, 14–15; an expanded version appeared in *Keats-Shelley Journal* 45 (1996): 23–43.

1. Keatsian vulgarity, in its many forms, has been ably documented in recent criticism. In this essay I mean to elucidate a cultural and geographic explanation for the force of a contemporary critical reaction to the less traditional aspects of Keats's poetry. The place to begin studying the many aspects of what was seen in 1817 as Keats's vulgarity is Lionel Trilling's "The Poet as Hero: Keats in His Letters," in *The Opposing Self: Nine Essays in Criticism* (New York: Harcourt, 1955) 5–17, where Trilling discusses Keats's appetitive "geniality" (a term that also has implications for my focus of Keats's domesticated nature), and John Bayley's exploration of the intricacies of Keatsian "gemein," or commonness, in "Keats and Reality," *Proceedings of the British Academy* (1962): 91–125. Bayley's study is followed closely by John Jones's *John Keats's Dream of Truth* (London: Chatto, 1969), which champions the poet's sensual "feel," and by Christopher Ricks's *Keats and Embarrassment* (Oxford: Clarendon, 1974). Most recently, Marjorie Levinson has broken sociopolitical ground, connecting Blackwood's charges of vulgarity to the social contexts from which they arose, in *Keats's Life of Allegory: The Origins of a Style* (Oxford: Blackwell, 1988). Levinson's argument that Keats's poetic ambitions were inseparable from his class aspirations forms a crucial background to this essay, which sees Keats's suburbanism as a reflection of his desire to have middle-class status.

2. On the ways in which a marriage of art and nature was advocated as a domestic ideal by Victorians such as Ruskin, Morris, and Scott, see Ellen Frank, "The Domestication of Nature," in *Nature and the Victorian Imagination*, eds. U. C. Knoepflmacher and G. B. Tennyson (Berkeley: University of California Press, 1977), 68–92.

3. F. M. L. Thompson, Introduction, *The Rise of Suburbia*, ed. F. M. L. Thompson (Leicester: Leicester University Press, 1982), p 12. Thompson's essay is particularly helpful in discussing the "cult of privacy and regulated domesticity" (13) and its relationship to the rise of suburban housing that took hold after 1815.

4. Alan Bewell goes into great detail about Keats's floral imagery and its connection not to Wordsworthian nature, but to an "incipient Victorian culture" that commercialized and textualized nature, in "Keats's Realm of Flora," *Studies in Romanticism* 31 (1992): 71–98. On the Victorian desire for suburban stability in the aftermath of Romanticism, see Walter L. Creese, "Imagination in the Suburb," and Andrew Griffin, "The Interior Garden and John Stuart Mill," in *Nature and the Victorian Imagination*, 49–67, 171–86.

5. The changes in landscape design that lead up to the aesthetic of suburbanism parallel the ornamented, intricate, and sensual descriptions of nature found in the poetry of the Cockney school; they are reflected in the architecture and landscape designs of Regency-period "Men of Taste." The designers of this period aimed to reform the picturesque aesthetic of Uvedale Price and Richard Payne Knight—an aesthetic suited to the high-art tastes and pocketbooks of the gentry—and the uniform and barren clumps and belts of "Capability" Brown by taking the ideals of the picturesque to practical conclusions that

could not have been realized in the vast estate gardens of the wealthy. The first designer to react to the fact that the "natural" garden had become as sterile as the formal garden that the picturesque aesthetic had aimed to correct was Humphrey Repton, in his *Theory and Practice of Landscape Gardening* (1802), who aimed to return to the original picturesque ideals of intricacy and luxuriance and put them to practical use in the smaller urban and suburban lots of the professional classes. One of the early followers of Repton's new style was Edmund Bartell, whose *Hints for Picturesque Improvements in Ornamental Cottages* (1804) emphasized luxuriance and profusion in smaller spaces over the vast, shaven lawns of the picturesque. See Donald Pilcher, *The Regency Style: 1800 to 1830* (London: Batsford, 1947), 17–46.

6. The social and political terms of Lockhart's critique of "The Cockney School" are discussed by Nicholas Roe in "Keats's Lisping Sedition," *Essays in Criticism* 42 (1992): 36–55. Roe argues that Lockhart politicized Keats negatively in order to stifle his poetry's "disturbing potency for his first readers" (53) and notes that Lockhart used Keats's suburban status, in addition to his affiliation with Hunt's liberal politics, to place his poetry in a "cultural limbo," which had much to do with subsequent portrayals of the poet as removed from "the world" (42). Kim Wheatley, in "The Blackwood's Attacks on Leigh Hunt," *Nineteenth-Century Literature* 47 (1992–93), 1–31, presents a fascinating account of how the class attacks on Hunt may be read as the fiction-making of Lockhart, a would-be Victorian novelist, who turned the amiable Hunt into a Gothic threat to the chastity of women and an effeminate corrupter of lower-class boys and his poetry into a prostitute threatening the literary morality of gentlemen everywhere.

7. Z., John Gibson Lockhart "On the Cockney School of Poetry, No. I," *Blackwood's Edinburgh Magazine* 2 (1817): 39.

8. Z., "On the Cockney School of Poetry, No. IV," *Blackwood's Edinburgh Magazine* 3 (1818): 521.

9. *Byron's Letters and Journals*, ed. Leslie A. Marchand (London: John Murray, 1973–82), 8:166.

10. Lord Byron, *The Complete Miscellaneous Prose*, ed. Andrew Nicholson (Oxford: Clarendon Press, 1991), 159.

11. F. M. L. Thompson, *Hampstead: Building a Borough, 1650–1964* (London: Routledge, 1974), 22–23.

12. John Scattergood presents the cultural contexts for Chaucer's suburban loci in the *Second Nun's Tale* and the *Canon Yeoman's Tale* to explain Chaucer's locating of radical religious activities and alchemy on the margins of the city and to show how he used the geographic unorthodoxy of the suburban location to enrich the confrontation, in the tales, between an established urban order and a suburban culture that was in constant moral, social, and religious flux. The fact that suburban areas were commonly used as repositories for impoverished and diseased members of society gives an additional cultural reference to Lockhart's portrayal of Hunt, in the third "Cockney School" article in particular, as "leprous," "vermined," "polluted," (453), "pestilential," and "infect[ed]" (455). See Scattergood's "Chaucer in the Suburbs," in *Medieval Literature and Antiquities: Studies in Honour of Basil Cottle*, ed.

Myra Stokes and T. L. Burton (Cambridge: Brewer, 1987), 145–62; Lockhart, "On the Cockney School of Poetry, no. 3," *Blackwood's Edinburgh Magazine* 3 (1818):453–56.

13. For a clear account of the rise of suburbia in mid-eighteenth-century England, see Robert Fishman, *Bourgeois Utopias: The Rise and Fall of Suburbia* (New York: Basic, 1987), and John R. Stilgoe, *Borderland: Origins of the American Suburb, 1820–1939* (New Haven, Conn.: Yale University Press, 1988).

14. F. M. L. Thompson, *Hampstead*, 20.

15. Nicholas Taylor, *The Village in the City* (London: Temple Smith, 1973), 39.

16. J. C. Loudon, *The Suburban Gardener and Villa Companion*, ed. John Dixon Hunt (1838; reprint, New York: Garland, 1982), 11. Loudon's text is a watershed for Regency landscape gardening, coming as it did after many design treatises aimed at reforming the tenets of the picturesque that set the cultural stage for the suburban aesthetic; after 1838, the Victorian middle-classes embraced suburbanism with gusto (see n. 5). Although Loudon, in *Country Residences* (1806), began by reproducing the picturesque designs of Price and Knight, he quickly adapted his aesthetic to follow that of Repton, Bartell, and many others who found the picturesque ill-suited to the practical and smaller-scale tastes of the burgeoning middle-classes. Among the many works that contributed to the influence of the Regency garden aesthetic are W. Robertson's *Designs in Architecture* (1800); John Plaw's *Sketches for Country Houses, Villas and Rural Dwellings* (1800); W. F. Pocock's *Architectural Design for Rustic Cottages . . .* (1807); and J. B. Papworth's *Rural Residences* (1818) and *Ornamental Gardening* (1823).

17. Ann Bermingham, *Landscape and Ideology: The English Rustic Tradition, 1740–1860* (Berkeley: University of California Press, 1986), 171.

18. Bewell, "Keats's Realm of Flora," 71–79.

19. Bermingham, *Landscape and Ideology*, 167–68.

20. Fishman (*Bourgeois Utopias*, 20–38) documents the rise of the cult of domesticity, seeing it as resulting from a combination of urban overcrowding and decay; the subsequent separation of work and home in the decentralization of the middle-class residence; and the Evangelical movement, which emphasized the sanctity of the home and family as a moral antidote to the rampant consumerism taking hold of pre-Victorian lives.

21. *The Poems of John Keats*, ed. Jack Stillinger (Cambridge, Mass.: Harvard University Press, Belknap Press, 1978). All quotations of Keats's poetry are from this edition; line numbers are given in text.

22. Cornelius Webb, *Glances at Life in City and Suburb* (London: Smith, Elder, 1836), 73–74.

23. See Walter Jackson Bate, *John Keats* (New York: Oxford University Press, 1966), 67.

24. Fishman, *Bourgeois Utopias*, 56.

25. Ian Jack, *Keats and the Mirror of Art* (Oxford: Clarendon Press, 1967), 130–35.

26. Bermingham, *Landscape and Ideology*, 168–69.

Poetic Voodoo in *Lamia*

Keats in the Possession of African Magic

DEBBIE LEE

I N THE FINAL and most shocking scene of Keats's *Lamia*, the "bald-headed philosopher" Apollonius destroys the wedding ceremony of young Lycius and his bride Lamia by gazing so intensely at Lamia that he reveals she is not the woman she seems to be:

> the sophist's eyes,
> Like a sharp spear, went through her utterly,
> Keen, cruel, perceant, stinging: she, as well
> As her weak hand could any meaning tell,
> Motion'd him to be silent; vainly so,
> He look'd and look'd again a level—No!
> "A Serpent!" echoed he; no sooner said,
> Than with a frightful scream she vanished:[1]

Apollonius's impaling gaze cuts to the heart of a "knotty problem" Keats had been pondering about the poet's role (I.160). In 1818 he wrote to Richard Woodhouse, "What shocks the virtuous philosop[h]er, delights the camelion Poet . . . because he has no identity—he is continually in for—and filling some other Body."[2] By connecting himself as poet to the chameleon, an animal identified by early nineteenth-century European explorers and travelers as a beautiful and mysterious reptile indigenous to Africa, Keats gives both shape and color to that state of "Negative Capability," or "being in uncertainties,

Mysteries, doubts" while "remaining content with half knowledge" (*L*1:193).

It comes as no surprise, then, that in early 1819, when Keats started *Lamia*, he chose an unknowable serpent-woman, who lay hidden in the "dusky brake" of an exotic island, to enact this chameleon transformation (I.46). For Keats, Lamia was mysterious in three senses. Not only serpent and woman, she was also African. According to *Lempriére's Classical Dictionary*, one of the sources Keats used for the poem,[3] "Lamiae" refers to "certain monsters of Africa, who had the face and breast of a woman, and the rest of their body like that of a serpent. They allured Strangers to come to them, that they might devour them; and though they were not endowed with the faculty of speech, yet their hissings were pleasing and agreeable."[4] Keats takes hold of or possesses Lamia's African mysteries and so re-enlivens his poetic imagination. At the same time, the poem sounds a cautionary note: British possession of African magic could be brutally destructive to both cultures.

I

The years 1818–20, when Keats conceived of *Lamia* and published it, mark a transitional period in Britain's interaction with Africa. This point midway between the abolition of the slave trade in 1807 and that of slavery in 1833 generated strikingly contradictory portraits of both Africans and West Indian slaves. For instance, Captain George Francis Lyon's account of his travels in northern Africa with his companion, the surgeon/explorer Joseph Ritchie (whom Keats had met), in 1818–20 is typical in presenting Africans as both trustworthy and treacherous.[5] In fact, during this period, most travel writing and discourse on slavery wrestled with the confusion and uncertainty inherent in the changing role of Africans and West Indian slaves in Britain's future economy. One thing was clear. The British would no longer be able to trade with Africa in human bodies. They therefore determined to understand African and slave culture—both how they could be endangered by it and how they might benefit from it. West Indian customs and Africa as a continent had proved impenetrable to Europeans, who had come to an increasing awareness that they possessed only partial knowledge. To the British there seemed only one course of action: to know more.

Just before beginning work on *Lamia*, Keats had expressed interest in those pursuing knowledge of Africa and mysterious African customs.

In January 1819, he wrote his brother George of a travel narrative describing the "discovery of an african Kingdom." Referring to Thomas Edward Bowdich's 1819 *A Mission from Cape Coast Castle to Ashantee*,[6] Keats views the narrative as an uncanny "romance" in which an English adventurer encounters foreign African customs:

> They have window frames of gold—100,000 infantry—human sacrifices—The Gentleman who is the adventurer has his wife with him—she I am told is a beautiful little sylphid woman— her husband was to have been sacrificed to their Gods and was led through a Chamber filled with different instruments of torture with the privilege to choose what death he would die without their having a thought of his aversion to such a death they considering it a supreme distinction—However he was let off and became a favorite with the King who at last openly patronized him, though at first on account of the Jealousy of his Minister he was wont to hold conversations with his Majesty in the dark middle of the night—All this sounds a little Bluebeardish— but I hope it is true. (L2:28)

Though dreadful African practices had long been observed and recorded by Europeans, Keats emphasizes in this letter that human sacrifice—a complete giving over of the self—is the result of the African–European encounter. For Keats, cultural exchange generates a tale whose rhythm defies stable identities, approximating a state of negative capability. The story of African–European encounter is one of mystery, uncertainty, and doubt, one neither wholly European nor fully African, located somewhere between "Bluebeardish" fiction and "true" fact. But for all their mystery and power, African–European encounters were fraught with the politics of domination and profit, as Keats ironically acknowledges in this passage. Thus, what one culture loses in identity, the other possesses in patronizing power.

Such a dangerous clash between light and dark cultures structures *Lamia* from the beginning. Keats situates the poem at the dawn of a history of conquests, or increasingly technological and tyrannical military takeovers, when the English fairies "drove Nymph and Satyr from the prosperous woods," while "king Oberon's bright diadem, / Sceptre, and mantle clasped with dewy gem, / Frighted away the Dryads and the Fauns" (I.2–5).[7] These conquests also get "whiter" in Keats's retelling,

as the satyrs—traditionally associated with dark-skinned people[8]—are
overtaken by Oberon, whose name comes from the Latin word *albus*,
meaning "white." The poem's early whiteness foregrounds Lamia's
dusky origins. She is both a "Proserpine" and an "Eurydice" (I.63,
248), dark distinctions no doubt stemming from the first Lamia's myth-
ological status as Zeus's Libyan mistress.[9] Further, like Aeneas's Dido,
Keats's Lamia pays a high price for her encounter with white culture,
which literally destroys her, turning her "deadly white" (II.276).

Lest we imagine such violent encounters as somehow natural or accidental, Keats figures the poem's proto-conquest as an act of self-interest
by a prodigal god. Hermes, who commissions himself to uncover the
secret bed of the lovely nymph, flies from "vale to vale" and "wood to
wood" (I.27), bent on "amorous theft" (I.6), to find the "unseen"
maid, whose freedom is inextricably linked to her invisibility (I.8). In
staging this conquest, Keats draws on exploratory travel writers who
insisted that though their activities involved a certain amount of "amorous" probing and "theft," the primary road to the control of Africa
lay in uncovering and possessing its secrets. Mungo Park's inaugural
address, for instance, burns with a "passionate desire to examine into
the productions of a country so little known." Through his observations, he pledges to "render the geography of Africa more familiar to
my countrymen" and thereby open "to their ambition and industry
new sources of wealth."[10]

Keats appears to profit from this new source of wealth as much as
any commercial industrialist. The wedding of Lamia and Lycius is the
poem's richest deposit of travel narrative descriptions taken from the
books Keats had read. Imported images that mimic both Park and Bowdich (who called the lushness and excessiveness of African vegetation
"romantic")[11] decorate Lamia's wedding banquet hall. "Mimicking a
glade" (II.125), the hall opens into "Two palms and then two plantains,
and so on, / From either side their stems branched one to one / All down
the aisled place" (II.127–30). This elaborate counterfeit equally mimics
the canopied valley described by Bowdich, "profusely covered with
pines, aloes, and lilies; and richly varied with palm, banana, plantain,
and guava trees" (B15). But Keats does not merely take hold of and
transplant tropical vegetation from travel literature. He draws in the
"dull catalogue[s]" and the intrusive scientific systems of naturalist and
colonist alike (II.233). The "charms" of Lamia's wedding hall—the
lushness of which literally overtakes part II of the poem—dissipate as

soon as the scientific Apollonius "force[s]" himself upon the "wealthy lustre" of the banquet room (II.229, 166, 173). Keats aligns Apollonius with the methods of the African explorer who would "Conquer all mysteries by rule and line, / Empty the haunted air, and gnomed mine— / Unweave a rainbow while it erewhile made / The tender-personed Lamia melt into a shade" (II.235–38).

Yet because Keats attempts to capture the charms of Lamia within the "rule and line" of his own poetic, he raises questions about what kind of inscription can possess African magic without sucking the life out of it. As the writing of the period demonstrates, through the discourse of either exploratory writing or poetry, Europeans who represented what they did not understand worked out, to varying degrees, a process of deadly possession or appropriation. African snakes and serpents, for example, were catalogued by scientific writers such as Bowdich, Captain John Stedman, and Joseph Ritchie as natural manifestations of the African landscape and therefore as fair game for not just observation, but dissection. Bowdich records the chameleon in a fairly standard naturalist description, rendering the reptile as part of what in Africa could be mined, categorized, and grossly appropriated.

With *Lamia*, Keats also takes up this chameleon quality, but to a different end. Unlike Bowdich's account of the reptile, Keats's poem is a Gordian knot of ambiguity to many readers because he refuses to "melt" or absorb her into the "shade" of his poetic (I.47).[12] Instead, he exposes her only to protect her (to some extent) from complete possession. When Hermes first lays eyes on the serpent, he finds her an excessive, magnificent creature:

> Vermilion-spotted, golden, green and blue;
> Striped like a zebra, freckled like a pard,
> Eyed like a peacock, and all crimson barred;
> And full of silver moons, that, as she breathed,
> Dissolv'd, or brighter shone, or interwreathed
> Their lustres with the gloomier tapestries—   (I.48–53)

While this passage in some sense participates in stereotypes that exoticize Africa, it also serves to highlight Lamia's destabilizing transformation when, "left to herself, the serpent now began / To change" (I.46–47). She is literally "undressed" of her colors and masked in white skin and human form, her entrée to the busy city of Corinth (I.160). From this point on, Keats marks her as "fair" (I.181, II.110) but never ceases to hint at the serpent coiled beneath that skin. "The serpent—Ha, the serpent! Certes, she / Was none" (II.80–81), he writes, declaring her both serpent and not serpent. He defines her as transformation and therefore with the process that undermined notions of a possessive, territorializing self of travel writers and poets alike, that self posited so confidently in Bowdich's account of Ashantee as well as in the final books of Wordsworth's *Prelude*.[13]

In contrast to both Bowdich and Wordsworth, Keats's poetry interacted with Africa in a way that caught the attention of William Hazlitt, who wrote about Keats and Africa to illustrate his concept of Romantic imagination. In an 1822 review of the art collection of "Fonthill Abbey" for *London Magazine,* Hazlitt expresses disappointment, because the collection's "frippery and finery" lacked the air of "impenetrable mystery" he had expected to find. He concludes that such mystery could better be found among the "wastes and wilds" of Abyssinia or, better, in a cultural exchange like the one in which "a volume of Keats's poems was carried out by Mr. Ritchie to be dropped in the Great [Sahara] Desert."[14] It turns out that in 1818, Keats had been following Ritchie's African travels, which Keats likened to those of Park (*L*1:198). Keats had sent a copy of *Endymion* to Ritchie, asking him to cast it into the heart of the Sahara.[15] Ritchie replied by letter in December 1818: "Endymion has arrived thus far on his way to the Desart, and when you are sitting over your Christmas fire will be jogging (in all probability) on a camel's back o'er those Afran Sands immeasurable."[16] There is something chilling about Ritchie carrying *Endymion* into Africa while carrying out plans for the British government to explore the continent in order to possess its most powerful resources. But the image of Ritchie tossing Keats's poetry into Africa and then declaring him "the greatest poetic luminary of the age to come" can be traced to Keats's own view of his poetic as something that could coexist with cultural difference.[17] For example, Keats (with his usual irony) wrote to his brother George that copies of *Endymion* commingled with the mysterious and unknowable worldwide: "One is in the wilds of america—the other is on a camel's back in the plains of Egypt" (*L*2:16).

Lamia further demonstrates Keats's awareness that questions of exploration and conquest are inseparable from questions of poetic imagination. By invoking the "rule and line" (II:235) of the explorer/colonist within the "wide expanse" (*On First Looking into Chapman's Homer*, 5) of his own poetic, Keats implies that the transformations of poetry can interact with cultural difference without annihilating it. The opening canto in *The Fall of Hyperion*, which Keats composed while he was writing *Lamia*, records an imaginative interchange between Keats's "fine spell of words" and the "shadows of melodious utterance," "sable charm," and the heavenly dreams of the "savage" (I.1–11). With Lamia, Keats casts doubt on ideologies that would impose a sovereign identity onto a space. He realizes that to inscribe the "sands of Africa" (*L*1:223) in the "dull catalogue of common things" (II.233) and to place the African serpent's chameleon transformations under the static view of the scientific writer or the possessive gaze of colonial authority is to kill them utterly.

II

Keats must have been aware that the question of Lamia's serpent nature and its symbolic value was itself a nexus for the meeting and interworking of cultures. For a Western audience, the serpent Lamia immediately suggests the smooth-talking reptile and the induction of evil into the world in Christian mythology. By making his serpent a woman, Keats combines Eve and the satanic slitherer. Her "serpent prison," where we find her at the outset of the poem, is just the reverse of the serpent that encases Satan in Milton's *Paradise Lost*. Keats sympathizes to some extent with this satanic colonial outcast, because like Lamia, Milton's serpent-as-transformed-animal seduces and has his legs, if not his entire body, dissolved by a greater force.

The serpent also had rich meanings for African and Caribbean societies in the early nineteenth century. Though many travel accounts characterized Africa as a "paradise," the serpent played a central role in African voodoo before and during European exploration and imposition. European writers record traces of the centrality and power of the serpent in Africa religion which was known as *Vaudoux*, obeah, or as some type of fetish worship.[18] For example, M.L.E. Moreau de Saint-Mery's 1797–98 account of Saint-Domingue is one of the most thorough of the period on the subject. He writes of the mysterious "cult of the serpent" led by the "pythonisse" or "*Vaudoux* mistress"[19] and emphasizes the serpent's non-European significance:

> *Vaudoux* signifies an all powerful and supernatural being upon whom depends all the events that take place in the world. . . . Knowledge of the past, the present, and the future, all these belong to this grass snake. (M. 1:64)

Yet, throughout European literature of the Romantic period, the value Africans and West Indians grant to the serpent is repeatedly represented as a locus of nervous uncertainty. It is at once an extremely powerful ritual to slaves and a completely baffling one to Europeans.[20]

Africans and snakes were brought together during the Romantic period most often in the debate on the slave trade. For example, the widely circulated tract *An Apology for Negro Slavery: or the West India Planters Vindicated from the Charges of Inhumanity* (1786) targets snake worship among other justifications for slavery. Before the Europeans came to Africa, the author alleges, "the people were immersed in the grossest ignorance, idolatry, and barbarism. They worshipped snakes . . . and other wild beasts imagining that the homage they paid them would hinder them from doing them any harm."[21] Given the Christian beliefs common to both sides in the slavery debate, African snake worship could only imply devotion to something evil. It did not take long for Africans who "worship serpents, and even reptiles and entertain very unbecoming and confused notions of Deity"[22] to become West Indian slaves "without any religion but that called *Obeah,* or belief in a demon."[23]

The belief that snake worship was an ever-present danger to white planters became inextricably related to its unknowability. In his 1819 edition of *The History of the West Indies* (the period's most widely read and respected history of the Caribbean), Bryan Edwards attempts to understand the practice by imposing European knowledge onto it, literally, by defining obeah through etymological meaning. He finds that

> a serpent, in the Egyptian language, was called Ob, or *Aub.* — *Obion* is still the Egyptian name for a serpent.—Moses, in the name of God, forbids the Israelites ever to inquire of the demon Ob, which is translated in our Bible, Charmer, or Wizard, Divi-

nator, aut Sorcilegus. The woman at Endor is called *Oub* or *Ob*, translated Pythonissa; and *Oubasois* . . . was the name of the Basilisk or Royal Serpent, emblem of the sun, and an ancient oracular Deity of Africa.[24]

Edwards unwittingly writes the serpent as a shared symbol for divergent cultures. He aligns both Europeans and Africans under the symbol of the serpent and acknowledges the different interpretive value given it in each realm. The beguiling serpent in "our Bible" is demonized, whereas the "Royal Serpent" of African cultures radiates fertility and life. Though African power originated with the snake, Europeans (including Edwards) remained in the dark about the nature of this power. Whereas some dismissed obeah as nonsense, others (e.g., the Jamaican surgeon Benjamin Moseley) claimed that its practitioners could cast spells that caused disastrous epidemics on plantations.

However little the English knew about their specific functions, they clearly linked obeah ceremonies and voodoo possession to slave rebellions, insurrections, and other threatening acts. Many islands even established laws and held "obeah trials" to prevent the practice. Keats's use of the African serpent or pythoness in *Lamia* may have caused readers to recall scenes of *obias* possession described by Captain John Stedman, whose travel book was not as popular as Edwards's *History* but would have been available to the educated reading public. Stedman called these scenes the "dance of the mermaid," performed by the "*Sibyls,* who deal in oracles" and then dance and whirl

> round in the middle of an assembly, with amazing rapidity, until they foam at the mouth, and drop down as convulsed. Whatever the prophetess orders to be done during the paroxysm, is most sacredly performed by the surrounding multitude; which renders these meetings extremely dangerous, as she frequently enjoins them to murder their masters, or desert to the woods.[25]

Stedman's account repeats Moreau's description of the *Vaudoux* mistress, who is possessed or mounted by the spirit through the serpent and who presides over the ceremony.

> All of a sudden, he takes the box where the serpent is, puts it on the ground where it mounts the *Vaudoux* mistress. As soon as

the sacred sanctuary is under her feet, she is instantly pythoness, she is filled with her god, she becomes disturbed, her whole body shakes with convulsions, and the oracle speaks through her lips. (M1:66)

Such anguished ecstasy, in fact, characterizes Lamia's spell-binding transformation:

> her elfin blood in madness ran,
> Her mouth foamed, and the grass, therewith besprent,
> Withered at dew so sweet and virulent;
> Her eyes in torture fixed, and anguish drear,
> Hot, glazed, and wide, with lid-lashes all sear,
>
> . . . .
>
> The colours all inflamed throughout her train,
> She writhed about, convulsed in scarlet pain: (I.147–54)

The Gordian contradictions of the woman mounted by her god through the serpent completely mystified European logic. For example, while the pythoness had power through possession, she was also, according to Moreau, "prone to more violent agitations" and delirium than any other practitioner (M1:67). These contradictions, inherent in the religious practices of slaves, help explain Lamia's inconsistencies. Her physical incarnations start to make interpretive sense: as a "palpitating snake" (I.45), she first appears trapped in a "wreathed tomb" (I.38), yet she is simultaneously incorporated into Hermes's imperial value system, emblemized on his "serpent rod" (I.89). She performs medical miracles by "unperplex[ing] bliss from its neighbor pain" and "dress[ing] misery in fit magnificence" (I.192, II.117). She lives in both freedom and slavery, enacting the "unconfined Restraint," the "imprisoned liberty" Keats claimed in *Endymion* as the "great key . . . to all the mazy world / Of silvery enchantment" (I.455–61). From within her "serpent prison-house," Lamia sends her spirit "where she willed," from the pearly bowers of the sea goddess to the "rioting blend" of teeming mortals (I:203, 205, 214).

In fact, the most puzzling aspect of *Vaudoux* or obeah possession (as far as Europeans were concerned) was its power to liberate and enslave its practitioners, what Moreau described as a "a system of both domination and blind submission" (M1:65). The paradox described so apprehensively by Moreau, Stedman, and others is at the heart of Lamia. Her voodoo-like crisis seems to manifest her freedom in several senses. She sloughs off her colorful skin and dark origins, possessed instead by "white arms," a "neck regal white," and a "new voice luting soft" (I.287, 243, 167). This possession by whiteness affords her social mobility. As a "lady bright" (I.171), she wins the love of Lycius, who gives her the opportunity to move from slave dwelling to the house of the master, from "love in a hut" to "love in a palace" (II.1, 3).[26] Such freedom, however, only serves to underscore the enslaving function of possession. Like the West Indian slaves she partially recalls, Lamia is entangled in the continual process of giving herself up. The core contradiction of the ritual, one that has a probable explanation in the realities of slavery, is that a person achieves power and dominance only through complete obedience and submission to the possessing spirit.[27] The crux of West Indian voodoo, the suicidal question for slaves, and the ultimate question for Lamia are the same: Once one is in the possession of a white body, where does the possibility of giving up oneself stop?

Possession by whiteness signified evil and death for the West Indians and West Africans alike. Bowdich records that during the Ashantee rituals he witnessed, "they spill a little liquor on the ground as an offering to the fetish; and on rising from their chairs and stools, their attendants instantly lay them on their sides, to prevent the devil (whom they represent as white) from slipping into their master's places" (B269–70). Captain John Adams is more explicit in summing up what most educated Britons knew about the difference between white and black devils. Evil may be black in Britain, but "the blacks," writes Adams, "invariably" represent "evil . . . to be of white color."[28] In Keats's poem, Apollonius, whose baldness literally means the "mark of whiteness" and whose "demon eyes" conjure images of the devil, exemplifies "British" possession's systematic and therefore most destructive side. When he arrives at the feast where Lamia is to become Lycius's possession in a marriage bond, Apollonius's "calm-planted step," his methodical "patient thought," and his exacting "eye severe" turn "poor Lamia" into properties that he can then "thaw," "solve[,] and melt" (II.157–63).

To escape the threat of such piercing whiteness, slaves cloaked their ceremonies with secrecy. According to Edwards, the Jamaican slaves threw "a veil of mystery" over their rituals to "conceal them from the knowledge and discovery of the White people" (E2:109), and Moreau observed the sacred oaths of secrecy taken by practitioners in Saint-Domingue. Ceremonies were thus conducted during the middle of the night as a kind of protective curtain that made slaves invisible to planters. Throughout *Lamia,* Keats likewise provides the "half-retired" serpent woman with a similar kind of nocturnal concealment (I.312). The entire narrative takes place in the protective covering of night, moving from "evening dim," to "wide-spreaded night," to "eventide," to "midnight" (I.220, 354; II.17, 84). When the poem and Lamia herself emerge from darkness on that bright "day" (II.107) of her wedding, she is married, revealed, and dissolved.

Keats's desire to reinvest the Western story (in both its biblical and Greek versions) of the serpent-as-transformed-animal with a newly charged exoticism is part of what could be mined in Africa. Thus, Keats's activity does parallel that of Bowdich, Park, and Ritchie in their attempts to gather aspects of the African terrain into their classificatory scheme. In this sense, they did take possession of what they saw as "natural" magic. However, Keats's text is vexed because, unlike the accounts of travelers and colonists, he not only took hold of the magic of Africa, but was taken by it. By choosing a sympathetic figure with African origins who enacts aspects of West Indian religious magic, Keats manages to celebrate the imaginative power of Africa, whose force comes from a reversal of colonial methods, from being the possessed instead of the possessor, from keeping power hidden instead of displaying it, and from working in darkness instead of panoptic visibility.

III

Analyzing Jeremy Bentham's politics of space and visibility in late-eighteenth-and early-nineteenth-century English culture, Michel Foucault observes the European preoccupation with eradicating darkness and creating a transparent society:

> A fear haunted the latter half of the eighteenth century: the fear of darkened spaces, of the pall of gloom which prevents the full visibility of things, men and truths. It sought to break up the patches of darkness that blocked the light, eliminate the shadowy areas of society, demolish the unlit chambers where arbitrary political acts, monarchial caprice, religious superstitions, tyrannical and priestly plots, epidemics and the illusions of igno-

rance were fomented. . . . The new political and moral order could not be established until these places were eradicated.[29]

This same British gaze oversaw the work habits and living style of West Indian slaves while it tried to make visible voodoo rituals and other covert activities where slave rebellions could be planned and executed. But by 1818 it was the continent of Africa itself that represented the most immediate area of darkness in the expanding British imagination. Though journals and newspapers printed any news of Africa, which the English public readily consumed, large areas of Africa remained unknown. The African Association, formed in 1788 for exploration of the mysterious interior, sent adventurers up Africa's most powerful rivers—the Niger, the Nile, and the Congo—to observe in excruciating detail African "character, manners, and habits" (B5); to probe the secrets of their military power and political structures; and to make visible the kinds and quantity of resources held there. The point was to inscribe Africa in the words of Englishmen for British spectating and speculation.

In much the same way, Lamia also becomes the object of various sets of "imperial eyes," to use a phrase suggested by Mary Louise Pratt.[30] As Pratt observes, for some African explorers, Park in particular, gazing was a reciprocal activity. Park recorded not only what he saw, but what saw him. The women he met in Bondou, for example, "rallied me with a good deal of gaiety on different subjects, particularly upon the whiteness of my skin . . . [which] they said, was produced when I was an infant, by dipping me in milk."[31] Keats, too, begins his poem with a type of reciprocal gaze.[32] Lamia strikes a bargain with Hermes through the power of her vision. The oath Hermes swears "by [her] eyes" transpires only when "she breathe[s] upon his eyes" (I.90, 124). This exchange gives Lamia volcanic vision—her eyes "in torture fixed, and anguish drear, / Hot, glazed, and wide, with lid-lashes all sear, / Flashed phosphor and sharp sparks, without one cooling tear" (I.150–52)—and turns her into the poem's first "seer." Like Milton's Eve in her newly born body, Lamia stops "by a clear pool" to see "herself escaped," but at the very moment she becomes conscious of her own freedom, she loses that freedom to the binding forces of the culture in which she is inscribed (I.182–83).

In Lamia's world, as in Keats's, reciprocity did not last long. Lamia's eyes are "ever watchful, penetrant" (II.33) when she lands at the border of Corinth, but within that border Lycius's eyes turn her into a mirror of colonial desire and Apollonius's gaze harpoons her. When Lycius first observes Lamia, he bends to her "open eye / Where he was mirrored small in paradise" (II.46–7). He falls desperately in love with her, literally consuming her with his eyes: "his eyes had drunk her beauty up, / Leaving no drop in the bewildering cup, / And still the cup was full" (I.251–2). A visual alcoholic, Lycius is instantly addicted, as he declares "Ah Goddess, see / Whether my eyes can ever turn from thee!" (I.225). Like the master whose identity comes from the work of the slave who is literally the source of his power, Lycius is "chain[ed]" to her so strongly that he predicts what his fate will be when she ceases to mirror him: "Even as thou vanished so I shall die," he moans (I.256). Indeed, he feels horror at Lamia's unsightly death precisely because she no longer reflects him. After Apollonius has impaled Lamia with his own "juggling eyes," the panicked Lycius

> gazed into her eyes, and not a jot
> Owned they the lovelorn piteous appeal
> More, more he gazed; his human senses reel;
> Some hungry spell that loveliness absorbs;
> There was no recognition in those orbs. (II.245)[33]

Keats also indicts the piercing vision of Apollonius. At Lamia's death, Lycius impugns Apollonius's eyes (eyes that hover between "unlawful magic" and "enticing lies"), warning that the gods will "pierce them on the sudden with the thorn / Of painful blindness" (II.279–82). In commanding the common Corinthians to "look upon that gray-beard wretch! / Mark how, possessed, his eyelids stretch / Around his demon eyes! Corinthians, see!" (II.287–89), Lycius punishes Apollonius by making a spectacle of his eyes, while the poem wraps up Lycius as the final imaginative exhibit.

Moreau warns of the disruptive nature of West Indians in connection with *Vaudoux,* wherein slaves would explicitly ask for "the ability to manipulate the spirit of their masters." More shocking is what he calls "the magnetism" created in white masters who gazed too curiously on this culture. In fact, "Some whites found spying on the mysteries of the sect and touched by one of the members who had discovered them are actually driven to dancing and consenting to pay the *Vaudoux* mistress a fee in order to put an end to this chastisement" (M1:68). Like Keats, who turns Lycius's addictive gaze into a "love trance" from which he cannot escape (II.241), Moreau records not only the white community's desire to gaze on the strange and powerful African customs, but also their fear of being caught and mastered by a practice they could not control.

Just as Keats's poem condemns a certain kind of seeing, it equally celebrates the unseen and explicitly links it to freedom. The nymph is "invisible, yet free / To wander as she loves, in liberty," Lamia insists during her interchange with Hermes (I.108–9). "She tastes unseen; unseen her nimble feet, . . . She plucks the fruit unseen, she bathes unseen" (I.:99). In the context of the island,[34] it is Lamia's power that keeps "her beauty veiled / To keep it unaffronted, unassailed / By the love-glances of unlovely eyes" (I.95–96). Lamia also demonstrates a desire to keep herself veiled and unassailed in her move to the Corinthian marketplace, which was, after all, both an imperial metropolis and the largest slave market in ancient Greece.[35] Given this fact, who can blame Lamia for hiding out, even during her first face-to-face encounter with Lycius, when he literally sees right through her as she stands "so neighboured to him, and yet so unseen" (I.240)? She dwells unseen in Corinth, and though the voyeuristic crowds try to look on, even "the most curious / Were foiled, who watched to trace them to their house" (I.395). This seclusion makes her suspect, yet for a time she maintains her invisibility and thus her power.

It is this focus on secret space destroyed by the consumptive context of the market, where bodies become possessions, that characterizes Lamia and Lycius's fateful union. As Marjorie Levinson notes, the reciprocity between Lamia and Lycius means that "each lover becomes to the other a property."[36] As they hide in their chamber, veiled by "midnight silence," their bliss is "too short / To breed distrust and hate, that make the soft voice hiss" (I.84, II.9–10). If she does not hiss, Lamia at least senses Lycius's mental return to the "noisy world," the very conditions that would reframe their experience and cause him to "desert" and "dismiss" her (II.43–45). Lycius destroys this context not simply by proposing marriage to Lamia (and by extension ownership of her), but by reconceiving of her as a "prize" that will make his "foes choke" and his "friends shout afar" (II.57–62).[37] Keats implies that if Lamia is brought into the daylight of Western representational systems that uphold distinctions based on color and value systems in which profit triumphs over love, her charms will disappear absolutely. Mutual passion and possession will turn to ownership, and the result will be dangerous, if not deadly.

Lamia's loss of self, identity, and power begins with Lycius's unveiling of her secrets. In his effort "to reclaim / Her wild and timid nature to his aim" (II.70–1), he insists on displaying her before the public in a wedding ceremony, even though Keats as narrator explicitly condemns this kind of visibility: "O senseless Lycius! Madman! Wherefore flout / The silent-blessing fate, warm cloistered hours" (II.148). For it is not merely the one traveler observing the beauty and magic of Africa who kills it, but the act of inscribing and publicizing such a place in representations for all to see. Lamia, like Africa, becomes the object of the gaze of an entire population. At her ceremony, "The herd approached; each guest, with busy brain, / Arriving at the portal, gazed amain" (II.150). When Apollonius, as a figure for the center of white culture and its imperial gaze, destroys Lamia by piercing her with the eye and learning her secrets, he merely finishes the job that Lycius started. Thus while Keats exposes Lamia to the demon eyes of Apollonius, he nonetheless admonishes those like Lycius, inclined to unsettle and display the vast treasure of African mysteries to "show to common eyes these secret bowers" (II.150). And though Apollonius reveals Lamia's mystery and leaves Lycius in a dead stare, Keats seems to warn against probing too deeply into the heart of her secrets.

Yet in his letter to Woodhouse in September 1819, Keats attempted to define *Lamia* as a poetic of possession, one in which the reader is also possessed by the serpentine tale. "I am certain," he wrote, "there is that sort of fire in it which must take hold of people in some way" (*L*2:189). Keats forces readers to take hold of the poem's main narrative through Lamia's trance and therefore through her affinity with African and West Indian religious magic. But not only do readers take hold of the poem; it takes hold of them. They come to identify with Lamia through an unsettling process whereby she shifts between mortal and goddess, snake and human, African and European, visible and invisible, freedom and bondage, possession and dispossession.

This is what must have happened to Woodhouse. A month after he read *Lamia*, Woodhouse was still so taken by Keats's spell-binding poetic that he wrote Keats's publishers about it. Specifically, he pondered how Keats could move from subject to object, throw his soul "into any object he sees, feels, or imagines" and so "speak out of that object, so that his own self will, with the exception of the mechanical part, be annihilated." Woodhouse's practical dilemma, one that Keats did not seem to consider, centered on how the poet as man could be stripped of identity. Woodhouse concluded "As a man he must have identity, but as a poet he need not."[38] Thus, while Keats uses Lamia to celebrate the poetic imagination through the magic and mystery of Africa, it is his colonial prerogative to possess and dispossess the magic of Africa in the "dreams of Gods," far from the whip, the chain, and the sugar plantation.

NOTES

I would like to thank Jerry Hogle, Joan Dayan, Alan Richardson, Susan Wolfson, and John Willinsky for their contributions to this essay. An abbreviated version of this chapter, "Certain Monsters of Africa: Poetic Voodoo in Keats's *Lamia*," appeared in the London *Times Literary Supplement*, October 27, 1995, 13–14.

1. *John Keats: The Complete Poems*, ed. John Barnard, 3d ed. (New York: Penguin, 1988), II.299–306. All quotations of Keats's poetry are from this edition; line numbers are given in text.
2. *The Letters of John Keats: 1814–1821*. ed. Hyder E. Rollins (Cambridge, Mass: Harvard University Press, 1958); 1:387. All quotations of Keats's letters are from this edition, abbreviated *L* in text; volume and page numbers are given in text.
3. Robert Burton's account of Lycius, Lamia, and Apollonius in *Anatomy of Melancholy*, which Keats published along with the poem, is its most obvious source. For a discussion of Burton's influence, see Jane Chambers, "'For Love's Sake': *Lamia* and Burton's Love Melancholy" *SEL: Studies in English Literature 1500–1900* 22 (1982): 583–600. George C. Gross discusses another possible mythic source of the poem in "*Lamia* and the Cupid-Psyche Myth," *Keats-Shelley Journal* 39 (1990): 151–65.
4. John Lempriére, *Lempriére's Classical Dictionary of proper names mentioned in ancient authors writ large*. (London: Routledge, 1984), 317.
5. Captain George Francis Lyon, *A Narrative of Travels in Northern Africa, in the Years 1818, 19, and 20; accompanied by geographical notices of soudan, and of the course of the niger with a chart of the routes, and a variety of coloured plates, illustrative of the costumes of the several natives of Northern Africa, by Captain G. F. Lyon, RN, companion of the late Mr. Ritchie* (London: John Murray, 1821). The most blatant example of Lyon's double-characterizing of Africans appears in Lyon and Ritchie's encounter with an African sultan. When informed of Ritchie's "proposed journey and plans respecting the interior," the African sultan extends "the most flattering promises of protection," promising to "act toward Mr. Ritchie as a brother, and assist him in all things to the utmost of his power" (4). At the same time, Lyon designates the king a duplicitous man, strongly implying that Ritchie's death is hastened by, if not caused by, the king's ill will (220).

6. Thomas Edward Bowdich, *A Mission from Cape Coast Castle to Ashantee* (London: John Murray, 1819); hereafter cited in text as B.

7. Barnard (n. 1) points out that "the idea that classical nymphs, satyrs, and gods were displaced by the fairies of English folk-lore is common in Elizabethan and seventeenth-century literature" (691).

8. See Frantz Fanon, *Black Skin White Masks,* trans. Charles Lam Markmann (New York: Grove Weidenfeld, 1967), 161.

9. At the time Keats was writing, on many maps of Africa "Libya" designated the space occupied by the Sahara desert.

10. See Mungo Park, *Travels in the Interior Districts of Africa, 1799.* (London: John Murray, 1817), 1.

11. The intertextuality between Romantic poetry and travel narratives during this period is evident simply on the level of description. For Bowdich, the "luxurious" vegetation of Africa created a "romantic park" (15). Thomas Beckford refers to the landscape of Jamaica as "a romantic valley" (*A Descriptive Account of the Island of Jamaica* [London: T. and J. Egerton, 1790], 27).

12. For critics who see the poem as a demonstration of ambiguity arising from various contradictions between philosophy and poetry, rationalism and imagination, good and evil, immortality and mutability, see M. R. Ridley, *Keats's Craftsmanship: A Study in Poetic Development* (1933; reprint, Lincoln: University of Nebraska Press, 1968); Jack Stillinger, *The Hoodwinking of Madeline and Other Essays on Keats's Poems* (Urbana: University of Illinois Press, 1971); Joseph C. Sitterson Jr., "Narrator and Reader in *Lamia,*" *Studies in Philology* 79 (1982): 297–310; Earl R. Wasserman, *The Finer Tone: Keats' Major Poems* (Baltimore: Johns Hopkins University Press, 1953, 1967); John Daniel Skirp III, "Intellect, Imagination and the Poet: An Interpretation of *Lamia,*" *Journal of Evolutionary Psychology* 7 (1986): 143–47; Timothy Pace, "'Who Killed Gwendolen Harleth'? Daniel Deronda and Keats's *Lamia,*" *Journal of English and Germanic Philology* 87 (1988): 35–48. Terence Hoagwood, in "Keats and Social Context: *Lamia,*" *SEL: Studies in English Literature 1500–1900* 29 (1989): 675–95, argues that critics who see the text in these kinds of dichotomies evade the social/political problems the text addresses. Readings that incorporate gender criticism often cite Keats's having a "gordian complication of feelings" for women (*L*1:342). See Margaret Hallissy, "Poisonous Creature: Holmes's Elsie Venner," *Studies in the Novel* 17 (1985): 406–19; Martha Nochinson, "Lamia as Muse," in *The Poetic Fantastic,* ed. Patrick D. Murphy (New York: Greenwood Press, 1989); Karla Alwes, *Imagination Transformed: The Evolution of the Female Character in Keats's Poetry* (Carbondale: Southern Illinois University Press, 1993). Susan Wolfson gives an excellent analysis of Keats's "gordian complication of feelings" with reference to his entire oeuvre in "Keats and the Manhood of the Poet," *European Romantic Review* 6 (1995): 1–37. The word "Gordian" in its mythic context also connotes the power of imperialism. As legend would have it, the intricate Gordian knot, originally tied by King Gordius of Phrygia, was cut by Alexander the Great on the promise that whoever could undo it would be the next ruler of Asia.

13. Critics regularly remark the poem's deterritorializing poetic. For example, John Barnard (*John Keats* [Cambridge: Cambridge University Press, 1987]) finds the poem "unsettled and unsettling" (120).

14. William Hazlitt, *London Magazine* 6 (1822): 406.

15. Stephen Coote, *John Keats: A Life* (London: Hodder & Stoughton, 1995), 117–18.

16. The letter is still in Haydon's journal (see *L*2:16). Ritchie's journey is recorded in Lyon's *Travels* (n. 5).

17. Letter written in 1818, printed by David Garnett, *New Statesman*, June 10, 1933, 763 (see *L*1:198).

18. See Alan Richardson, "Romantic Voodoo: Obeah and British Culture, 1797–1807," *Studies in Romanticism* 32 (1993):3–28. In this groundbreaking work, Richardson points out that during the Romantic period, the term "'Obeah' tended to signify whatever forms of supernatural beliefs and religious practices the British encountered among the slaves" (5). The word "Obeah," in its various spellings, probably of Ashantee origin, appears most often in connection with slave rituals, but Moreau de Saint-Mery (n. 19) referred to the "*Vaudoux*" practices of Saint-Domingue in 1797–98. For a full history the origin of "voodoo," its Dahomey origins, and its West Indian manifestations, see Melville J. Herskovits, *Life in a Haitian Valley* (New York: A. Knopf, 1937). Modern historians distinguish between obeah, voodoo, and myalism. See Barbara Bush, *Slave Women in Caribbean Society 1650–1838* (Indianapolis: Indiana University Press, 1990), 73–76. In her work on Haiti, Joan Dayan employs the word "*vodoun* rather than 'voodoo' in order to distinguish the Haitian religion from the lurid images of mud baths, bleeding chickens, and black magic evoked by the work in its more common form" ("The Crisis of the Gods: Haiti after Duvalier," *The Yale Review* [1988], 300).

19. M.-L. E. Moreau de Saint-Mery, *Description de la partie francaise de Saint Domingue*, 2 parties (Paris: Chez Dupont, 1797–89), 1:68; hereafter cited in text as M. For a postcolonial treatment of Moreau, see Jean Price-Mars, *So Spoke the Uncle,* trans. Magdaline W. Shannon (Washington, D.C.: Three Continents, 1990).

20. For the most compelling work on the history and function of West Indian voodoo or vodoun, see Dayan, "The Crisis of the Gods" (see n. 18); Dayan, "Haiti, History, and the Gods," in *After Colonialism: Imperial Histories and Postcolonial Displacements,* ed. Sherry B. Ortner, Nicholas B. Dirks, and Geoff Eley (Princeton: Princeton University Press, 1995), 66–97; and Dayan, "Vodoun, or the Voice of the Gods," *Raritan* 10, no. 3 (1991), 32–57. I am grateful to Dayan, who first suggested this line of inquiry to me.

21. [Author unknown], *An Apology for Negro Slavery: or, The West India Planters Vindicated From the Charges of Inhumanity* (London: J. Stevenson, 1786), 10.

22. Robert Renny, *A History of Jamaica* (London: J. Cawthorn, 1807), 165.

23. [Author unknown], *The State of Society in Jamaica: In a Reply to an Article in Edinburgh Review No. LXXV* (London: James Ridgeway, 1825), 12.

24. Bryan Edwards, *The History, Civil and Commercial, of the British West In-*

dies. 5 vols. 5th ed. (London: T Miller, 1819; reprint, New York: AMS, 1966), 2:107; hereafter cited in text as E.

25. Captain John Gabriel Stedman, *Narrative of a five years' expedition against the Revolted Negroes of Surinam, in Guiana on the Wild Coast of South America; from the year 1772 to 1777 elucidating the History of that country and describing its production viz, quadrupeds, Birds, Fishes, reptiles, Trees, Shrubs, Fruits, and Roots; with an account of the Indians of Guiana and Negroes of Guinea,* (2nd ed., corr. London: J. Johnson, 1813), 2:272–73.

26. The dwellings of Africans and slaves on plantations were notoriously called "huts" in all travel and abolitionist literature of this period.

27. See Erika Bourguignon, *Possession* (San Francisco: Chandler & Sharp, 1976), 48.

28. Captain John Adams, *Sketches taken during ten voyages to Africa, between the years 1786 and 1800* (London: Hurst, Robinson, 1822; reprint, London: Johnson Reprint, 1970), 65.

29. Michel Foucault, *Power/Knowledge,* trans. Colin Gordon, Leo Marshall, John Mepham, and Kate Soper, ed. Colin Gordon (New York: Pantheon Books, 1980), 153.

30. Mary Louise Pratt, *Imperial Eyes: Travel Writing and Transculturation* (London: Routledge, 1992), esp. 69–85.

31. Park, *Travels in the Interior,* 29.

32. Pratt (n. 30) argues that "reciprocity . . . organizes Park's human-centered, interactive narrative," but this dynamic is simply an idealization of "Park's expansionist commercial aspirations" whereby Park not only looks at and speculates on Africans, but also "repeatedly portrays himself as subjected to the scrutiny of the Africans" (80–81).

33. Marjorie Levinson's Marxist reading draws a parallel between Lamia's blank eyes and Moneta's eyes, which are "like two gold coins" (*Keats's Life of Allegory: The Origins of a Style* [New York: Basil Blackwell, 1988], 268). But even equating Lamia with the gold coin of Keats's day would have linked her to Africa and the slave trade. The "guinea," in which all goods were advertised, literally means "negro land" and takes it name from the fact that it was originally issued in Guinea gold. A good portion of the British slave trade took place on the Guinea Coast.

34. As Gordon K. Lewis explains in *Main Currents in Caribbean Thought* (Baltimore: Johns Hopkins University Press, 1983), the area around the Mediterranean is often compared to the Caribbean, primarily because both civilizations grew up as seaborne empires surrounded by awesome masses of water. Lewis goes into detail about how similarities in geography and climate have influenced the politics of both. These were observed even during the Romantic era by at least one interested writer. Olaudah Equiano comments in his slave/travel narrative: "I was surprised to see how the Greeks are, in some measure, kept under by the Turks, as the negroes are in the West Indies by the white people" (*The Life of Olaudah Equiano,* [1789; reprint, Coral Gables, Fla.: Mnemosyne, 1989], 1:90). Another discussion of possible African influences in Crete may be found in Martin Bernal's *Black Athena: The Afroasiatic Roots of Classical Civilization,* 2 vols. (London: Free Association

Books, 1987). Bernal speculates that Greek culture and mythology, especially as it originated on Crete, was influenced in major ways by Egyptian, Levantian, and North African religion and society.

35. Corinth was the center of worship for the patron goddess Aphrodite, for which the Corinthians built a magnificent temple housing thousands of slaves and prostitutes for the use of strangers. For historical accounts of slavery in ancient Greece and Rome, see Thomas Wiedemann, *Greek and Roman Slavery* (London: Routledge, 1981; reprinted 1992).

36. Levinson, *Keats's Life of Allegory*, 277.

37. Levinson states, "In order to constitute Lamia as a property (as opposed to something of the order of a natural resource), Lycius must first establish his ownership. He must publicly and legally secure his goods, hence his insistence on marriage, as on a very public reception" (ibid., 278). Coleman O. Parsons ("Primitive Sense in Lamia," *Folklore* 88 [1977]: 203–10) notes that Lycius's "indulging" in public invites his rivals to seize what is being enjoyed. Bruce Clarke ("Fabulous Monsters of Conscience: Anthropomorphosis in Keats's Lamia," *Studies in Romanticism* 24 [1985]: 555–579) also sees that much of the interaction of the poem is based on ownership and property, so that "Hermes and Lamia together compose an allegory for the participatory exchange of goods in free commerce, the counterpart of theft and dispossession" (569).

38. *Romanticism*, ed. Duncan Wu (Oxford: Blackwell, 1994), 713. Woodhouse also wrote notes to himself along these same lines; see *The Keats Circle*, ed. Hyder E. Rollins, 2 vols. (Cambridge, Mass.: Harvard University Press, 1965), 2:57–60.

Keats and the Critical Tradition

The Topic of History

———————◆———————

TERENCE ALLAN HOAGWOOD

You will suspect that examination of the conditions under which
works are created and their effect will try to usurp the place of
experience of the works as they are. . . . This approach will seem
especially distressing to you in the case of lyric poetry. The most
delicate, the most fragile thing that exists is to be encroached
upon and brought into conjunction with bustle and commotion,
when part of the ideal of lyric poetry, at least in its traditional
sense, is to remain unaffected by bustle and commotion. . . . Can
anyone, you will ask, but a man who is insensitive to the Muse
talk about lyric poetry and society?[1]

TRADITIONALLY, WHEN the subject of history has come up in
Keats studies (as in literary studies generally), the words "background" and "context" have often arisen.[2] Scholars narrate a historical
frame in which to place Keats's work for interpretive purposes. But
influential Romanticists have been pointing out that there is also a historical frame around Keats critics. For example, if we were to describe
the meaning and value of Keats's poetry in our own cultural moment,
would we take into account the preponderance of institutional uses of
the poems? Whereas in the nineteenth century Keats's poems were marketed with appeals to pleasure, now they are marketed by a machinery
of course requirements, as every editor of anthologies understands. The
name "Keats" was at one time a signifier of "the Cockney school of
politics"; at another time a signifier of "the pure and serene artist"; and

at another time a purely verbal structure, a well-wrought text in itself, preferable to material history; in our time, the name "Keats" has shrunk (we may as well admit it) into a segment on a syllabus produced for occupational reasons.[3] Whatever else it is, professional discourse on Keats is an occupational action, performed in institutional settings that are organized by requirements, rewards, and punishments; to some degree, perhaps, these things condition and determine how much (and even what) we say about Keats.

There is an inside story to Keats studies; this is a story of conceptual discourses among people inside the institutions of professionalized criticism. And there is an outside to this profession, where life in general is going on, all the while. The study of Keats has some relationship to this larger story. To historicize Keats studies in terms of the inside story would be to make a narrative of literary history, inside the tradition of professionalized commentary. It is also possible to tell the history of Keats studies in terms of its outside story. In the nineteenth century, how did commentary on Keats fit in the larger scheme of social life? How does it fit in that larger scheme now? John Gibson Lockhart suggested that Keats's poetry was a danger to the community; Thomas Carlyle suggested that it was a machine for personal hedonism;[4] for some publishers, the poems have been commodities; and I have met more than one person (so have we all) who thinks of Keats's poetry chiefly in terms of his or her occupational future.

Thus two kinds of criticism treat the topic of history: some historical studies of Keats tell an inside story, narrating what Keats thought or said about history and historical topics, including politics.[5] In contrast, the outside story of Keats's poetry in historical context concerns other things. Grant that a writer means something subjective, as in a romantic lyric; a critic can ask, What is the historical, political, or social meaning of the writer's doing such a thing?[6] Adorno suggests that the social dimension of a work of art is not a matter of the work's being literally about social issues at all. The conventional expectation that a lyric poem will be autonomous of historical circumstances "is itself social in nature":

> It implies a protest against a social situation that every individual experiences as hostile, alien, cold, oppressive, and this situation is imprinted in reverse on the poetic work: the more heavily the situation weighs upon it, the more firmly the work resists it

by refusing to submit to anything heteronomous and constituting itself solely in accordance with its own laws. The work's distance from mere existence becomes the measure of what is false and bad in the latter. In its protest the poem expresses the dream of a world in which things would be different.[7]

The meanings of poems that turn away from social issues are determined by the social issues that they evade. From this outside-story point of view, the poet's conscious intention is never enough to explain what is meaningful about the poem: "the lyric work of art's withdrawal into itself, its self-absorption, its detachment from the social surface, is socially motivated behind the author's back."[8]

Because I have cited Adorno, it may be a good idea to notice the widespread but false belief that in his *Aesthetic Theory,* Adorno uses the word "autonomy" in a way that is somehow consistent with the notion of a "poem itself," independent of social and material determiners, as that notion was formulated by W. K. Wimsatt and Monroe C. Beardsley, among others.[9] Understandably, that notion has been attractive to professors of English literature, but its attribution to Adorno is nonetheless false: for Adorno, all "linguisticality means collectivity," even when a patch of language tries to denote a private subjectivity, as a lyric often does. Adorno writes in *Aesthetic Theory* that "social antagonisms are not erased in art, but go on impinging on it"; art has an "illusory quality," which is, in Adorno's argument, a function of its pretending "to be an in-itself" when it is not and cannot be an in-itself. As he argued in the essay on lyric poetry that the lyric poem "is socially motivated behind the author's back," so in *Aesthetic Theory* he writes that "autonomy, art's growing independence from society . . . is tied up with a specific social structure." The "autonomy" that Adorno discusses is not some supposed independence of contingent social facts, but rather the economic arrangement whereby modern poets typically act as entrepreneurs, rather than as paid agents of the church or state; "before the French Revolution artists were retainers; today they are entertainers." But for Adorno "art is always a social fact," not because it takes up social themes explicitly, but, instead, as in the case of lyric poetry, "art criticizes society just by being there": "What is social about art is not its political stance, but its immanent dynamic in opposition to society." The oppositional politics of art, in Adorno's view, is not what a work states about politics, but rather the work's desire-driven projection of a different and better world—albeit a fragile, dreamed, and momentary one. In Adorno's account, even the most apparently escapist art is social, because it is a sign of the inadequacy of modern, administered society to actual human need.[10]

Josiah Royce pointed out in 1892 that "humanity depends, for its spirituality and its whole civilization, upon faiths and passions that are in the first place instinctive, inarticulate, and in part unconscious."[11] Royce associates the unconscious origin of these meanings with the fact that meanings are social, rather than personal, in their formation:

> As man is social, as no man lives alone, as your temperament is simply the sum total of your social "reflex actions," is just your typical bearing toward your fellows, the great philosopher, in reflecting on his own deepest instincts and faiths, inevitably describes, in the terms of his system, the characteristic attitude of his age and people.[12]

Thus Royce's nineteenth-century account—so different in many other ways—resembles Adorno's twentieth-century account in this way: both writers characterize meanings as socially determined. In this view, meanings are not limited by intentions, even when the poet means them to be, and they are not personal, even when the poem pretends to be; again, "art is a social act." These larger meanings are what we could not learn if all we knew were what Keats meant—these are the meanings "behind the author's back," larger than those contrived in the artifice of lyrical and singular illusion. The artist's intention cannot exhaust meanings, because, as Nietzsche said aphoristically in 1886, "the intention is merely a sign and symptom that still requires interpretation."[13]

Royce's observation expresses a method called "Historicism" in Wilhelm Dilthey's sense of the word, which in turn descends from Friedrich Schleiermacher. Schleiermacher's hermeneutic philosophy involves centrally a method of studying a historically removed language system and social system that are far larger than what any individual writer intended.[14] As Adorno would do much more than a century later, Schleiermacher observed that a language system produces meanings that are social rather than personal and historically specific rather than abstract.

What we as historicist interpeters say about works and authors applies with equal force to our own work: we, too, are located in the flux of time, place, and change that we call history, just as Keats was. It is not simply that Keats's mind and our minds contain sociohistorical thoughts, but rather that historical reality contained Keats's mind, and it contains our minds too. Our own interpretations, like the texts we interpret, represent historically specific structures of thought and feeling whether we are aware of them or not.

Jack Stillinger and Jerome J. McGann have shown, influentially, how bibliographical analysis can unfold an outside story: circumstances of the print trade, publishers' decisions, and the ordinary purposes of business affect the production of poems, and their meanings, and yet these things usually lie outside the story that is told in the poem.[15]

In an important review essay that appeared in 1985, Stillinger wrote that there may be good reason that little has been said about Keats's social and political views.[16] He was referring to inside-story politics, that is, what Keats said or wrote about politics in the explicit and intentional sense. This subject was also explored by Carl Woodring in his widely read book, *Politics in English Romantic Poetry*.[17] However, there is nonetheless much to say in terms of the outside story. If a political unconscious, or historical anxiety, or class anxiety, or the ordinary purposes of business did condition or determine the production of a poetry of pleasure and beauty and removal—in short, if such determiners did produce an illusion of a treasured aesthetic autonomy from the dirty world—then, at the level of authorial intention, politics and material history are part of the dirty world that the poet is deliberately avoiding. The poem's evasion bears witness to the dirty world that the poem evades. Inside the story, it is not history or politics about which the aesthete is concerned; outside the story, such aestheticism has a historical function and is susceptible to historical explanation.

At the level of theme, of course, there have been many studies of Keats's inwardness; for example, Leon Waldoff asked, How are we to conceive of imagination's relationship to the deepest patterns of feeling and thought in the poetry and the poet's psyche?[18] There have also been many studies contrasting Keats's sense of the visionary imagination, or idealism,[19] against his sense of reality, or his sense of the value of reality. Such studies may look at first like outside-story criticism, contrasting Keats's concept of inwardness with his concept of external reality. But I would suggest that both terms in that binary opposition are concepts. Thematic criticism about Keats's inwardness and thematic criticism about his sense of reality are equally inside-story explanations. The task of the conceptualizing and thematic critic is to explain what Keats wrote in terms of what he personally thought.

Expositions of what Keats thought formed the common sense of Keats criticism for so long (and so recently) that I will pause for a moment to illustrate the point that I am trying to make here. In 1968, Stillinger published the following influential explanation of what Keats thought:

> Keats's significant poems center on a single basic problem, the mutability inherent in nature and human life, and openly or in disguise they debate the pros and cons of a single hypothetical solution, transcendence of earthly limitations by means of the visionary imagination. If one were to summarize the career in a sentence, it would be something like this: Keats came to learn that this kind of imagination was a false lure, inadequate to the needs of the problem, and in the end he traded it for the natural-ized imagination, embracing experience and process as his own and man's chief good.[20]

Stillinger's emphasis on "earthly limitations" and "experience and pro-cess" seemed refreshingly realistic a decade or two after Wasserman's metaphysics and after a century and more of pseudo-Platonic apprecia-tions of the idealism of *Endymion*. Nevertheless, Stillinger did not men-tion reality. He mentioned Keats's thoughts about reality. His points of reference are internal to Keats's mind, though what Keats is said to have thought *about* is reality. Hence, that passage, or rather the book in which it appeared, is one of the most influential statements of the inside story in Keats criticism.

In contrast, an externalizer might take the words "social," "histori-cal," and "cultural" to imply a range of meanings beneath and beyond the consciously political meanings of, for example, topical or polemical works, such as Keats's poems *Written on the Day That Mr. Leigh Hunt Left Prison* and *To Kosciusko*. One is reluctant to recommend many new writing projects on Keats: the works of many other Romantic-period writers still need to be studied (e.g., I know of no book about the poetry of Charlotte Dacre), and already any serious student of Keats, setting out on a critical project, finds him- or herself in the posi-tion of the Sorcerer's Apprentice, besieged by too much critical help. If one wishes to write on one of Keats's odes, for example, about a thousand separate studies present themselves. However, I think there is still important and rewarding work to be done, and so I shall mention what I think are some promising possibilities.

Bibliographical scholarship remains to be done, and to be brought to bear upon interpretation. For example, independently both Paul Magnuson and Jeffrey Cox have been writing about *Ode on a Grecian Urn* in the context of the periodical in which it was first published, *Annals of the Fine Arts*.[21] Keats studies would be enriched by a detailed, comprehensive study of the *Examiner* as a contextual field in which several of Keats's poems appeared (independently, Nicholas Roe and I, among others, have been writing about Keats's work in this connection).[22]

Although Keats's politics have been the subject of studies for more than fifty years, studies of other kinds of historical contexts would be valuable even now. In his bibliographical essay of thirteen years ago, Stillinger said that "there are practically no specialized studies focusing on Keats's early education, his reading at Clarke's school"; I understand that Nicholas Roe has been working on that set of questions, and Keats scholars are looking forward to his work with some excitement. Stillinger also said back then that "much more could be done toward our understanding of how Keats's nonposthumous poems got into print," and his own important book of 1991, *Multiple Authorship and the Myth of Solitary Genius*, does much to show how that kind of work can be done. Recent books such as Karla Alwes's *Imagination Transformed: The Evolution of the Female Character in Keats's Poetry* have helped to provide explanations of "Keats's ideas about and depiction of women," which Stillinger also called for in 1985; one can hope that other scholars and critics will further pursue these issues.[23]

Bibliographical research and historical scholarship are likely to continue to collaborate to make more of the poems' meanings more evident. For example, Earle Weller's *Keats and Mary Tighe* (1928) prints Tighe's *Psyche* with extensive annotation consisting chiefly of phrases in Keats's poetry that resemble phrases in Tighe's. Recent discussion of the relationship of Keats's work to Tighe's is characterized by inside-story criticism, that is, accounts of Keats's thoughts and attitudes about Tighe and her work and women in general.[24] To move outside the question of what was in Keats's mind, it might be instructive to compare the way in which Tighe's poem got into print with the way in which Keats's poems got into print. Their different material arrangements, I would suggest, express different purposes and produce different meanings. For example, Tighe was not seeking personal or family income when she wrote, rewrote, and published her book; Keats did seek income, among other things, from the production of his last great book, and that concern affected his work profoundly, as McGann and Stillinger have persuasively shown.

I shall mention only one more example of the sort of criticism informed by bibliographical work that can, I think, still contribute constructively to understandings of Keats's poems, as densely overwritten by criticism as they are. The first book in which Keats's major odes appeared, *Lamia, Isabella, The Eve of St. Agnes, and Other Poems. By John Keats, Author of Endymion* (1820), includes *Hyperion, A Fragment.* It also includes, in the front matter, an "Advertisement" from its publishers, Taylor and Hessey, which is typographically emphasized because it is the only text on its page. The publishers announce in the advertisement that *Hyperion* "was printed at their particular request, and contrary to the wish of the author." The meanings contributed to the poetic book by the inclusion of *Hyperion* are thus antiauthorial meanings, but nonetheless they are important in helping to define the book and its effects on both its contemporary readership (including Shelley, who admired it most of Keats's works) and its later readership, including ourselves. The inclusion of *Hyperion* changes the meaning of the book in a number of ways: the longer poems in the volume are the three verse romances mentioned in the book's title and then the Miltonic epic *Hyperion;* this multiplicity of generic codes makes the book a sampler of inherited styles. The book's artifice, eclecticism, and sheer literariness are made more extreme by this juxtaposition of the *Hyperion* fragment with the verse romances. Yet none of these additions to the meaning of the book is authorial. The book says that these meanings are, in fact, produced against the poet's intention.

Even outside specifically literary evidence, a historical vantage can open visions of Keats's work fruitful for interpretation. For example, Charles Cowden Clarke's memoir of Keats suggests an approach to the question of Keats's response to some historical conflicts that is still promising. Clarke writes of Keats's association with Leigh Hunt and of the hostility that Keats's *Poems* of 1817 elicited from reviewers because of that association: "the word had been passed that its author was a Radical; and in those days of 'Bible-Crown-and-Constitution' supremacy, he might have had better chance of success had he been an Anti-Jacobin." Clarke distinguishes the time in which he writes this memoir from the time in which Keats wrote his poems: "Men may now utter a word in favour of 'civil liberty' without being chalked on the back and hounded out."[25] He suggests an outside-story approach: circumstances outside the poem determine the content and even the style of what is inside the poem. If there is sedition in Keats's *Poems*, Clarke defines some reasons for its relatively oblique articulation in that book. If Clarke represents accurately the determining power of suppression that constrained poets and the press at the time, those conflicts and their historical suppression should count among the meanings of those poems.

In the poetry of our own time, Reed Whittemore has written, in *The Trouble Outside*, a narrative that comically and sadly develops the concept of the outside story. The poem is about an inner death suffered by an orderly librarian named Miss Prunewhip. "Inside all is order, magazines, books, periodicals all in order," Whittemore writes,

> But outside on the sidewalk, under the trees, by the curb
> All is not in order, not at all, not Prunewhip's order.
> The leaves are not in order, and not on file; nor the faces,
> No, the faces, in disorder, and the leaves, in disorder,
> Swirl brazenly in the air, uncarded, unclassified.
> It is outside Miss Prunewhip that the inside has died.[26]

What this poem suggests about the outside world may be equally true of poems, including Keats's poems, and their meanings. It is probably outside the poems' strictly verbal features—outside their textual nuance—that their real-life meanings are found and made.

NOTES

1. Theodor Adorno, "On Lyric Poetry and Society," in *Notes to Literature*, ed. Rolf Tiedemann, trans. Shierry Weber Nicholsen (New York: Columbia University Press, 1991), 37. Adorno's essay was first a lecture—"Rede ueber Lyrik und und Gesellschaft"—for RIAS Berlin, and it was first published in *Akzente*, 1957.
2. One example is Marilyn Butler, *Romantics, Rebels and Reactionaries: English Literature and Its Background 1760–1830* (Oxford: Oxford University Press, 1981).
3. Z. [John Gibson Lockhart], "On the Cockney School of Poetry, No. IV," *Blackwood's Edinburgh Magazine* 3 (1818): 109; Oscar Wilde in his American lecture on Keats as quoted by George H. Ford, *Keats and the Victorians*

(New Haven; Conn.: Yale University Press, 1944), 104; Cleanth Brooks, "Keats's Sylvan Historian: History without Footnotes" (1942); reprinted in Brooks, *The Well-Wrought Urn: Studies in the Structure of Poetry* (1947; reprint, London: Methuen, 1968). To my knowledge, the most conspicuous reduction of Keats's poetry to transparent vocationalism is *Approaches to Teaching Keats's Poetry,* ed. Walter H. Evert and Jack W. Rhodes (New York: Modern Language Association, 1991), which includes advice about how to proceed in a classroom.

4. In a letter to his mother, Carlyle wrote, "The kind of man that Keats was gets ever more horrible to me. Force of hunger for pleasure of every kind. . . . Away with it!" (quoted by Lawrence and Elisabeth Hanson in *Necessary Evil: The Life of Jane Welsh Carlyle* [New York: Macmillan, 1952], 369).

5. See, for example, June Q. Koch, "Politics in Keats's Poetry," *Journal of English and Germanic Philology* 71 (October 1972): 491–501; Butler, *Romantics, Rebels and Reactionaries,* 138–54; David Bromwich, "Keats's Radicalism," *Studies in Romanticism* 25 (1986): 197–210; Nicholas Roe, "Keats's Lisping Sedition," *Essays in Criticism* 42 (1992): 36–55; and the essays by many hands gathered in *Keats and History,* ed. Nicholas Roe (Cambridge: Cambridge University Press, 1995).

6. Critical studies that have taken this external vantage on Keats in history include Jerome J. McGann, "Keats and the Historical Method in Literary Criticism," *Modern Language Notes* 94 (1979): 988–1032, reprinted in McGann, *The Beauty of Inflections* (Oxford: Oxford University Press, 1985); Terence Allan Hoagwood, "Keats and Social Context: *Lamia,*" *SEL: Studies in English Literature 1500–1900* 29 (1989): 675–97; Daniel P. Watkins, *Keats's Poetry and the Politics of the Imagination* (Rutherford, N.J.: Fairleigh Dickinson University Press, 1989); and Hoagwood, "Keats, Fictionality, and Finance," in *Keats and History,* 127–42.

7. Adorno, "On Lyric Poetry and Society," 40.

8. Ibid., p. 43.

9. Wimsatt and Beardsley, *The Verbal Icon: Studies in the Meaning of Poetry* (1954; reprint, London: Methuen, 1970).

10. Adorno, *Aesthetic Theory* (London: Routledge and Kegan Paul, 1983), 240, 241, 242, 320, 321.

11. Royce, *The Spirit of Modern Philosophy* (Boston: Houghton, Mifflin, 1892), 11.

12. Ibid., 8–9.

13. Nietzsche, *Beyond Good and Evil: Prelude to a Philosophy of the Future,* trans. Walter Kaufmann (New York: Random House, 1966), 44.

14. Schleiermacher, "Outline of the 1819 Lectures" [from *The Hermeneutics*], trans. Jan Wojcik and Roland Haas, in *The Hermeneutic Tradition: From Ast to Ricoeur,* ed. Gayle L. Ormiston and Alan D. Schrift (Albany: State University of New York Press, 1990), 85–99. See also Wilhelm Dilthey, "The Rise of Hermeneutics," trans. Fredric Jameson, also in *The Hermeneutic Tradition,* 101–14.

15. See, for example, Jack Stillinger, "Keats's Extempore Effusions and the Question of Intentionality," in *Romantic Revisions,* ed. Robert Brinkley and Keith

Hanley (Cambridge: Cambridge University Press, 1992); Stillinger, *Multiple Authorship and the Myth of Solitary Genius* (New York: Oxford University Press, 1991); McGann, "Keats and the Historical Method in Literary Criticism"; and McGann, *The Textual Condition* (Princeton: Princeton University Press, 1991): "A study of textuality grounded in paleography, bibliography, and the sociology of texts" is important *for interpreters*, and not merely bibliophiles or editors, because "the meanings we may imagine for the poems . . . are a function of all these matters, *whether we are aware of such matters when we make our meanings or whether we are not*" (12).

16. Stillinger, "John Keats," in *English Romantic Poets: A Review of Research and Criticism*, 4th ed., ed. Frank Jordan (New York: Modern Language Association, 1985), 665–718.

17. Woodring, *Politics in English Romantic Poetry* (Cambridge, Mass.: Harvard University Press, 1970).

18. Waldoff, *Keats and the Silent Work of Imagination* (Urbana: University of Illinois Press, 1985), xi. Another study of Keats that is informed by psychoanalytic concepts is Marjorie Levinson's *Keats's Life of Allegory* (Oxford: Blackwell, 1988), which includes class consciousness among its points of reference: "The psyche that motivates my John Keats is a dynamic reflection of social configurations" (33); Levinson's stated purpose is "to read the meaning of a life in the style of a man's writing, and then to read that writing, that style, and that life back into their original social context" (6).

19. Most influential in this genre of criticism was Earl R. Wasserman, *The Finer Tone: Keats's Major Poems* (Baltimore: Johns Hopkins University Press, 1953).

20. Stillinger, "Imagination and Reality in the Odes," in *The Hoodwinking of Madeline and Other Essays on Keats's Poems* (Urbana: University of Illinois Press, 1971), 100; this essay was first published as the introduction to *Twentieth-Century Interpretations of Keats's Odes*, ed. Stillinger (Englewood Cliffs, N.J.: Prentice-Hall, 1968).

21. Magnuson, "Ode on a Grecian Urn" (paper presented at the meeting of the Keats-Shelley Association at the convention of the Modern Language Association, San Diego, December 1994); Jeffrey N. Cox, "Cockney Classicism: Keats's Urn in Context," in manuscript.

22. Roe, "Keats's Lisping Sedition"; Roe, "Sedition in Keats's *Poems, 1817*"; Hoagwood, "Keats and Social Context"; Hoagwood, "Fictionality and Finance."

23. Stillinger, "John Keats," 716–17. Roe, *John Keats and the Culture of Dissent* (Oxford: Clarendon Press, 1997). Alwes, *Imagination Transformed: The Evolution of the Female Character in Keats's Poetry* (Carbondale: Southern Illinois University Press, 1993).

24. Weller, *Keats and Mary Tighe: The Poems of Mary Tighe with Parallel Passages from the Work of John Keats* (New York: Modern Language Association, 1928). Greg Kucich, "Gender Crossings: Keats and Tighe," *Keats-Shelley Journal* 44 (1995): 29–40. Kucich concludes that Keats responded to Tighe's work by "cultivating a feminine poetics for one work" but in the same poem reverting to "masculine poetic practices, reinforced by anxious

denials of female influence." Kucich's conclusions are propositions about Keats's attitudes: "recognizing this level of tension in Keats's particular inter-actions with the texts of female writers should move us away from any cate-gorical conclusions about his gender position, any singular classifications of him as a colonizer or a supporter of the feminine" because he had "conflicted relations with women" (39).

25. Charles Cowden Clarke, "Recollections of John Keats" (1861), reprinted in Charles and Mary Cowden Clarke, *Recollections of Writers. By Charles and Mary Cowden Clarke* (New York: Charles Scribner's Sons, n.d. [1878?]), 141.
26. Whittemore, *The Trouble Outside,* in *Fifty Poems Fifty* (Minneapolis: University of Minnesota Press, 1970), 10.

Prophetic Extinction and the Misbegotten Dream in Keats

HERMIONE DE ALMEIDA

M Y SUBJECT IS the interrelation of Romantic evolution theory and Romantic dream theory in the two *Hyperion* poem fragments.[1] I focus in particular on the novelty of the concept of extinction during the period and its connection to contemporary Romantic notions about the misconceived or misbegotten creations of the mind. My specific illustration is the first dream recounted in the first *Hyperion* fragment. This disturbing dream anchors Keats's long poetic attempt to tell the story of the Titans' fall from power, or life intensity, to extinction (a story that he was to characterize in his letters as mythic prehistory, a Grecian abstraction, and a "new Romance" and then, in the later fragment's subtitle, as "A Dream").[2] The dream also serves to situate the Titans' history within a fossil-strewn natural geography and, at the same time, amid the shifting time sequences of several dreamscapes.

The dreamer is Hyperion, the only Titan who has not yet fallen. The hour is near midnight, an inspecific time located equidistant from a twilight long past and a dawn reluctant to become the future. The sun god sits motionless and alone in a singular place of darkness within his "palace bright." Incense, teeming up from the sacrifices of men to the "sun's God," clouds the airy brilliance of his palace; it obscures the god's piercing vision and stifles the very spirit of divinity that it would honor. Instead of reassuring Hyperion of his godly rank, "the spicy wreathes / Of incense" bear a novel "Savour of poisonous brass and metal sick" to the miserable god's "ample palate"; without homage the fragrant wreathes remind Hyperion precipitously of his fellow Titans' wreathless fate and of his own sole and "unsecure" position as the only "one of the whole mammoth-brood" who still keeps "His sov'reignity, and rule, and majesty." Hyperion's palace of "orbed fire," despite being "Bastion'd with pyramids of glowing gold" and securely "harbour'd in the sleepy west," is no sanctuary or safe haven. Rather, it is a place filled with dark shadows and "omens drear" fashioned specifically to "frighten and perplex" a sleepless god. Not "prophesyings of the midnight lamp," nor death knells, nor the "gloom-bird's hated screech," nor the dog's howl, "But horrors, portion'd to a giant nerve," assail Hyperion's senses as he waits each night for the hour of dawn. He sees or thinks he sees in his blind agitation "eagle's wings, / Unseen before by Gods or wondering men"—inaugurous birds that darken his palace of light. He hears or thinks he hears "neighing steeds . . . / Not heard before by Gods or wondering men"—disruptive nightmares that trample the order and quietude of his domain (I.164–200). These nightly visitations, glimpsed and heard fleetingly, are recurrent and unremitting. Moreover, they assault Hyperion while he is awake and at home, under conditions where he should be most secure: "into my centre of repose, / The shady visions come to domineer, / Insult, and blind, and stifle up my pomp" (I.243–45).

Against this backdrop of premonitions and visitations from earlier nights, directly within the "great main cupola" of his "own golden region" of the West, upon an empty and echoing "mirrored level," Hyperion's waking dream now takes dark form and shadowy substance.

> O dreams of day and night!
> O monstrous forms! O effigies of pain!
> O spectres busy in a cold, cold gloom!
> O lank-eared Phantoms of black-weeded pools!
> Why do I know ye? why have I seen ye? why
> Is my eternal essence thus distraught
> To see and to behold these horrors new?
> Saturn is fallen, am I too to fall?
> Am I to leave this haven of my rest,
> This cradle of my glory, this soft clime,
> This calm luxuriance of blissful light,
> These crystalline pavilions, and pure fanes,
> Of all my lucent empire? It is left

Deserted, void, nor any haunt of mine.
The blaze, the splendor, and the symmetry,
I cannot see—but darkness, death and darkness.

(I.221–42, 257)

Mirror-faced, Hyperion's dream addresses the forms and shadows that
give it substance as other dreams—dreams of day and night, monstrous
forms, effigies of pain, busy spectres, and lank-eared phantoms. From
within his waking dream, Hyperion finds these forms to be at once
familiar and previously seen—and horrors new. The forms crowd the
reflecting surface of the dream even as the crystalline pavilions and pure
fanes of its lucent empire are left deserted and without reflection. When
the disturbed Hyperion attempts to escape the confines of his dream by
asking, "why / Is my eternal essence thus distraught . . .?," "a heavier
threat" holds "struggle with his throat," and he is given another, even
more constricting dream-vision: "at Hyperion's words the Phantoms
pale / Bestirr'd themselves, thrice horrible and cold," and "A mist"
arises, "as from a scummy marsh" from off the mirrored level (I.255–
62). Yearning to see "the blaze, the splendor, and the symmetry" of a
perfected Titan empire, the overwrought god sees instead the shadows
of his own distraught mind made visible as "darkness, death and darkness." The doubled vision of his dream leaves the "bright Titan"
"phrenzied with new woes," "in grief and radiance faint," and lost upon
"a dismal rack of clouds" located somewhere "upon the boundaries of
day and night" (I.290–304). Although Hyperion is "a primeval God,"
he cannot disturb the "sacred seasons" or speed the coming of day.
Once his dream ends and its speeding timescape fades, Hyperion finds
he must still wait "full six dewy hours" for the dawn to come—must
wait without hope and in a condition of half-knowledge: he is blind to
all but the images of his dream, and he is able to sense only the premonitions of gloom-birds and nightsteeds that hover on the peripheries of
his mind's empire.

Hyperion's dream foretells the Titans' future, a future that is only
partly comprehensible to Hyperion, because he remains a god, but that
in time will comprehend him also into its consequential end for the
Titan story. Earlier lines of the poem recount how the immortal giants
fell from power and became like mortals in their emotions and misperceptions. The specific vision here of Hyperion's seemingly misbegotten

dream is of what will become of the Titans *after* they have all fallen from power, that is, of their free fall from life, and the ability to create and replicate, to extinction.[3]

Titanic Hyperion dreams in prophecy of the coming extinction of his species. The prospect is overwhelming and horrific, a specialized version of how the concept of extinction overwhelmed and horrified a Romantic age. Earlier centuries had confined the use of the term "extinction" to sources of natural energy, such as fire, light, and volcanoes and, by analogy, individual lives, personal aspirations, and (in the legal sense) noble families without descendants.[4] The giant fossils of extinct creatures uncovered by geologists in Europe and the Americas in the latter part of the eighteenth century provided indisputable evidence of the wholesale and random obliteration of entire species and types; they proved with actual and tangible substance a new and terrifying concept of absolute end. Extinction was a fact—and a nightmare that was to haunt a century (the "evil" dream of a demented Nature at war with herself, indifferent to her own creations and her own history, as Tennyson described it in *In Memoriam:* "'So careful of the type?' but no, / From scarped cliff and quarried stone / She cries, 'A thousand types are gone: / I care for nothing, all shall go'").[5] Romantic natural philosophers, scientists, and poets were the first to face this nightmarish fact in all its implications for human creation, human history, and human consciousness. As early as 1777 Joseph Priestley speculated that generic extinction governed matter and spirit, that "Every faculty of the mind . . . is liable . . . to become wholly extinct before death."[6] When Keats proposed in 1817 in *Endymion* that the excavated giant fossils "Of beast, behemoth, and leviathan" were of the Titans' "vintage" (III.129–36), he acknowledged the consequence of a mythic story finding its tangible verity in natural history. He envisioned briefly the reality of Hyperion's dream.

To Keats, extinct species were the "families of grief" "roof'd in by black rocks" that "waste in pain / And darkness for no hope" he describes in the second *Hyperion* fragment (*Fall of Hyperion* I.461–63). The lank-eared phantoms, skeletal spectres, and hollow effigies that people Hyperion's dream in the first fragment are futuristic images of the actual subsistent bulk or the geological matter that the Titans will become once they are extinct and part of a prehistoric landscape of behemoth fossils and bone shells. Hyperion's dream-vision of the future of his mythic race seen through the lens of natural history reveals a naturalistic prophecy of imminent extinction for his fellow Titans, for himself, and, far worse, for the very form of consciousness with which they each conceive and dream of themselves. The "darkness" Hyperion encounters near the end of his dream is a dim consciousness or darkness visible, not of death or mere mortality, but of absolute end—not the death of one nightingale or the fading of birdsong to a single consciousness, but the dying out of Titan song itself. Not only will there be no "hymns of festival," no "silver stir / Of strings in hollow shells," no "Beautiful things made new, for the surprise / Of the sky children," as Saturn laments (I.127–34), but there will be none to remember these sounds and none remaining to tell their tale. This, then, is Hyperion's nightmare of Titan natural history; it is not that history is conceived as nightmarish because it is internalized and personal (as it is in Byron's *Cain* and in Stephen Dedalus's history-ridden psyche) but that the nightmare becomes the impersonal, actual unfolding of a too-natural history.

Hyperion's nightmare of natural history encapsulates the multiple paradoxes of the *Hyperion* fragments whose declared region of narrative lies somewhere between the dissembling dream, the fictional event, and the scientific fact and in which "Nature's law" is to be explained as both "monstrous truth" and healing "balm," even as the unfolding of this inexorable "eternal" law is to transpire within the timeless and disruptive spaces of dream-fiction (II.181; I.65; II.228, 243). In this "epic" project of far too many dreams, wherein all the Titans lie immobile and dreaming "in thousand hugest phantasies"; where Saturn, their king, wishes to awake from his "icy trance" but cannot; where Thea, the mother of Hyperion, urges dreaming sleep as the ideal solution to an inconceivable end; where Hyperion dreams and senses but cannot see impending doom; and where even Apollo, the agent of new order, would postpone the consequences of the vision of terrible beauty given him by Mnemosyne (II.13; I.20, 68–69; III.91–94), Keats attempts no less than to view the prehistory of the primeval past through the immediate and deflective lens of contemporary dream-vision. The poem's titular transformation in revision to something he called *The Fall of Hyperion: A Dream* highlights the radical novelty of his experiment in subjecting an immortal species and the mythic space in which it dwells to the laws of natural history that govern mortal life and human consciousness. Keats makes a prophetic dream of mythic prehistory by casting the known legend and emerging natural history of an ancient breed of giants as a synoptic pattern of their own dreams of themselves and, later, as a telescoping dream-vision of these dreams as it is induced by one of these giants, Moneta, and shown as transpiring within her skull as a high tragedy and fiction most true, yet borne by a mortal poet.

Composed during twelve months of Keats's most intense creative period (between October 1818 and September 1819), the *Hyperion* fragments are an important touchstone for Keats's thinking on subjects such as the nature of history (especially given the new contexts of natural history); dreaming (especially given the new, medical contexts of consciousness); and creation, both natural and poetic.[7] Several immediate events from Keats's personal life gave impetus to his decision to tell the story of the Titan behemoths through a mortal consciousness' dream of their passage to extinction: his walking tour of the north of England where he saw dreamscapes of sublime ruins and natural monuments of rock and water; his early return home from the tour with a sore throat to nurse his consumptive and dying brother, Tom; his first meeting with Fanny Brawne; the most serious of the review attacks on the poetry of the Cockney school and Mr. John Keats, apothecary; and his reading of Count Buffon and other English and European natural historians from Erasmus Darwin to Jean-Baptiste Lamarck, Georges Cuvier, and Alexander von Humboldt, and use of Romantic theories of the evolution of mind for his formulations on the development of poetic perception.[8] Because of his training as a physician within the ferment of the London scientific circles, Keats would have had to conceive of human history and any poetic attempt to recount it first in terms of natural history and the concepts of evolution of the natural historians of his time.[9] Out of this necessity would have come his decision to tell the story of the Titans as an analogy of natural history or as a dream of this history drawn from images of what a physician or naturalist might imagine to have transpired within the fading mind or "hollow brain" of a prehistoric giant at the moment of extinction (*Fall of Hyperion* I.275–81).

Several things dovetailed in Keats's mind when he saw the connections between the evolutionary moment—be it of fulfillment, fresh perfection, or radical extinction—and the always present timescape and fragmentary nature of human dreaming as described and documented by the philosophers of mind of his time. Certainly for Keats there was a connection to be found between the evolution of creatures in nature and the evolution of dreams in the human mind; both were subject, moreover, to the same momentous consequences of chance, interruption, and the accidental immediate passage from natural reality. Characteristically, and because of the connection he saw between the making of organic creatures and dream images, where other Romantic naturalists might have addressed the potential of organic advance and scrutinized the fossil remnants of the evolutionary past with retrospective vision (or "retrospective prophecy" to use Thomas Huxley's phrase)[10] to predict the course of future development or speciation, Keats focused on the underside of evolutionary theory as he understood it—on the fact of extinction. Keats's *Hyperion* poems are about the consequences of generic extinction in a natural world and the consequences of recounting history and dream, or even rendering meaning to each of these purported counters, given such a natural world. Whereas the naturalists focused on the long geological time of natural history, the poet focused on the brief moment of natural history when time stopped or was disrupted, as happened in human dreaming. He tells natural history from the perspective of the soon-to-be extinct creature, turns this perspective into a metaphor for human consciousness, and then uses the occasion to question storytelling and creative dreaming in poetry.

From naturalists such as Buffon, whom he read in Barr's translation, and Erasmus Darwin (who paraphrased everybody), Keats learned that life began in the ocean, the mountains of earth were made of sea shells, the earth began eons before 4004 B.C., and the breadth of geological time (natural prehistory) that preceded human history was incalculable. From Cuvier and Lamarck (by way of William Nicholson's *Journal of Natural Philosophy, Chemistry and the Arts* and Darwin's paraphrase), Keats learned of the fossils of extinct species found in Germany and South America; of the terrifying novelty of these discoveries for the meaning of created life; and of the catastrophic, revolutionary events that could and would disturb the repetitive complacency of natural creation to bring forth radical variations and permanent destructions of entire life-forms. From Lorenz Oken and Fredrich Schelling (by way of von Humboldt's travel diaries), Keats learned that the creative activity of nature and of mind was one evolutionary pattern of development, wherein the entire animal kingdom could be classified as individual representations of the five senses through which the human mind perceived nature and wherein (even though the mental or spiritual was antecedent to the natural) organic nature and perceptual vision mirrored one another in their stages of evolutionary self-realization.

Among the evolutionists, Lamarck bears particular note, since it was he who declared evolution to be "the dream of nature" (one source, no doubt, of the "evil dreams" of Tennyson's Nature). He proposed to his Romantic age the novel idea that natural organisms could respond to environmental need and direct evolution for better or worse through appetency or longing (a kind of organic dreaming). Through this biological version of Romantic aspiration, successfully acquired characteristics could become hereditary organs in future generations, and unsuccessful aspirations could occasion the extinction of a species. The fossil malformations would be enduring signposts of unrealized creatural dreamings to future generations of naturalists puzzling over the lacunae in the patterns of evolution. Schelling contributed a visionary addendum to this idea when he proposed that the failed aspirations of extinct life, be they the malformations of organic life or the misperceptions of spiritual life, be read with a unique retrospective prophecy so as to envision from the remnants of aspirations unrealized the promised forms of future creations of life and mind.

Extinction was necessary for the impetus of creation. Hence, Romantic evolution faced forward, but its meaning could only be known in retrospect. The "dead hand" of Lamarckian matter, composed of the husks and shells of former perfected beings, was an essential creative roadblock in the path of evolving life's fresh perfections. As a corollary to the concept of evolution, extinction disrupted the dreamlike stasis and unconscious replication of nature to spur sudden new creations. The dream of aspiration in organic nature and in the perceiving mind, regardless of whether its products were malformed species or misperceptive visions, was vital to fulfillment and comprehension in the future. The Romantic evolutionists' retrospective vision of fossils and failed visions in nature and in mind thus could be either a nightmare (of the past) or a prophetic dream (of a future most true). All this bears particular relevance to the dream-visions that form and deform the natural history of the Titans as it is recounted by Keats in his *Hyperion* poems.

In their hypotheses on the nature of human dreaming, Romantic physicians and philosophers of mind noted all of the familiar characteristics of dream: the fragmentation, the disjointed associations, the recurrence of image and event, the seemingly heightened senses and double vision of the dreamer, the archetypal patterns of various dream species, the circumstances under which dreaming was most likely to occur, the occasions when dreams were most likely to be meaningful, the disjunctions of episode and subject, the contraction and expansion of time during a given sequence, and the overall velocity of dream time. The absence of any sense of recountable history during the experience of dreaming, with the confusion of past and present within an always-present dreamscape, was an absorbing subject for the theorists of mind, especially in its implications for the imagination. Popular claims of a prophetic or divinative power in dreams also received extensive (and skeptical) attention from these theorists, and the knowledge of futurity in dream was placed within the powers of ordinary cognitive reasoning and an innate sixth sense. Beliefs such as the notion that early-morning dreams are always true were rationalized likewise by noting that the will was indeed most active and the senses least deceptive near the end of sleep.[11]

The primary focus of dream theory of the period was on the interpretive symptomology of dreams. Perhaps as a result of the triumph of mechanistic physiology in the new medical age, dreams were classified as the consequences of the health or disease of the body and, often, of the mind. Whereas the sleep of health was considered to be sound, refreshing, pure, and virtually dreamless, except for the occasional vision that was pleasant and unremembered, impure and disturbing dreams were seen as symptomatic of a distempered body, perturbed mind, or both. Medical observers read in the ascending intensities of patients' bad dreams, from the common dream of fanciful nonsense to the terrifying nightmare and sustained delirium of vision, the symptomatic signs of ill health ranging from passing indigestion or malarial fever to the terminal afflictions of cancers and consumptions. Unpleasantly vivid dream images and strange and unforgettable dreams were believed to be the first and only prognostic sign to precede the onset of major physical disease. Hospital case studies of the period record in particular the dreams patients experienced just before their terminal illnesses manifested physical form. Moreover, because dreams were believed to be influenced by "the prevailing temper of mind" that prefaced them, the sudden ability to recall unpleasant dreams in full and horrific detail was taken to be a medical sign not just of grave physical malady, but of a pending general derangement of the mind and perception.[12]

From all this we must conclude that Hyperion dreams very badly. His dream occurs during a moment of imperfect sleep at midnight—not early morning—when his will is least reliable and his senses are most deceptive. It has the intensity of a nightmare and the sustained vision of serious delirium. His "temper of mind" immediately preceding the dream is influential with "omens drear" (II,169). The dream itself takes place in a "cold gloom" and is attended by a black "mist" replete with images of the dispossessed Titans as fossilized hollow effigies and the rotting "lank-eared" vegetation of "black-weeded pools" (I.229–30)— the traditional Hippocratic dream symbols of an excess of black bile and putridity in the body and the presence of the cold phlegm found in brain disease. Hyperion's total recall of this dream and his obsessive need to repeat it (with all of the symptoms of a dissociated body and mind) as a mirror image from *outside* his body signal to us not just that he shares the physical dis-ease of his extinction-bound fellow Titans (who are described to us as lying bound within a sick ward, bruised, in pain, racked by nervous palsy, and emotionally disturbed [II.1–28]), but also that the onset of a far greater perceptual illness has occurred, a psychic affliction portioned appropriately, as it always is in nature, to a giant's nerve.

Because Hyperion is "still" extant and therefore least afflicted by the sickness of extinction that has felled the other Titans, the dream that he has of Titanic woe far exceeds their dreams of dis-ease and disjuncture in the extent of its premonitions and in the import of its prophecy. We should not wonder that Hyperion is frenzied by new woes as yet unknown to the other members of his giant species (I.299). His dream is a product of true but failing Lamarckian aspiration: like other creatures in nature who sought to advance their species by revealing greater appetency and aspiration, which, even as it showed them to be the vanguard of a new subspecies, failed and so occasioned the end of their entire species, Hyperion seeks to rescue his immortal Titanic race from the immobile subsistence in which they lie.[13] He aspires to dream for them in "hugest" desire, to obliterate their huge past with a prophetic vision of a more magnificent future. With a perceptive interpretation of his dream he would, furthermore, unwrite or disrupt their history to expunge recent events from their communal past. Hyperion's aspiration, because of his status as the only member of the giant species that is yet unfallen, is at once a mark of advancement in the species and the key to their imminent obsolescence: he dreams better than they do, with more prophetic image and greater perceptual depth, but because he is also afflicted with Titan sickness he nevertheless dreams badly, with less comfort, and far worse and farther into the future.

Indeed, it could be said that because Hyperion—in a moment of advanced but misbegotten perception—dreams unnaturally of his brothers as unknown and terrifying monsters and hulks and phantoms of prior life, he occasions the monstrous end of his and their immortal history in natural mortal extinction. No wonder Hyperion can neither accept nor forget the monsters engendered by his own mind under the stress of omens drear during a dream of futurity too dreadful to be unreal. The generation of monsters was a subject of recurring and ghoulish fascination for the early nineteenth century. Benjamin Bablot's notorious treatise on the effects that pregnant women's imaginations and desires could have on their fetuses' physical features and personalities (*Dissertation sur le pouvoir de l'imagination des femmes encientes,* 1788) and James Augustus Blondel's remarkable summary of prevailing speculations on the prior imaginative creation of the forms of birthmarks and physiognomic misfeatures of newborn children (whereby the horrifying visions experienced during pregnancy—either real encounters with madmen and murderers or nightmares of tigers and monsters—could be imprinted upon the fetus [*The Strength of Imagination in Pregnant Women Examin'd,* 1727]) were two of several Enlightenment pseudoembryologies that survived to haunt the Romantic age of science and medicine.[14] Researchers who studied the living examples of pygmies, polydactyls, and other mutants (which were first made the subject of evolutionary inquiry by Pierre Maupertuis in his *Vénus physique,* 1745), physicians (e.g., John Haighton) who encountered freak embryos and monstrous births in the obstetric wards and in the brine-filled jars lining the walls of operating theaters in London hospitals like Guy's, natural historians (e.g., William Lawrence and Joseph Henry Green) who viewed the extraordinary collection of skeletons, giant skulls, Siamese twins, and other embryonic freaks in John Hunter's Museum, and theorists of mind (e.g., Dugald Stewart and Robert Macnish) who pondered the creation and induction of dreams, all puzzled over whether human physical creation could be influenced by psychosomatic impressions intensely created and intensely felt first by the dreaming imagination.

Buffon had noted the extensive "sympathies" that existed between mother and unborn child and deduced that any stress-induced commotion in the maternal blood could well deform fetal growth.[15] Erasmus

Darwin proposed that the sex of a child was decided by the images in its father's mind at the moment of conception.[16] Goethe, in his novel of mental adultery in which a child is born with the features of absent lovers (*Die Walverwandtschaften*, 1809), ascribed blame for congenital monstrosity of body to the imaginative misconduct of both parents. Mary Shelley, in her novel of creation turned miscreation through retroactive misperception of the self (*Frankenstein*, 1818), returned to the ancient speculation (recapitulated by Ambrose Paré in *Of the Generation of Man*, in which he declared that just as begetting parents "deluded by nocturnal and deceitful apparitions" could imprint with "force into the Infant conceived," so could "the force of the imagination . . . be so powerful in us, as for the most part, it may alter the body of them that imagine")[17] that creatures could become monsters retroactively through the force of imagining themselves as monsters or the force of others' imagining them as such.

Thus do Keats's *Hyperion* fragments show themselves to be the product of Romantic speculations on the misbegotten. From the Titans' perspective, their fate or fall from power is accidental, unnecessary, reversible, and misbegotten. From Hyperion's as-yet-unfallen perspective, his dream of their extinction is unreal, untrue, outside giant time (which is endless), and misbegotten. From the perspective of Apollo, the future inheritor of the kingdom, he himself is misbegotten because the dream-vision offered him by Mnemosyne embodies his painful future in an unknown and terrifying past. For the poet of *The Fall of Hyperion*, his retrospective vision of the Titanic dreams that Moneta half-remembers, which he witnesses through the opaque brain and brittle bones of the giant's skull and which he must contain and preserve in an all too mortal consciousness, is none other than the natural historian's reversing or retrospective vision of the generation of the misbegotten.

"Real are the dreams of Gods, and smoothly pass / Their pleasures in a long immortal dream," the poet warns us in *Lamia* (I.127–28). Real gods have real dreams that are timeless, smoothly pleasurable, unremembered because there can be no retrospection in the present immediacy of the dreamscape, and without need of interpretation. Real gods do not dream of themselves as the monsters past of a future natural history. Real gods are their own dreams of themselves; their immortal condition precedes history and warrants no further consciousness. Not so for the Titans of Keats's *Hyperion* poems: upon ceasing to be real gods, they become part of mortal time, history, and the evolutionary cycles of natural species and dream species. They fall into history and the terrible knowledge that comes with natural process; their terminal sickness of body invades their perceptions; they become conscious of their dissociated selves and of the spaces between their dreams and their realities; they require outside consciousnesses to quarry out their selves and interpret their stories; their impure sleep produces a most various species of dreams which, far from maintaining the familiar ever-present time of the dreamscape, presage and deceive with a sense of futurity and pastness. Natural time in the natural history of the Titans—and this is the only way in which the real dream of gods and the actuality of the Titans' dreaming condition coalesce—is collapsed into the geological moment before extinction (which is the real timescape of Hyperion's dream) and the geological moment after extinction (which is the proposed timescape of Apollo's yet-to-be-written dream-vision at the end of the first fragment). The prehistory or tale, "Too huge for mortal tongue or pen of scribe," of a mythic species and the long geological account of "Nature's universal scroll" of life and death (I.159, 151) are then viewed through the telescopic dream time of the second *Hyperion* fragment; both contract thus into the visualization of a moment of consciousness as it passes within a mortal human mind. The poet's fleeting and fragmentary dream-vision in *The Fall of Hyperion* is also an evolutionary "moment big as years" (I:64), and Hyperion's dream and Apollo's projected vision are reduced telescopically to a single "humanized" picture (II.2) of the pause between the moment before and the moment after extinction. The poet of Titan fall sees for a second: like Adam near the end of *Paradise Lost,* he is given a vision of the future that is already past, and he has one moment of prophecy that is necessarily retrospective and too late.

"We cannot properly be said to be conscious of our own existence;—our knowledge of this fact being necessarily posterior, in the order of time, to the consciousness of those sensations by which it is suggested."[18] This assertion by Dugald Stewart of the interpretation of the self's existence is no less true of the interpretation of dreams and of life-forms. "I am gone / Away from my own bosom: I have left / My strong identity, my real self, / Somewhere between the throne, and where I sit / Here on this spot of earth. Search, Thea, search!" Saturn pleads (I.112–16), sadly recognizing that there will be no recovery of self or place by him and that such recovery will occur only through the retrospective search and disruptive interpretation of others. So also did the natural historians of the Romantic period realize that they could know a species in the totality of its completion only through the retrospective search and prophetic interpretation of the extinct life-forms that had preceded it. So also does Hyperion realize that he cannot reconstruct and return his fellow Titans to their former existence through the imaginative images of his dream; that his attempt to re-create them after the dream merely intensified their alienation of form; and that his dream of prophecy of Titan future must remain without interpretation, misbegotten and misbegetting to his own perception. So also can Keats first propose, in the face of the deadlock of ideas confronting him, that poetry alone can search out and tell the "true" story of the telescoping dream of Titans dreaming and falling and then declare the prophetic interpretations generated by this to be mortal, disruptive, reverse-faced, and timebound (*Fall of Hyperion*, I, 8–15, 199–202).

For Keats, as for Lamarck, extinction makes evolution and new creation possible—in nature's dream as well as in the poet's dream. In the same way that suddenly extinct matter breaks the unconscious and pure stasis in nature's dreaming complacency to spur new creation (albeit at high cost to those extinct "families of grief"), the impurities of sleep and mortal dreaming produce the flash vision of past as future seen within the echoing spaces of a behemoth's fossilized skull:

> As I had found
> A grain of gold upon a mountain's side,
> And twing'd with avarice strain'd out my eyes
> To search its sullen entrails rich with ore,
> So at the view of sad Moneta's brow,
> I ached to see what things the hollow brain
> Behind enwombed
> (*Fall of Hyperion* I.271–77)

The extinct matter "rich with ore" within Moneta's mountainous brow drives the poet to seek out the random "grain[s] of gold" amid fossil sands, to glimpse the terminal history and know the disintegrating consciousness of the Titans, to experience a golden-grained dream-vision of high tragedy enacted in the present that concerns at once the Titans' past and the poet's future. For Keats, extinction brings a novel and particular meaning—and the momentary or always-present timescape of dream—to history. Dream interrupts the flow of what history seeks to record; it disrupts with simultaneity and fragmentation all notions of sequence and accuracy in much the same way that natural history pre-empts and disrupts with geological time all prevailing (and merely human) notions of history. The auguries of history and of dream thus become subject to the same brief and compelling uncertainties and the same randomness of chance active in natural evolution.[19]

In the *Hyperion* poems, immortal and certain mythic history and natural and unpredictable (but nevertheless inexorable) evolution are condensed into the flash dream or brief vision of a fading giant's consciousness as this is granted, for one second, to the mortal senses and perceptions of a dying poet. The agent granting this vision, "sad Moneta," is a Keatsian version of the goddess of memory. Her "immortal essence" (I, 249) has become subject to natural pattern or the interruptions of matter and mind, and her "hollow brain" *contains* the dreams of the Titans and so reveals their certain membership among the extinct giants whose memories must spill like the husks of former life into nature's indifferent and ahistoric vacuum. This history is certainly the dark and timebound underside of Romantic organicism and its faith in developmental process. It is a history too natural and too short, a mean rendering of William Blake's eternity, a narrow and terrifying version of the end of history postulated by Hegel. Hegel saw the end of history as a merger of natural individuations and individual consciousnesses into a consciousnesses of a higher order, a magnificent and abstract—albeit tragic and estranged—return home of history that presupposed the annihilation of individual stories.[20] In *Hyperion*, the Titans' consciousness of their fall and the imminent presence of new and more sensitive life to replace them presumes the end of their "immortal" history and brings home the occasion of their extinction in mortal or natural time. The consciousness of the poet of *The Fall of Hyperion* that his prophetic dream-vision is *only* a dream, a dream already ended in an unrecoverable past, ensures that their story will be lost in mortal time and that memory either cannot return home or returns with estrangement and end. History in the *Hyperion* poems is neither grand and Hegelian nor giant and Titanic. It is natural, interrupted and brief, and like a dream, seen only in its moments of ending.

NOTES

1. *The Poems of John Keats*, ed. Jack Stillinger (Cambridge, Mass.: Harvard University Press, Belknap Press, 1978). All quotations of Keats's poetry are from this edition; line numbers are given in the text.

2. *The Letters of John Keats: 1814–1821*, ed. Hyder E. Rollins (Cambridge, Mass.: Harvard University Press, 1958), 1:168, 207.

3. In the dream-visions of *The Fall of Hyperion*, this evolutionary consequence has already transpired. See my discussion of Romantic evolutionary theory in *Hyperion* and other poems in *Romantic Medicine and John Keats* (New York: Oxford University Press, 1991), 219–311.

4. The *Oxford English Dictionary* cites "That fyre was extincte . . . ," "Duke Turgesius was perished and extincte" (*Higden* [Rolis] [1430–50], I:219), and "the more they lyght them [candellys] the more were they extyncte" (*Golden Legend* [Caxton] [1483], 176).

5. *Tennyson's Poetry*, ed. Robert W. Hill (New York: Norton, 1971), *In Memoriam*, 55–56.

6. Joseph Priestley, *Matter and Spirit* (London, 1782), 1:56.

7. The concept of history, according to Raymond Williams, evolved from a diffuse and diffusely applied term referring to an account either of imaginary events or of events supposed to be true, to the fifteenth-century sense of the term as a formal and enduring organized knowledge of real past events. The major change (or changes) in this concept of history took place over the hundred years of upheaval in Europe that stretched between the Augustan age (and its concern with the maintenance of past and prevailing culture) and the Romantic age (and its fascination with revolutionary endeavor for the future). Williams asserts,

> It is necessary to distinguish an important sense of *history* which is more than, though it includes, organized knowledge of the past. It is not easy either to date or define this, but the source is probably the sense of *history* as human self-development which is evident from e18C in Vico and in the new kinds of *Universal Histories*. One way of expressing this new sense is to say that past events are seen not as specific histories but as a continuous and connected process. . . . Moreover, given the stress on human *self-development, history* in many of these uses loses its exclusive association with the past and becomes connected not only to the present but also to the future. In German there is a verbal distinction which makes this clearer: *Historie* refers mainly to the past, while *Geschichte* (and the associated *Geschichtsphilosophie*) can refer to a process including past, present and future.

Raymond Williams, "History," in *Keywords: A Vocabulary of Culture and Society* (New York: Oxford University Press, 1976), 119–20.

8. From Keats's March 24, 1818, letter to James Rice and his March 25, 1818, letter to John Hamilton Reynolds, we know that he was reading Buffon and other evolution theorists during the spring of 1818. I refer here to his letter of May 3, 1818, in which he describes human life and mind as "a large Mansion of Many Apartments" (1:275–83). For a discussion of Romantic evolution theories in this letter, see my *Romantic Medicine and John Keats*, 257–60.

9. Significant to my discussion of Keats is the contribution to this new and comprehensive *developmental* sense of history by the sciences, and specifically by

the physical sciences, of the revolutionary period. Late eighteenth-century physics contributed the idea of universal activity to the prevailing concept of history: history thereafter could be seen as encompassing not just the past phenomena of human life, but also those of the natural world. (Michèl Foucault's proposal that natural history found its "locus in the gap that . . . opened up between things and words" expresses a version of this development.) This notion that every part of the universe had its history in turn paved the way for the new Romantic sciences of biology and comparative zoology to manifest the historic attitudes of their disciplines and instill ideas of evolutionary development, process, and extinction into the age's ever-widening concept of history. The organic world and the creatures within it were now known to be subjects of a natural and historical (albeit dimly perceived) process of development called "evolution"; they had a natural history, over and above specific natural processes, that encompassed past and future and together formed part of a universal history. Romantic natural historians could now scrutinize the patterns of past life available to them as fossil remnants and, with novel retrospective vision, attempt to predict the course of life's future developments. Biology came into existence at the turn of the century, and the term "biology" was coined in 1802 by the natural philosopher G. R. Treviranus in his *Biologie, oder Philosophie der lebenden Natur* (1802–22). See "History" in *Encyclopaedia Britannica*, vol. 13 (1910): 527, on the contribution of the notion of universal activity by the new physics and on the historical "attitude of mind" contributed by the doctrine of evolution. See also Foucault, *The Archaeology of Knowledge*, trans. A. M. Sheridan Smith (New York: Pantheon, 1972), 129–30. See also Williams, "Evolution," in *Keywords*, 104:

> What then happened in biology was a generalization of the sense of *development* (fully bringing out) from immature to mature forms, and especially the specialized sense of *development* from "lower" to "higher" organisms. From lC18 and eC19 this sense of a general natural process—a natural history over and above specific natural processes—was becoming known.

10. See my discussion of T. H. Huxley and the meaning of "retrospective prophecy," in *Romantic Medicine and John Keats*, 225–27, 247–49, 283–84, 302–6. Primary works on the general subject of Romantic evolution would be Buffon's *Histoire naturelle* (1749–1804), Darwin's *Zoonomia* (1801), Cuvier's *Mémoires sur les epèces d'éléphants vivants et fossiles* (1800), Lamarck's *Philosophie zoologique* (1809) and *Histoire naturelle des animaux sans vertebres* (1815–22), Oken's *Gundriss der Naturphilosophie* (1802) and *Lehrbuch der Naturphilosophie* (1809–11), and Schelling's *Von der Weltseele* (1798) and *Erster Entwurf eines Systems der Naturphilosophie* (1799).

11. "Our dreams in the morning have greater variety and vivacity, as our sensibility increases, than at night when we first lie down," Erasmus Darwin notes in *Zoonomia: or The Laws of Organic Life* (London: J. Johnson, 1801), 1:302; Robert Macnish theorizes that early morning dreams might have more

verity because the mind is more rational at that time (*The Philosophy of Sleep* [1830; reprint, New York: William Pearson, 1835], 10).

12. See Dugald Stewart, *Elements of the Philosophy of the Human Mind* (Philadelphia: William Young, 1793), 288, 570.

13. I use the word "subsistence" in Coleridge's sense as the passive residual life that is polar to active "existence." See "Hints Toward a More Comprehensive Theory of Life" in *The Complete Works of Samuel Taylor Coleridge,* ed. W. G. T. Shedd (New York: Harpers, 1863), 1:376–88.

14. See also Marie-Hélène Huet, *Monstrous Imagination* (Cambridge, Mass.: Harvard University Press, 1993), for an account of the Western myths concerning monstrosity and the maternal imagination.

15. See Bentley Glass's discussion of this idea in "Maupertuis, Pioneer of Genetics and Evolution" in *Forerunners of Darwin: 1745–1859,* ed. Bentley Glass, Owsei Temkin, and William L. Straus Jr. (Baltimore: Johns Hopkins University Press, 1959), 77–78.

16. Erasmus Darwin, *Zoonomia,* 1:412.

17. Ambrose Paré, *The Works of that Famous Chirugeon Ambrose Parey,* trans. Thomas Johnson (London: Mary Clark, 1678), 596.

18. Dugald Stewart, *Outlines of Moral Philosophy,* 2d ed. (Edinburgh: William Creech, 1801), 19.

19. See Carl Woodring's discussion of the Romantic ironies in Darwinian evolution in *Nature into Art: Cultural Transformations in Nineteenth-Century Britain* (Cambridge, Mass.: Harvard University Press, 1989), 173–203.

20. Georg Hegel, *Phenomenology of Spirit,* trans. A. V. Miller (1807; New York: Oxford University Press, 1997).

Keats and the Aesthetic Ideal

DAVID BROMWICH

WHAT FOLLOWS IS the reiteration of a commonplace that was once a part of the truth about Keats that went without saying. It now seems far along in the passage from things not said to things not known; and I come back to it in the belief that it belongs to an adequate historical account of the reasons why people cared for his work. It ought to be numbered, too, among the reasons why the few who read difficult poetry today still care for his.

T. S. Eliot, praising Keats's letters for their wisdom about poetry, wrote in *The Use of Poetry and the Use of Criticism:* "There is hardly one statement of Keats about poetry, which, when considered carefully and with due allowance for the difficulties of communication, will not be found to be true; and what is more, true for greater and more mature poetry than anything that Keats ever wrote."[1] I am not sure that Eliot could have said what he meant by "mature," but he quoted from Keats's letters the following celebrated passage:

> One thing that has pressed upon me lately, and increased my
> Humility and capability of submission—and that is this truth—
> Men of Genius are great as certain ethereal chemicals operating
> on the Mass of neutral intellect—but they have not any individu-
> ality, any determined character—I would call the top and head
> of those who have a proper self Men of Power.[2]

This observation Eliot called "the result of genius"—a careful and curious description. In what circumstances could a remark about a quality of mind itself exemplify that quality, as if a demonstrable acquaintance with the thing were proof of participation in it? Eliot believed that genius in a work of art did resemble the action of certain ethereal chemicals, having nothing of individuality or determined character or proper self. He also believed that this idea was so difficult to communicate and to recognize that the presence of the idea argued, as it were, the presence of the chemicals. This may have seemed particularly true as he looked back on an age dominated by "large self-worshipers." The result of genius in Keats's letters is the allegory, neither quaint nor charming, in which Keats felt pressed to offer his conception of genius. It is a result in the literal sense of a springing back, a jumping away from the sensations it recollects.

Another name for the wisdom Eliot found in the letters of Keats is the aesthetic sense of poetry. A poem, on the view Keats was working out, emerges from the pains and pleasures of life, but these do not come to us frankly professing their value as sensations; the poem refuses to associate the value of what is made of the experience with its utility for the experiencer. More than any other English poet, it is Keats who represents this view of art; he is its prophet and its first and exemplary instance. One can find expressed in the dicta of Robert Frost and Wallace Stevens, and in the criticism of Valéry, a comparably intense awareness of what is anomalous about the discipline of art, but in Keats this comes with an emphasis not to be found elsewhere: that for the work of art to exist, something must have been sacrificed. Indeed Keats is so closely associated with the aesthetic idea of poetry that the fate of his work seems bound up with it; in a time that has grown imperceptive or hostile toward this aspect of poetry, we might expect the reputation of Keats to be one of the first casualties. He would still survive, from the sheer interest of his life, as a type of the youthful genius; but that is a different thing.

Several other passages from Keats's letters bear a family resemblance to the one Eliot chose, and if the aesthetic idea is counted as vital in Keats they have to be weighed heavily. His best known but not his most translatable formula is the one about "negative capability," that is, "when a man is capable of being in uncertainties, Mysteries, doubts, without any irritable reaching after fact & reason" (L1:193). This is a mood of susceptible imagining that can lead to poetry, because it does not settle in certainty or any wish for enlightenment or edification. It seems a mood of nervous (not irritable) unease, whose peculiarity is that it never tends to resolve itself into satisfaction.

Keats does not specify the sort of fact and reason to which the poet should be indifferent. But one may feel that a particular distaste ("we hate poetry that has a palpable design upon us" [L1:224]) served as a motive for the proposal of negative capability. Keats was setting himself against the moralism of Wordsworth, but his words have a wider application. A poem should not impose itself on a realm of action or intention outside the poem; that is getting credit on the cheap, and Keats deplores it as one might deplore any vulgar mixing of virtues, as when a politician tells you what a good husband he is. "A poet is the most unpoetical of any thing in existence; because he has no identity" (L1:387). The distinction of the poet is stressed to the point of irony, as if being "most unpoetical" he acquired a claim to perfect ordinariness of an antithetical kind; much as Kierkegaard would say the good man always serves in his station anonymously, out of uniform.

Finally, in a late letter to Shelley, Keats wrote explicitly against a rival understanding of art:

> A modern work it is said must have a purpose, which may be the God—an artist must serve Mammon—he must have "self concentration" selfishness perhaps. You I am sure will forgive me for sincerely remarking that you might curb your magnanimity and be more of an artist, and "load every rift" of your subject with ore. . . . My Imagination is a Monastery and I am its Monk. (L2:322–23)

To generalize, the artist stands apart from our understanding of power or identity, and he does so in exchange for something that "it is idle to pause to call much or little so long as it contributes to swell the volume of consciousness."[3] Sensations are not nursed up for their own sake, as Pater would say they must be: they are neither enjoyed nor suffered, but rather are absorbed for the sake of self-concentration or an intensification that changes their character. This again is a kind of abstraction—a pulling away from its origin that does not render the mental object less definite. Poetry that has a palpable design moves in the opposite direction; it drives toward its origin, and lets us see the author's hand on the materials, guiding our response; it makes sure of our sympathies, by leaving no doubt what the author's are and how pleasing our conversion will be. "His heart is in the right place" will always be the sentiment of response to poetry that has a palpable design, even when it means the right wrong place, as Keats said about Byron.

If we try to hold in a single thought these observations on poetry, what traits do they suggest as defining the modern work of art?

1. The work seeks out objectification—of a subject matter that lay undigested in experience; of the author's anger or envy or enthusiasm; of data about the world that have found no other calculus. Objectification, in this sense of the word, does not relate directly to form or meaning. It has nothing to do with what the work of art refers to or what it says. It is rather a way of establishing how it wants to be taken.

2. We are made to feel a deep and at the same time impenetrable relation between the work and its author. When Flaubert said that he was Madame Bovary, he was executing a dandyish stroke of wit or paradox within the aesthetic mood at the expense of that mood, and one can suppose that some way under his remark was an unsparing self-diagnosis. Yet, in any regime other than the aesthetic, such a comment will hardly seem witty or poignant. It is what every author can say, and the reader is always free to take it literally: "The opinions expressed by the characters in this book are necessarily the opinions of the author."

3. The work does not exist in order to present admirable or imitable models for the reader, models of personal style or ethical conduct. When the reader is drawn to say of a fictive hero, "I want to be like him," it is a sure sign of the presence of inferior work: this was a remark of Lionel Trilling's, and a very Keatsian one. The work of art tends toward neither identification nor antagonism.

4. Belief is of no consequence. Kierkegaard said that the motto of the Christian is "As thou believest, so it comes to pass; or As thou believest, so art thou; to believe is to be."[4] The artist of Keats's type has escaped the force of this imperative, being, by choice and calling, nothing himself. Eliot felt more ambivalence than Keats regarding this element of the aesthetic discipline, because he had got from T. E. Hulme and from weightier sources the conviction that what modern society and the arts alike demanded was the solidity of objective institutions. The aesthetic ideal of Keats does not try to do justice to both sides of this question. It stops at the thought that very good doctrine can make very bad po-

ems: a fact that was never hidden from any intelligent critic, but that had never been stressed so single-mindedly.

5. Art carries a suggestion of completeness that brings out by implication the incompleteness of common life. (This contrast is not unique to Keats. If, instead of "completeness" and "incompleteness," one were to speak of "unity" and "disunity," the thought would sound closer to Coleridge.) The claim to point to something that is not in the world, something that is nevertheless real rather than fantastic, is part of the meaning of objectification. One is making a thing whose surface does not change, a thing that does not participate in the technological urge to treat every piece of the world as malleable. But the gesture is performed in a worldly medium of contingencies that will affect the shape of the result. A fragment, wrote Theodor Adorno, is "a work that has been tampered with by death,"[5] and the sense that accident, fate, and mortality are metaphors for each other, the meaning of which is proved on the author's pulses, must find a way of being figured in the work itself, in its manner of presentation and withdrawal. The divergence of aim from end, the break of perspective by which a sylvan history is changed to a cold pastoral, is regarded by the work of art with the pathos of distance.

6. The work of art attempts to give no account of itself. As Stevens once said in a letter (June 3, 1941): "What I intended is nothing."[6] This is not quite the same as saying that poetry makes nothing happen.

Earlier I borrowed from Adorno without acknowledgment the idea of the objectification of a work of art as a process distinct from the cult of immediacy or the fetish of perfection. This double contrast I find extremely useful, and it is related, I think, in ways Adorno is not often explicit about, to the power he thinks one can discern of a shape or a line or a melody to pick itself out of a swarm of stimuli once it has passed into history. Art, in the phrase that Adorno liked to borrow from Stendhal, is a *promesse de bonheur*. This means, among other things, that the work of art is a token of a happiness that can never become a promise kept to the artist. And it suggests a modernist sense for the scattered remarks by Keats regarding the discipline of posterity, a sense quite opposed to the monumentalist tenor of similar sounding remarks in renaissance and classical criticism. In an early verse letter to his brother George, after a series of images from fancy and reverie, Keats turned on himself and said (with what can seem complacency), "These

are the living pleasures of the bard: / But richer, far, Posterity's reward"
[*L*1:107]. To evoke posterity is mawkish if it means to weep on your
own grave with the help of an unfalsifiable chorus. This has long been
the spirit in which many people have read Keats, admiring his presump-
tion because he was young and pardoning both his anxiety and trustful-
ness because he peopled his afterlife with presiders chosen in such good
taste. The interest of posterity for him was less human and less consoling. There are times when the fact and reason of the present appear so
tidal an onrush that they threaten to carry off any possible imagining
of a future. All that throng of worthy or energetic purposes, of fashions
that exert an unchallengeable command, were a provocation that Keats
wrote his letters to steel himself against. Posterity was often, for him,
the name of a power of resistance and in that regard one of the necessary motives of abstraction.

NOTES

1. T. S. Eliot, *The Use of Poetry and the Use of Criticism* (London, 1933), 101.
2. *The Letters of John Keats: 1814–1821*, ed. Hyder E. Rollins (Cambridge, Mass.: Harvard University Press, 1958), 1:184. All quotations of Keats's letters are from this edition, abbreviated *L* in text; volume and page numbers are given in text.
3. Henry James (*Literary Criticism: European Writers and the Prefaces* [New York: Library of America, 1984], 998) wrote this eloquent encomium much in the spirit of Keats:

   [Turgenev's] sadness has its element of error, but it has also its larger element of wisdom. Life *is*, in fact, a battle. On this point optimists and pessimists agree. Evil is insolent and strong; beauty enchanting but rare; goodness very apt to be weak; folly very apt to be defiant; wickedness to carry the day; imbeciles to be in great places, people of sense in small, and mankind generally, unhappy. But the world as it stands is no illu-sion, no phantasm, no evil dream of a night; we wake up to it again forever and ever; we can neither forget it nor deny it nor dispense with it. We can welcome experience as it comes, and give it what it demands, in exchange for something which it is idle to pause to call much or little so long as it contributes to swell the volume of consciousness. In this there is mingled pain and delight, but over the mysterious mixture there hovers a visible rule, that bids us learn to will and seek to understand.

4. Soren Kierkegaard, *The Sickness unto Death,* trans. Walter Lowrie edition (New York: Anchor, 1954), 224.
5. Quoted in the editors' epilogue, T. W. Adorno, *Aesthetic Theory,* ed. Gretel Adorno and Rolf Tiedemann, trans. C. Lenhardt (London, 1984), 493.
6. *Letters of Wallace Stevens,* ed. Holly Stevens (New York, 1970), 390.

The Dog Did Not Bark

A Note on Keats in Translation

GEORGE STEINER

THE MATTER OF TRANSLATION plays a very minor role in Keats's work. The contrast with, say, Coleridge's translations of Schiller or with Shelley's translations from Homeric and Platonic Greek, from Calderón or from Goethe's *Faust* is manifest. There is, famously, the 1816 sonnet *On First Looking into Chapman's Homer*, not only a tribute, distinctive at the time, to Chapman, but a lasting statement of the shock of recognition that can come of translation. The sonnet is hardly among Keats's best. Its oddly ambiguous opening line—"Standing aloof in giant ignorance"[1]—summarizes the unfamiliarities of a very young, largely self-taught, and quintessentially English poet in respect of foreign tongues and literatures. The incomplete *Translated from Ronsard*, dated 1818, is jejune. This leaves the April 1819 sonnet *On a Dream*, a brief evocation of the Paolo and Francesca episode in canto V of Dante's *Inferno:*

> Where in the gust, the whirlwind, and the flaw
> Of rain and hail-stones, lovers need not tell
> Their sorrows, —pale were the sweet lips I saw,
> Pale were the lips I kiss'd, and fair the form
> I floated with, about that melancholy storm.

(Where "flaw," signifying a sudden gust or spell of stormy weather, is indeed fine.)

A meager harvest. The classical mythology that crowds and overcrowds Keats's poetry is, as we know, derivative. It draws on secondary sources and iconography. Where a Hellenistic romance or Italian novella provides the underlying scripts (as in *Lamia*, in *Isabella*) English-language versions interpose. The immediacies of imitation, both metrical and topical, which attach important works by Byron and Shelley to their precedents in Goethe or Dante are not available to Keats. It is via his perceptions of Milton that Keats comes closest to an occasional willed Latinity and to technical-grammatical effects not natively English. Normally, he is as thoroughly "at home" as was Jane Austen (the part played in these two lives by Winchester seems emblematic). It has often been remarked that many of Keats's most "Grecian" turns are deployed in an English setting and pastoral (e.g., the "beechen green, and shadows numberless" of the nightingale Dryad and the perhaps unconsciously revealing "Cold Pastoral!", which characterizes not burning Hellas but Hampshire in May). *Ode to Psyche* says it all when it invokes "Olympus' faded hierarchy!" Keats always remained of England, English.

There can be informing symmetries in the life of letters. It is as if the art of translation reciprocates Keats's essential indifference to it. Unless I am altogether in error, he is not only the least translated of the major English romantics, but among the least translated of the major English poets.[2] By contrast, Byron and Shelley elicit numerous echoes in other languages, notably across Europe and Russia. Byron is, obviously, a commanding presence in European history and sensibility. The adjective "Byronic" is crucial to certain moods, postures, styles of rhetoric, and self-dramatization in French romanticism (consider Berlioz); in Goethe's estimate and legacy (cf. the "Byron-elegy" in *Faust* II); in Italy; in Greece; in revolutionary Poland; and in Russian literature from Pushkin to Nabokov. Shelley's romantic Neoplatonism, his radical libertarian eloquence, and the debt he owes to Aeschylus, Sophocles, and Dante, in turn, generate translation.

But it is not only his immediate peers who far exceed Keats in creative reception. It is the Coleridge of *The Rime of the Ancient Mariner*, prodigally rendered in other languages, and it is, after Keats, Browning and Swinburne (the latter, it may be to our current surprise, turns up ubiquitously and is the object of loving translation by such masters as Stefan George). I emphasize that I may be mistaken, having access to only a very few other languages. But a look at the relevant bibliographies and library holdings does seem to confirm that Keats is translated rarely, if at all. The challenge is evident: why should this be?

Could the crux be that of intrinsic difficulty? In the practice of translation, "difficulty" is a grossly subjective and intuitive notion. One man's perplexity is another man's ease. English poetry of a lexical, grammatical, and metrical complexity far exceeding that to be found in Keats, has been superbly translated. One need allude only to Pierre Leyris's versions of Gerard Manley Hopkins, to Yves Bonnefoy's transfers of Donne, and to the delightful wagers won in Steegmuller's capture for French of Lewis Carroll and Edward Lear. Enzensberger has now "smuggled" Lear into German. Formal difficulties have never inhibited—indeed they have stimulated—poetic translation.

Is the fundamental problem more awkward? To almost everyone participating in this conference, Keats's stature is, I imagine, self-evident. Even if one qualifies Middleton Murray's celebrated placement of Keats beside Shakespeare, his inclusion in the best, most representative of poetry in the language is hardly open to question. Is this the case abroad? Judgments across languages and cultures are notoriously varied, even discordant. Byron's poetry, *Don Juan* in particular, is canonic in Russian responses as it hardly is at home. Until our midcentury, Swinburne seemed to informed opinion, to imitative intimations in France and Germany, a much greater master than he did to modern English bards or reviewers. That *Middlemarch* stands paramount among English novels remains, even for attentive taste on the continent, something of a secret. Charles Morgan was acclaimed in France as a classic; current German rankings set Lawrence Durrell foremost among recent English novelists.

Unless I mistake the evidence, which admittedly is difficult to quantify, Keats's standing in European literacy and literatures remains honored, but only fitfully, as it were, "in the observance." (A partial, but instructive analogy would be Hölderlin's place in Anglo-American awareness, the recent "breakthrough" of Hölderlin into French having occurred under the particular aegis of the French obsession with Heidegger.) Conceivably, Keats is viewed from across the Channel as the author of a small number of anthology exhibits, unquestionably stellar but of a very particular tenor. The brusque alternation between pathos and sublimity, between economy and lushness, between visionary authority and poor taste, poses obstacles, as it did to Keats's immediate contemporaries, not all of whom were malevolently myopic. Might it be that the special "parochialism" of Keats, which is so inseparable from his personal condition, is gauged more accurately at a distance than it is on home ground? There may well be those, particularly among poets and would-be translators, who locate the indispensable Keats, the Keats who does justify invocations of Shakespearean humanity and strengths, not so much in the poems as in the incomparable letters. (I share this intuition or misprision.)

But motives for "absence" are always elusive. The history of literary translation abounds with hazard. The discovery of a writer by another, the resolve to proclaim such discovery by means of critical comment and translation, can arise from pure chance. The elective affinity is often made visible only in retrospect. Where Baudelaire and Mallarmé launch Poe on his dazzling gallican career (for Valéry, Poe's *Eureka* is the most important philosophical text of the nineteenth century), T. S. Eliot recuperates Laforgue and Corbière. It may simply be the case that no translator of sufficient prestige and critical influence has, so far, taken on the challenge of Keats on any comprehensive scale. The brief examples I have found for your consideration make this point (though very incompletely).

1. Charles Merivale, an eminent Victorian divine, theologian, academic, Roman historian and author of numerous Latin poems, issues his *Keatsii Hyperionis libri tres* (2d ed.) in 1863. This *versuum fasciculum* is, in more senses than one, analogous with the translation into Greek of Milton's *Comus* by Merivale's friend and patron, Lord Lytelton. It appears to have been in the perspective of Milton's Latinity that Merivale transposes Keats's "Miltonizing" Hellenism. Take the illustrious twenty-four lines in book I of *Hyperion*, which depict Thea's speech and appeal to Saturn. "Those green-rob'd senators of mighty woods" speak to the Latin as the ultra-Keatsian "tranced summernight" does not. "Branch-charmed by the earnest stars" is indistinctly lush; the "superinclinatibus astris" provides only harsh echo. But the Virgilian-Tennysonian "Sic veniunt, abeunt, divinae murmura vocis" does justice to the original. Merivale flinches from the trope, at once out of Wordsworth's repertory and Chateaubriand's, of that "natural sculpture in cathedral cavern"; but homes in well on Saturn:

> Tum fracti morbo gemitus, et balba loquela;
> Barbaque populeae ceu frons tremit horrida sylvae.

These lines do counterpoint the consonantal force and tremors of Keats's "Shook horrid with such aspen malady."

Or look at the difficult passage, both so Miltonic and so Keatsian, in II.116–28. The assonance, the onomatopoeia in Keats's roarings of winter are not difficult to match: "Sunt montanorum fera murmura pinetorum." Far more demanding is that piece of divine semiotics, when a God signals how he means "to load / His tongue with the full weight of utterless thought." Here Merivale's "Mentis inexpressae molitur gutture pondus" reflects not only Keats's motion, but the touch therein of pretentiousness, of labored striving after intellectual and rhetorical effect. The absolute challenge is that implicit in Keats's invocation and mimesis of Saturn's organ-voice: "when other harmonies, stopt short, / Leave the dinn'd air vibrating silverly." (A line-and-a-half that seems to me to crystalize both the sensory precision and freshness of Keats's observations and the unsteadiness of executive means, so often adverbial—that "silverly.")

> Organon ingeminat numeros, aliosque sonores
> Excipit, et teneris quassum rapit aëra chordis.

These lines capture not only the deployment of "organ-stop" vowels from sonorous *o* to acute *i*, but also the necessary vibrato in "rapit aëra chordis."

As he translates, Merivale, no doubt unconsciously, grows more and more Vergilian. Thus in III.355–59—which themselves read like an imitation of the *Aeneid* ("When the prow sweeps into a midnight cove")—

> In pale and silver silence they remain'd,
> Till suddenly a splendour, like the morn,
> Pervaded all the beetling gloomy steeps,
> All the sad spaces of oblivion,

(where the explicit Miltonic echo shades into the Vergilian):

> Sic illi argenteum taciti pallere colorem;
> Donec ibi splendor subitus, ceu mane corusco,
> Pervasit clivos saxis pendentibus omnes,
> Et contristatae nebulis spatia omnia Lethes.

This closing verse momentarily elevates Merivale's Keats above the status of a *curio*.

2. But it is just this word that applies to Rudolf Borchardt's translation of *La Belle Dame sans Merci*, made between 1918 and 1923 and first published in the anthology *Englische Dichter* in 1936:

> *La belle dame sans merci*
>
> Ah was befiel Dich, Ritters Knab,
> Bleich and allein daß Du streichst herum?
> Die Rohre sind dürr all um den See,
> Und die Vögel stumm.
>
> Ah was befiel Dich, Rittes Knab,
> So hohl und blickend solcher Pein?
> Der Hamster hat sein Scheuer bestellt,
> Und der Herbst ist ein!
>
> Ich seh die Lilj ob Deiner Brau
> Von Herzweh feucht und Fiebers Hauch,
> Und auf der Wang die Rose welkt
> Zusehends auch!
>
> Ich fand ein Fräulein im Gereut,
> Ein Feenkind, ganzer Schönheit Bild,
> Ihr Haar war lang, ihr Fuß war leicht
> Und ihr Aug war wild.
>
> Ich macht ein Kränzlein für ihr Haupt,
> Armspange dazu und duftgen Bort,—
> Sie blickt' auf mich, als liebte sie,
> Und gewann mich dort.
>
> Ich saß sie auf mein schreitend Roß,
> Und andres sah ich nicht Tag lang,
> Denn seitwärts bog sie sich und fand
> Einen Feeensang.
>
> Sie fand mir Würz von süßem Schmack
> Und Honig wild, und Manna-Tau'n,
> Und ernst in fremdem Laut sprach sie:
> Ich lieb Dich traun.
>
> Sie nahm mich in den Elfengrund
> Und weint' sich dort zu Tode schier;

Ihre wild wilden Augen schloß ich dort
Mit Küssen vier.

Und lullte sie mich dort in Schlaf,
Und träumt´ —ah was sich nie verliert—
Den letzten Traum, den ich geträumt,
Wo der Berghang friert.

Ich schaute Könige und Prinzen fahl,
Fahl Kriegsvolk, totfahl Mann für Mann,
Die schrien: La belle dame sans merci
Hält Dich in Bann!

Ich sah erhungert ihren Mund
Von grauser Warnung aufgegiert,
Und ich erwacht und fand mich hier
Wo der Berghang friert.

Und darum hause ich hier noch fort
Bleich und allein und ich streich herum,
Ob die Rohre auch dürr all um den See
Und die Vögel stumm.

Borchardt is a neglected but fascinating figure: poet, philosopher, writer of fiction, crucially involved in the aesthetics of Stefan George and Hofmannsthal and in the spiritual collapse of the Austro-Hispanic ideals of European *civilitas*. Persuaded that German-language literatures lacked their *Divina Commedia,* Borchardt rendered the entirety of Dante's epic into what he took to be the medieval Middle High German that a contemporary of Dante among German *Minnesänger* would have used. It is a bizarre, monumental enterprise almost unique in the history and theory of poetic translation. Occasionally, it reaches uncanny heights of interpretative recreation.

With a few conventional, Coleridgian exceptions—"faery" (which is also, of course, Spenserian) and "elfin grot"—Keats's *La Belle Dame* is not a pastiche of the medieval, nor was it meant to be. It is characteristic of Romantic antiquarianism and prepares the Pre-Raphaelites. Its spell, its eerie desolation, lies in the versification, in the off-beat cadence of the fourth line in each clipped stanza. Keats plays with consummate control on hushed sibilants and the liquid sounds of watery sadness. Borchardt's resolute archaism, his transposition of Keats into medieval

German does programmed violence to the psychological indirection of the original. It is Borchardt who has "a palpable design upon us." "Riter Knab" "ob," "traun," and the syntax point to Borchardt's philological medievalism, rather than to Keats. Nonetheless, Borchardt mimes the rhythm admirably and finds haunting solutions. "Der Herbst ist ein!" has a terminal sorrow, a promise of winter even beyond the original. "Gereut" is, again, decorative-archaic, but the singular in "ihr Aug war wild" matches, perhaps outstrips, Keats. If "Berghang" magnifies, and thus adulterates, Keats's deliberately morose "hill's side," the almost homophonic "fahl" and "totfahl" (for "pale" and "death-pale") could not be better. This is true also of the closing quatrain. "Hause ich hier noch fort" embodies the gray open-endedness of "so-journ here." Once more, "dürr" seems to recuperate the distant common course of the fricative in Keats's "wither'd."

Given Borchardt's immersion in Greek mythology and his Platonic aesthetics of beauty and truth, it is to be regretted that he did not turn his hand to some of Keats's odes. What we find instead is Browning, Swinburne, and Edna St. Vincent Millay.

3. Keats's presence in Italian does seem to surpass that in other European languages and literatures. The catalogue refers us to a number of collections in translation in the early part of the century, to a cluster in the 1920s, to an *Ottone il Grande* in 1938, and to several more recent *Poesie* and *altri scritti poetici*. This relative prodigality allows us to compare two Italian translations of *Ode on a Grecian Urn*: one by Silvano Sabbadini (1986) and one by Franco Buffoni (1989).

Sabbadini retains Keats's stanzaic form; Buffoni comes nearer to blank verse. Neither seeks to render Keats's intricate rhymes. The respective openings show a seemingly inevitable facsimile of vocabulary. Here is Sabbadini:

> Tu, ancora inviolata sposa della quiete,
>   Figlia addotiva del tempo lento e del silenzio,
> Narratrice silvana, tu che une favola fiorita
>   Racconti, più dolce dei miei versi,
> Quale intarsiata leggenda di foglie pervade
>   La tua forma, sono dei o mortali

And Buffoni:

> Tu, per sempre inviolata sposa della quiete!
> Tu, figlia del Tempo lento e del Silenzio,
> Narratrice silvestre, che più de poesia
> Sai dire e dolcemente un racconto fiorito:
> Quale leggenda intarsiata di morali o di dei,
> O di dei e mortali, ti pervade

So close in idiom yet rather different in effect. Sabbadini aims for the rounded, in woven motion, for the *ralentando* in Keats. Buffoni's anaphoric, somewhat dramatized and pounding pace stresses Keats's rhetoric. The final stanza compacts both Keats's genius and sometimes startling vulgarity (that "Attic . . . attitude" sequence). Our two translators rightly avoid it. Buffoni translates:

> Attica forma! Dolce dispozione
> Di uomini e fanciulle nel marmo ricamati,
> Di rami d'albero e d'erba calpestata!
> Tu, silenziosa immagine! Sgomenti il pensiero
> Come l'eternità. Fredda pastorale!
> Quando l'età avrà perso questa generazione
> Tu resterai e tra nuovi dolori amica sarai
> Al' uomo, gli dirai che "belezza è verità
> E verità bellezza; e questo tutto quel che sappiamo
> Al mondo, e tutto quel che dobbiamo sapere."

Sabbadini translates:

> Oh, forma attica! Posa leggiarda, con un ricamo
>   D'uomini e fianculle nel marmo,
> Coi rami della foresta e le erbe calpestate—
>   Tu, forma silenziosa, come l'eternità
> Tormenti e spezzi la nostra ragione. Fredda pastorale!
>   Quando l'età avra devastato questa generazione,
> Ancor tu ci sarai, eterna, tra nuovi dolori
>   Non più nostri, amica all'uomo, cui dirai
> "Bellezza è verità, verità bellezza,"-questo solo
>   Sulla terra sanete ed è quanto basta.

"Quanto basta" is, to be sure, a disaster. But Sabbadini's concisions— "nel marmo," and "verità bellezza"—and his "devastato" for Keats's blighting "waste" do seem to me more faithful than Buffoni's oratorical options to the ode.

Buffoni's *Vigilia Di San Marco* finely conveys the hushed chill of the original:

> Tutta era tenebre e silenzio
> Rotto soltanto dal passo fermo
> Di chi tornava a casa più tardi
> Oltre I recinto della cattedrale.

Or note the Roman heat of his "coppa colma di caldo Sud" in *Ode to a Nightingale*. Striking, as well, is the expressly Dantean quality of Sabbadini's *Ode sull'Inodolenza*, with its "Come mai ombre, non vi riconnobi," for Keats's "How is it, shadows, that I knew ye not?" which could, indeed, be out of Dante.

4. There is not much to go on in French: a mediocre *Poèmes choisis* by Albert Laffay in 1952 and Alain Suied's translation of the odes followed by *La Belle Dame* in 1994. Academic in the unfavorable sense. Thus in the closing stanza of *To Autumn*:

> Où se sont-elles enfuies, les chansons du Printemps?
> Ne les recherche pas: toi aussi tu as ta musique,
> Tandis que des nuages striés fleurissent le jour
> Qui doucement meurt, et vermeillent les toits de chaume;
> Les petites éphémères en choeur se lamentent
> Parmi les saules de la rive, soulevés ou retombant
> Au diapason du vent léger;
> Et les agneaux déjà sevrés bêlent sur toutes les collines;
> Les grillons des haies chantent; et l'on entend
> Le rouge-gorge siffler haut dans le pré,
> Et les hirondelles rassemblées trisser dans le ciel.

The initial reiteration is missed (and this in the language of Villon). The characteristic Keatsian touch of robustness amid the flowering languor—those "stubble-plains"—is transformed into postcard thatched roofs. "Éphémères" may be lexically and zoologically correct, but it totally conceals the mock-heroic domesticity of the "small gnats." "Diapason" is translationese. "Hilly bourn"—again the earthy counterpoint so vital in Keats—is passed over. The "soft treble" is evaded, and the lightness of motion in Keats's "gathering" is made static in "rassemblées."

A similar ponderousness and lexical imperception obtains in *La Belle Dame*. Nothing, for instance, is more horrific in the key of Gothic fantasy than Keats's "With horrid warning gapèd wide"; nothing is more bureaucratically tame than "Ouvertes pour d'horribles avertissements."

It may be that Paul de Roux's *Hypérion,* published as an elegant *plaquette* by *La Dogana* (Geneva, 1989), is among the more successful of translations from Keats. Let us consider just a few words and phrases of the identical passage from Book I that we earlier examined in Merivale's Latin version.

"Extatique" overloads "trancèd," but is validly Keatsian. Why Roux translates "earnest stars" as "jalouses étoiles" is puzzling. But the somber "slowing-down" in the source text is finely mimed by "une graduelle et douce rafale solitaire." The rather neoclassical "front superbe" corresponds well with Keats's statuesque vision. And "prodigué" matches "had shed." I find "et vît son royaume en allé," with its lightly heightened idiom, faithful to Keats. Only "maladie du tremble," in its bathetic literality, is a letdown. Let me conclude with the sonorous passage from II. 300–305. Here Roux manages some remarkable echoes. Keats's "The ponderous syllables, like sullen waves / In the half-glutted hollows of reef-rocks, / Came booming thus" yields the following for Roux:

> Les pesants syllabes, comme de sombres vagues,
> Parmi les anfractuosités glougloutantes des récifs,
> Arrivaient en tonnant.

No doubt, there is much that I have missed or do not have access to. Neinz Piontek's "poetische Eindeutschung" (a barbaric formula) of Keats in 1960 has its advocates and was reissued in 1995. The Russian domain is obviously important. Versions of *Endymion* and *Ode to Autumn* by Pasternak may represent the one instance of Keats translation by a major master. There are also admired versions by Marshak. An issue of the *Keats-Shelley Journal* in 1995 surveys renderings into Japanese. A very brief visit suggests to me that there could be a handful in Albanian, where Byron's ghost looms large.

Nonetheless, I offer the tentative finding that Keats has been only fitfully and poorly translated into the principal European tongues. His poetry has not drawn the great translators who, from Valéry to Leyris, from Stefan George to Celan, from Montale to Quasimodo, have made of our century one of the summits in an exact art. That virtuoso of hermeneutic inquiry, Sherlock Holmes, may be our best guide to the case when he reminds Dr. Watson that what requires explanation is indeed the fact "that the dog did not bark." Or not very loudly.

Notes

1. *The Poems of John Keats*, ed. Jack Stillinger (Cambridge, Mass.: Harvard University Press, Belknap Press, 1978). All quotations are from this edition.
2. The first "imitation" of "ce jeune et charmant génie" by Philarète Chasles appears in the *Revue des Deux Mondes* in 1848. A brief selection appears in Dutch in 1888. A passage from *Endymion* is included in a French anthology in 1890. Six poems are rendered into German by Gisherte Freiligrath in the collection *Englische Dichter* (1898). Ettore Sanfelice's *Poemetti E Odi di Jŏhn Keats* are issued in Messina in 1901. The sonnets are rendered into prose in 1904. The Mercure de France publishes Paul Gallimard's extensive translation in 1910. Fragments appear in a Spanish anthology in 1918. The Duchesse de Clermont-Tonnerre labors for Keats in French between 1907 and 1922. Three sonnets, *La Belle Dame* and *Ode on a Grecian Urn* appear in Norwegian in 1932. This is a very incomplete list, but it may illustrate my point: not only are translations few and dispersed, but they do not enlist major poets or translators.

On First Looking into John Keats's Letters

PHILIP LEVINE

I FOUND THE WORK of John Keats in my twenty-first year, and it has guided and inspired me ever since. I count as the work not only the poems and the amazing letters but the life as well, which I encountered in the biographies of Sidney Colvin and Amy Lowell and later in those of Aileen Ward, Robert Gittings, and Walter Jackson Bate. I also found suggestions of the work of the living man in hundreds of relevant pages of the writings of those who made up the "Keats Circle," pages I pored over in the stacks of the Wayne University library in Detroit in my hunger to devour this early hero.

My formal education, such as it was, was bequeathed to me by the Detroit public schools, and I believed then and still believe they did well by me. Math, history, French, chemistry, physics, English composition, literature, and physical education were all taught with rigor and skill. It was not, however, until my junior year in high school that I encountered a poem that seemed relevant to the life that I'd experienced or the one I believed was waiting for me. My literature teacher, Mrs. Paperno, a small, dark-haired, intense woman, read to the class one day a short poem by Wilfred Owen. "Did you all hear that?" she asked in her most severe voice, and even the football players in the class nodded their assent, for Mrs. Paperno commanded respect from all of us. The poem was *Arms and the Boy:*

> Let the boy try along this bayonet blade
> How cold steel is, and keen with hunger of blood;

Blue with all malice, like a madman's flash;
And thinly drawn with famishing for flesh.

Lend him to stroke these blind, blunt bullet-leads,
Which long to nuzzle in the hearts of lads,
Or give him cartridges whose fine zinc teeth
Are sharp with the sharpness of grief and death.

For his teeth seem for laughing round an apple.
There lurk no claws behind his fingers supple;
And God will grow no talons at his heels,
Nor antlers through the thickness of his curls.

How Mrs. Paperno divined the power this poem had over me I do not know, but as the class broke up at the end of the hour she offered to loan me the little collection of Owen's poetry if I promised to bring it back on Monday. I promised, and the book was mine for an entire weekend. World War II was still raging in Europe and the Pacific, and seventeen-year-olds expected to complete high school and enter the military. What we were supposed to feel about this, I gathered from the talk of my elders, my classmates, and the movies I saw, was some sort of profound inner swelling of the organs of patriotism. Of course that was not what I felt at all; I was simply horrified at the thought of being maimed or killed or being forced to maim and kill others. In poem after poem, Owen authenticated my own response to the carnage I might have to participate in. He had been there, he had seen it, and finally died from it. His poems, which seethed with his disgust for the Great War, as it was then known, went a long way toward assuring me that my response to the thought of battle was not insane.

Like many young people I had been writing something I hesitated then and would hesitate now to call poetry, though what else it might have been I don't know. Perhaps I should just call it bad poetry. These compositions were relatively short—I could recite any one in less than ten minutes (they were never written down)—they were unrhymed, and not in any fixed metrical pattern. Their rhetorical structures were based largely on the more adventurous sermons I heard on the radio on Sunday mornings. Their most common subjects were simple and present: rain, wind, earth (dirt, that is), snow, the night sky, the thickly clustered trees in the undeveloped, wooded blocks near our house, and the birds that thrived there. No doubt part of the intensity of pleasure I derived from composing these first poems during my nightly sojourns came from the fact that I avoided what bothered me most in my daily life: family life, anti-Semitism (which flourished in the Detroit of that—Father Coughlin's—era), sex, and the waiting war. I leaped immediately to a "higher" level and was conscious even then that every poem flung out at the night sky was an effort to use, perhaps luxuriate in, my separateness and possibly to bridge the great moat between me and all other living creatures. Of course like many beginning poets my age then, and perhaps now, I avoided the beneficial influence of the poetry of others, at least until my encounter with Wilfred Owen; but even his stylistic influence on me was minimal, for I found his rhythmic structures and his experiments with rhyme daunting. What I grasped for and fumbled with was his richly textured phrasing. His "The shrill, demented choirs of wailing shells" became something like my "The night wind's wail dies daily into prayer." Bad as these early efforts were at least now they had the model of true poetry.

Then quite suddenly the following summer the war ended, and I was allowed to consider alternatives to the military. I enrolled in Wayne, the city university of Detroit, and it was there I quickly encountered the poets who would have the most significant influence on my writing and thinking. For almost two weeks Stephen Crane became my model:

> *I saw a Man Pursuing the Horizon*
>
> I saw a man pursuing the horizon;
> Round and round they sped.
> I was disturbed at this;
> I accosted the man.
> "It is futile," I said.
> "You can never—"
>
> "You lie," he cried,
> And ran on

It took me a day to do a passable imitation of *I Saw a Man Pursuing the Horizon* and the other little gnomic poems and ten more days to tire of them; it was just too easy. Then T. S. Eliot became my lord and master until, in my second semester, I encountered his jew (with a small *j*) in the poem *Gerontion*, squatting on a windowsill, "spawned," if you will, in some Belgian whorehouse. Then it was the leftist, pre-Munich poetry of Auden and Spender, and later Hart Crane, whose impenetrability convinced me not only of his greatness, but of the wisdom of my own aesthetic, which might have been described as "Make it obscure," which comes quite naturally when so little of your world is clear to you.

Then came one of the crucial decisions of my life in poetry: the choice between Dr. Gene Sax and Professor A. D. Wooly, that is, the choice between the fashionable poets of that hour—Hopkins, Yeats, Eliot, Pound, and Stevens—taught brilliantly by Dr. Sax, the most elegant and seductive tenured member of the English department, and the all but forgotten stars of a previous era, the Romantic poets, taught with fading fervor by old Professor Wooly, whose lifework in scholarship was a small portion of the editing of the complete letters of Horace Walpole.

Tall, lean, costumed like a banker, Dr. Sax taught with a subdued theatricality. He used no notes but employed the blackboard ceaselessly as he paced back and forth before the front of the class, stopping every few moments to add lines or arrows to his diagram of the day's poem, or, if the poem were as dense as Yeats's *Byzantium*, an entire class period could be consumed with the explication of a single passage. (In 1947 the New Criticism was not all that new, but it had only recently made its way to Detroit.) I sat watching my classmates scribbling into their textbooks as the poem itself disappeared beneath a maze of notes and connecting horizontal and vertical lines. I think we all went away from these breathtaking performances convinced that a poem worthy of the name was at least as inscrutable as the Rosetta stone. What would we find in our anthologies when we got home? Certainly not the poem, for that had been replaced by a complex and brilliant tapestry woven by Dr. Sax. I never figured out why Sax could draw seventy-five students, including a scattering of the most elegant and depressed women on campus, long-haired lionesses who sat glumly in their tailored suits seemingly mesmerized by Sax's verbal dexterity. The assignments were small, rarely as many as a half-dozen poems, and Dr. Sax was far too occupied with his explications to find out if any of the poems had been read by the students.

Professor Wooly, on the other hand, thought nothing of assigning sixty pages of poetry for a single meeting. The class was expected to digest all of The Lyrical Ballads between Monday and Wednesday and to pay special attention to the famous preface. Whereas Sax chainsmoked Camels as he paced the classroom, Wooly sat, head down, drawing on an unlighted pipe and read aloud key passages from the assigned pages. His commentaries scarcely needed to be noted; they went something like, "This goes to the heart of the matter," or "Here is the poet at the height of his powers." He once stated that Coleridge never wrote a bad line, and then seemed so stunned by the boldness of his assertion that he sat in silence for a long minute before the dozen of us who had survived the three-week rampage through Wordsworth. A large rumpled man with a great head of gray hair going white, he would sit silently at his desk when the hour ended, as though lost in thought or exhausted by our presence as we took leave of the room in silence.

Even now it seems unlikely that I would have dropped Dr. Sax's class and stuck with Professor Wooly's. As unsophisticated as I was in my second year of college, I knew this was not superior classroom teaching, for I had encountered that in high school. It may have had something to do with Wooly's patience: he seemed willing to wait for as long as it took for us to realize the majesty and power of the poetry he was bustling us through. Perhaps I felt I couldn't desert the other eleven students or perhaps it was Professor Wooly I could not desert, for there was something genuine and dear about his befuddled manner. I'm sure I appreciated the lack of a performance, for already I had discovered how common performers were in the university. I sensed an unstated faith on Wooly's part that if we welcomed these poems into our hearts and minds they would achieve themselves without an insistence on his part. The case was sealed when, after a quiet reading of *Frost at Midnight,* Wooly looked up at the class and said, "There is something here for each of us." I believe it was in the "for each of us," the acknowledgment that in the face of Coleridge's genius we were all merely humble workers in the fields of poetry.

After a sideways glance at Southey that lasted only a single meeting, we raced first through Byron and then Shelley and, with four weeks left in the semester, arrived at young John Keats and his first tentative efforts at poetry, the imitations of Spenser. It suddenly appeared as though Professor Wooly had tired of his own method; perhaps he had a special fondness for Keats, or as an experienced teacher he may have been responding to the unstated urgings of the class. At any rate, the pace of our reading slowed drastically. It is possible he recognized the special place Keats could occupy in the spiritual lives we were in the process of creating. We were twelve young and not-so-young men and women from the city of Detroit, from working-class or lower-middle-class backgrounds. The class met in the late afternoon, and some members hurried to it after finishing the day shift at one of the local factories. Even our costumes revealed that. With Keats there was an immediate affinity we had not felt before. Wordsworth and Coleridge seemed to have stepped as poets directly into their maturity—in Words-worth's case, even middle age—at the beginning of their careers. Shelley and Byron were nothing if not exotic aristocrats, and they rode far above us, above even the clouds of industrial garbage that hovered over our university. In important ways, Keats was one of us: young, uncertain, determined, decently educated at mediocre schools, and struggling both to survive and to believe in the necessity of his art. He was what one of us might have been, had one of us been phenomenal John Keats.

From the moment I first read *On First Looking into Chapman's Homer.* I was hooked:

> Much have I travell'd in the realms of gold,
>   And many goodly states and kingdoms seen;
>   Round many western islands have I been
> Which bards in fealty to Apollo hold.
> Oft of one wide expanse had I been told
>   That deep-brow'd Homer ruled as his demesne;
>   Yet did I never breathe its pure serene
> Till I heard Chapman speak out loud and bold:
> Then felt I like some watcher of the skies
>   When a new planet swims into his ken;
> Or like stout Cortez when with eagle eyes
>   He star'd at the Pacific—and all his men
> Look'd at each other with a wild surmise—
>   Silent, upon a peak in Darien.

The poem expressed perfectly my own response to the great Romantic poetry I was reading for the first time and—to use Keats's expression—feeling on my pulse as I had felt no poetry before. I was dazzled by the fullness of expression, the daring of the figures, the sheer audacity of the conception, and the sonnet form fulfilled to perfection. The truth was, half of me never believed it at all: I was a skeptical, big city boy. But another part of me cared not at all about belief, for the language itself was so delicious that I read and reread the poem until, without trying, I'd memorized it. How could poetry be better than this? I asked myself, and as I read deeper into his work the answer came to me.

I do not know if Professor Wooly knew that my ambition was to become a poet; I'd shared this hope with very few people. Detroit was not Greenwich Village, Cambridge, or even Berkeley; it taught you not to advertise all of your ambitions. Its stance was ferociously masculine, and most of its citizens seemed to have little interest in or tolerance for the arts or for what might be described as "artistic behavior." Even half the women I went to Wayne with carried themselves as though they yearned to become professional bowlers. My guess is that Wooly, like Mrs. Paperno before him, divined certain needs in me and did his best to meet them, for like her he proved to have an extraordinarily generous nature.

It must have been concern for my spiritual nature that prompted Professor Wooly one late afternoon as the last of daylight faded across his desk to hand me a volume of the letters of Keats opened to the page concerned with what the poet called "The vale of Soul-making." Keats distinguishes between the "sparks of the divinity in millions" that are not yet souls and the souls they become when they "acquire identities" and "each one is personally itself." He goes on to ask how the sparks become individual identities and answers with a question: "How, but by the medium of a world like this?" While I read on in a state bordering on amazement, the professor cut an apple into eight nearly equal segments which he laid out on his desk between us. In what I read, a man barely older than I was attempting to account for the function of pain and suffering in the creation of the human spirit. For a brief moment I had a vision of the whole person I might become in "a world like this," and in that moment I found, to use his words, "the use of the world" for probably the first time in my life. "I will call the *world* a School," Keats had written, "instituted for the purpose of teaching little children to read—I will call the *human heart* the *hornbook* used in that School—and I will call the *Child able to read*, the *Soul* made from that *School* and its *hornbook*. Do you not see how necessary a World of Pains and troubles is to school an Intelligence and make it a Soul?" For a moment I saw. Nothing I had read before had so potently lifted the gloom that hovered over my small portion of Detroit. In my excitement, I reached for a slice of Wooly's apple and popped it into my mouth. A silence. Wooly sighed almost imperceptibly and, being the gentleman he was, offered me a second perfect eighth, which I had the good sense to decline. Like Mrs. Paperno before him, Professor Wooly loaned me the volume for the weekend. I remember with what care I held the book under my arm on the long bus ride back to my apartment, and how I hoped that in the days to follow some of its wisdom might pass into me. Perhaps it did.

This was 1948, some ten years before Americans of my generation would set about the creation of a body of poetry that would later be labeled "confessional" and even longer before those poets' acts of self-destruction, but the models were already there Had not the most gifted boy wonder of the American century, Hart Crane, shown us all that the true poet was the poet *manqué*? That year Detroit itself would welcome Dylan Thomas, then the most dazzling wordsmith in the English-speaking world, but it was not the gaunt, tousled bard of the photographs who mesmerized us with his voice but a bloated, stained, lurching, tiny version of W. C. Fields to whom the tall and elegant women flocked. My mentor-to-be, John Berryman, would later claim that what the poet required above all else was a wounding so terrible that he or she could only barely survive it. The accepted belief was that the poet wrote out of the source of his agony until he could no longer endure and then came the leap from the stern of a ship bound to New York City or from a bridge spanning the Mississippi. Imagine my relief and surprise when Professor Wooly handed me a volume of the letters opened to the following passage: "Whenever I find myself growing vaporish I rouse myself, wash, and put on a clean shirt, brush my hair and clothes, tie my shoestrings neatly, and in fact adonize as I were going out—then all clean and comfortable I sit down to write. This I find the greatest relief." A poet writing out of his joy in the world and in himself, out of what Coleridge had called his "genial spirits." What a relief for me after all the talk of creative mutilation. It seemed quite suddenly I could be both a poet and a person, dare I say a mensch, even in a world like ours, that is, if I were able to create such a person out of what I'd been given.

What did I make of Keats's famous "Negative Capability" letter? When only twenty-two years old he had written his two brothers that in a "disquisition" with a friend "several things dovetailed in my mind, and at once it struck me what quality went to form a Man of Achievement, especially in Literature, and which Shakespeare possessed so enormously—I mean *Negative Capability,* that is, when a man is capable of being in uncertainties, mysteries, doubts, without any irritable reaching after fact and reason." If I understood him fully I did not take him to mean I could stop thinking and live the rest of my life as a cabbage or even take too seriously the thrush, who in Keats's own sonnet advises the young poet not to fret after knowledge. Wooly, good academic that he was, had already drawn my attention to the letter in which the poet stated he meant to follow Solomon's direction and "get wisdom—get understanding." Keats had written that there was but one way for him: "the road lies through application, study, and thought." By this time, even at age twenty, certain things were clear to me. One was that Keats was a genius and I was not, and so I would have to apply myself with even greater dedication than he if I were to write anything worthy of a human life. Another was that his early poems— like the early poems of Hart Crane, which I already knew—gave not the least hint of what was to come. Great poet that he was, Keats did not spring fully formed from the mind of God. Though not as hopeless as mine, his first efforts were poor, and what finally mattered was that he had done just what he had set out to do, he had made himself a poet and he had done this while living "in uncertainties, Mysteries, doubts, without any irritable reaching after fact and reason." In other words, according to Keats, if my intentions were to become a poet, my ability to write in a world I did not understand and from which I did not demand final answers might prove to be an asset rather than a defect of character. At that time I lived among men and women my own age or slightly older who often took my refusal to search after "fact and reason" as a sign of sloth or indifference. I had known it was part of who I was but had not assigned it a label. My friends would become the mathematicians, historians, philosophers, and linguists of my generation. Gifted with Negative Capability and Keats's map of the road toward poetry, I might set out with realistic hopes. Unlike Lord Byron or Shelley, I was not the scion of a great family. Like Keats, I was descended from ordinary people; in my case, ordinary people with extraordinary minds and imaginations. This lack of class or family with a capital F could, I realized even then, prove to be a virtue, for it meant that, like Keats, I could not live apart from the daily difficulties of the world. I had somehow to support myself and those I might become responsible for. I could regard these circumstances as a terrible distraction, the Alps that stood between me and the poetry I might write, or like Keats I could regard them as an opportunity to become an adult; I could regard them as part of the material out of which I might build my character and, later, my poetry. I chose to try to follow the model I found in his letters and in his life. Unlike Keats, I was gifted with good health; I lived long enough to bless the needs that placed me in the company of the men and women who became my poetry.

For the final meeting of Professor Wooly's class, there was no reading assignment, and when the dozen of us assembled we had no idea what to expect. Somewhat shyly he thanked us for our attention and our good work. "I know this poetry has gone out of fashion, which should tell you the value of fashion," he said, "for there is no poetry more necessary for the growth of our spirits." He announced that he had saved this period to read a few things to us, though he assured us that he knew he was not a gifted reader of poetry. Nonetheless he read the *Ode to Psyche* and the great late ode *To Autumn* with remarkable authority, for in truth he had a deep and resonant voice, and when he slowed the pace of his reading he could be an impressive reader. He then opened a volume of the Buxton Forman edition of the letters and read to us from the October 1818 letter to Richard Woodhouse in which the poet discusses the lack of identity of the poet. "What shocks the virtuous philosopher, delights the camelion Poet," and he looked up at us with a delighted smile, and went on. "A Poet is the most unpoetical of any thing in existence; because he has no Identity," and finished with Keats's assurance to Woodhouse that he meant to do the world some good, though that might have to wait for his maturer years, for first he had to reach "as high a summit in Poetry as the nerve bestowed upon" him would suffer. Professor Wooly closed the book. "Keats has told us," he said, "that he has no sense of his own identity; he is constantly filling some other body possessing an unchangeable attribute, some creature of impulse, and yet each of us in this room has an overwhelming sense of the identity of John Keats, who has entered our lives through his writing for as long as we live." He bowed his head for a moment. "Isn't that remarkable! He requires us, his readers."

Though the semester ended, my reading of Keats did not. I was deep into the Colvin biography, and I read on to the end watching those terrible months unfold. I can still recall completing the book in a brightly lit annex of the Wayne library and feeling as though something enormous had been stolen from me, from all of us who love poetry, and feeling also the terrible injustice of a world that produces a poetic genius of this quality once a century and then takes the life before that talent is fulfilled. I thought then, as I've thought so many times since,

of the poems that might have been ours and the enormous literary reputation that might have been his, had he lived his three score and ten. It
is curious and wonderful to realize that the man who has served as my
mentor and model all these years was one third my present age when
he passed from poetry. Wonderful, too, it seems to me, that I found
him at Wayne, a campus of seedy old homes and temporary buildings
bursting with the new students the postwar years deposited. Rereading
his poems, his letters, his life now, I'm not sure what I regret the most.
I think it was the denial of his simple daily life, for who else have I
encountered through life or books who lived that life with such intensity and fullness? I think, too, of the loss of his daily human contact
with all those he would have encountered. Hard to imagine the power
and grace his presence would have conferred on those he would have
touched. At times I hear it as an unseen wave of genial caring breaking
forever on the farthest human shore. But what he left us and what we
will celebrate as long as our language survives is unique, for even
though he lived to be only twenty-five years old, he is with all of us, an
extraordinary human soul animating us still.

NOTE

After being delivered at the John Keats Bicentennial Conference, this essay was
first published in *DoubleTake* 4 (spring 1996): 137–41.

CONTRIBUTORS

M. H. ABRAMS, Class of 1916 Professor of English (Emeritus) at Cornell University, is the author of numerous books, including *The Mirror and the Lamp* (1953) and *Natural Supernaturalism* (1971), two of the most admired and influential works of Romantic scholarship in this century, and *Doing Things with Texts* (1989).

WALTER JACKSON BATE, Arthur Kingsley Porter University Professor of English (Emeritus) at Harvard University, is the acknowledged dean of Keats scholars and the author of the massive biography *John Keats* (a Pulitzer Prize–winner in 1964) as well as *The Stylistic Development of Keats* (1958). He has also published biographies of Coleridge and Samuel Johnson and *The Burden of the Past and the English Poet* (1970).

EAVAN BOLAND, an Irish poet, is Lane Professor in the Humanities at Stanford University. Her numerous books include *An Origin Like Water: Collected Poems* (1996), *In a Time of Violence* (1994), and *Object Lessons: The Life of the Woman and the Poet in Our Time* (1996).

DAVID BROMWICH, professor of English at Yale University and author of an important chapter on Keats in his *Hazlitt: The Mind of a Critic* (1983), is also author of *A Choice of Inheritance: Self and Community from Edmund Burké to Robert Frost* (1989) and *Politics by Other Means: Higher Education and Group Thinking* (1992).

HERMIONE DE ALMEIDA is the Pauline Walter Professor of English and Comparative Literature at the University of Tulsa and the author of *Byron and Joyce through Homer: Don Juan and Ulysses* (1981) and *Romantic Medicine and John Keats* (1990). She also edited *Critical Essays on John Keats* (1990) and coedited *Playing the Harlot; or, Mostly Coffee* (1996), an unpublished novel by Patricia Avis.

TERENCE ALLAN HOAGWOOD, professor of English at Texas A&M University, is the author of *Prophecy and the Philosophy of Mind: Traditions of Blake and Shelley* (1985), *Skepticism and Ideology: Shelley's Political Prose and Its Philosophical Context from Bacon to Marx* (1988), *Byron's Dialectic* (1993), *Politics, Philosophy, and the Production of Romantic Texts* (1996), and various articles analyzing Keats from a historicist perspective.

ELIZABETH JONES has published articles in the *University of Toronto Quarterly* and *Studies in Romanticism*. Her paper for the conference was also published in the London *Times Literary Supplement* and a longer version appears in the *Keats-Shelley Journal*.

DEBBIE LEE teaches at Washington State University and is coeditor of an eight-volume series called *Slavery, Abolition and Emancipation: Writings in the British Romantic Period*, which will be published in 1999. Her paper for the conference was also published in the London *Times Literary Supplement*.

PHILIP LEVINE, professor of creative writing at New York University and professor emeritus at California State University at Fresno, is the editor of *The Essential Keats* (1987) and the author of sixteen volumes of poetry, including *What Work Is*, which won the National Book Award in 1991; *New Selected Poems* (1993); and *The Simple Truth*, which won the Pulitzer Prize in 1995.

DONALD H. REIMAN, who coedits *Shelley and his Circle* at the Pforzheimer Library, is vice president of the Keats-Shelley Association. He is also the author or editor of numerous influential books on Romanticism, including *Percy Bysshe Shelley* (1969), *The Evidence of the Imagination: Studies of Interactions between Life and Art in English Romantic Literature* (1978), and *Intervals of Inspiration: The Skeptical Tradition and the Psychology of Romanticism* (1988).

ROBERT M. RYAN, professor of English at Rutgers University, Camden, was a co-director of the conference and is the author of *Keats: The Religious Sense* (1976), the first book-length study of the poet's religious ideas, as well as of *The Romantic Reformation: Religious Politics in English Literature, 1789–1824* (1997). From 1978 to 1995 he reviewed publications on Keats for the annual *Romantic Movement Bibliography*.

RONALD A. SHARP, John Crowe Ransom Professor of English and associate provost at Kenyon College was a codirector of the conference. He is a former editor of *The Kenyon Review* and the author of *Keats, Skepticism, and the Religion of Beauty* (1979), *Friendship and Literature* (1986), and a forthcoming book on Keats and friendship. With Eudora Welty he edited *The Norton Book of Friendship* (1991), and with Nathan Scott he edited *Reading George Steiner* (1994).

GEORGE STEINER, Extraordinary Fellow at Churchill College, Cambridge University, and professor of English and comparative literature (Emeritus) at the University of Geneva, was the first occupant of the Lord Weidenfeld Professorship of Comparative Literature at Oxford University. A regular contributor to *The New Yorker* for a quarter century, Steiner is the author of four books of fiction and more than a dozen influential books of cultural and literary criticism, including *Language and Silence* (1967), *After Babel* (1975), *Antigones* (1984), *Real Presences* (1989), and *No Passion Spent: Essays 1978–1995* (1996).

JACK STILLINGER, Center for Advanced Study Professor of English at the University of Illinois, wrote the definitive study of the texts of Keats's poems (1974), which led to the publication in 1978 of his now standard edition of the poetry. He is also the author of *The Hoodwinking of Madeline, and Other Essays on Keats's Poems* (1971), *Multiple Authorship and the Myth of Solitary Genius* (1991), and *Coleridge and Textual Instability: The Multiple Versions of the Major Poems* (1994).

AILEEN WARD, Albert Schweitzer Professor of the Humanities at New York University (Emerita), is the author of *John Keats: The Making of a Poet,* which won the National Book Award in 1963, of *The Unfurling of Entity: Metaphor in Poetic Theory* (1987), and of a forthcoming biography of William Blake.

SUSAN J. WOLFSON, professor of English at Princeton University, is the author of *The Questioning Presence: Wordsworth, Keats, and the Interrogative Mode in Romantic Poetry* (1986), *Formal Charges: The Shaping of Poetry in British Romanticism* (1997), and a number of articles on Keats that focus on issues of gender and cultural reception.

INDEX

Entries for works by Keats are indexed by title without attribution. Literary works by others are indexed under the author.